THE
FIRST
FLEET

Rob Mundle

ABC
Books

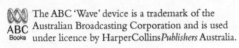 The ABC 'Wave' device is a trademark of the Australian Broadcasting Corporation and is used under licence by HarperCollins*Publishers* Australia.

First published in Australia in 2014
This edition published in 2017
by HarperCollins*Publishers* Australia Pty Limited
ABN 36 009 913 517
harpercollins.com.au

HarperCollins*Publishers*
Level 13, 201 Elizabeth Street, Sydney NSW 2000, Australia
Unit D1, Apollo Drive, Rosedale, Auckland 0632, New Zealand
A 53, Sector 57, Noida, UP, India
1 London Bridge Street, London, SE1 9GF, United Kingdom
2 Bloor Street East, 20th floor, Toronto, Ontario M4W 1A8, Canada
195 Broadway, New York NY 10007, USA

National Library of Australia Cataloguing-in-Publication data:

Mundle, Rob, author.
  First Fleet / Rob Mundle.
  ISBN: 978 0 7333 3544 0 (paperback)
  ISBN: 978 1 4607 0062 4 (ebook)
  Phillip, Arthur, 1738-1814.
  First Fleet, 1787–1788.
  Convict ships.
  Transportation of convicts – New South Wales.
  Penal colonies – New South Wales.
  Voyages around the world.
  Australia – History – 1788-1851.
  Australian Broadcasting Corporation.
994.402.

Cover design and illustration by Matt Stanton, HarperCollins Design Studio
Cover image by shutterstock.com
Paintings of the ships of the First Fleet by Frank Allen, www.frankallen.com.au
Typeset in Bembo Std by Kirby Jones
Maps by Map Illustrations www.mapillustrations.com.au
Printed and bound in Australia by McPherson's Printing Group
The papers used by HarperCollins in the manufacture of this book are a natural, recyclable product made from wood grown in sustainable plantation forests. The fibre source and manufacturing processes meet recognised international environmental standards, and carry certification.

To Arthur Phillip, the brave sailors and first settlers who, through unyielding courage and determination, overcame adversity and founded our great nation

Adieu Adieu my Native Land

Shackle Draggers. Allport Museum of Fine Arts, Tasmanian Archive and Heritage Office.

Contents

AUTHOR'S NOTE

Roald Amundsen, the Norwegian explorer, famously acknowledged the role of sailors in history's great endeavours and adventures when he said: 'We must always remember with gratitude and admiration the first sailors who steered their vessels through storms and mists, and increased our knowledge of the lands of ice in the South.' This is equally true of the officers and crew of the eleven-ship convoy which sailed to Sydney Cove, Port Jackson in 1787–88 – which we have come to call the First Fleet.

I am not an historian, nor an academic, but having sailed countless thousands of nautical miles in my life, in everything from skiffs to maxi yachts, inshore and offshore, I consider myself a competent sailor and a man of the sea. So, in researching this latest maritime story of the First Fleet, I realised there was an opportunity to provide a sailor's perspective of the 'passage to Botany Bay', as George B. Worgan, the Surgeon of *Sirius*, described it. As I ventured down this path, it increasingly struck me that this was the story of one of the great undertakings of the modern world, and it was as much the story of professional sailors in their day-to-day workings on individual ships, battling all that nature could hurl at them – from disease to possible shipwreck – as it was grand plans and strategic visions by politicians and authorities.

I have sailed out of Portsmouth and covered the length of the Solent, experienced a savage force-10 storm in the Atlantic, and been on the waters of both Rio de Janeiro and Cape

Town. These experiences placed me in the wake of the First Fleeters and gave me an appreciation of what they endured. Moreover, the research I undertook for my book about the tragic 1998 Sydney to Hobart yacht race (*Fatal Storm*) gave me a vivid understanding of what the Fleet might have experienced south of the Equator. The conditions those yachts faced were as bad as it can get in the depths of the Southern Ocean.

As I wrote my way more deeply into this powerful story my admiration for the achievement of Captain Arthur Phillip, and all those under his command grew proportionately. They had been directed to voyage to, and settle in, the unknown. It was one hell of a trip, and success did not come easily.

In crafting my story I have been able to combine my knowledge of the sea with information in the actual journals of First Fleet crew members and officers, and their various observations of the day-to-day workings of their individual ships, covering everything from the handling of the vessel in the widest range of weather conditions through to life below deck for the sailors and the shackle draggers (convicts). On many occasions I was pleased to be able to expand on a brief journal entry (those few words that are akin to an eighteenth-century Twitter post!) simply because it was obvious to me, through my sailing experience, what the fine detail of the moment was that lay behind those logs. As a consequence, I found myself in awe of what skilled sailors these men were in keeping their ships safe. It really was the era of ships of wood and men of steel.

Of course, the basic storyline for this book came from the coal face – the journals and letters of many of the key players, and some of the lesser known men in the fleet – characters who provided inspiration, perspective and colour. My methodology in constructing the core of the story relating to the voyage was to compare and contrast the individual journal entries so I could form a picture of a particular day or moment; then render that with my own sailor's perspective (or creative licence). Of considerable benefit to my writing was Jacob

Nagel's journal held by the State Library of New South Wales, which was edited by John C. Dann and published by New York's Grove Press (1988); and Governor Arthur Phillip's own documents. This situation might be compared with an artist blending colours – I had the formality of Phillip's account and the salty-seadog yarn from Nagle.

I acknowledge the critical role of the State Library of New South Wales and its magnificent First Fleet collection in the creation of this work. Of the contemporary records which survive documenting the First Fleet, the original private-manuscript journals written by those who actually sailed with the expedition occupy a central place in the library's collection; and we can all enjoy access to them via the web. The library proudly holds the world's largest collection of original First Fleet journals and correspondence. Of the eleven known journal manuscripts, nine are held in the Mitchell and Dixson Library collections of the State Library of New South Wales (sl.nsw.gov. au), including those by John Hunter, Second Captain; Philip Gidley King, Second Lieutenant; William Bradley, First Lieutenant; Jacob Nagle, a seaman; and George Worgan, surgeon, all serving on the *Sirius*; Ralph Clark, Second Lieutenant of Marines on the *Friendship*; James Scott, Sergeant of Marines on the *Prince of Wales*; John Easty, Marine private on the *Scarborough*; and Arthur Bowes Smyth, surgeon on the *Lady Penrhyn*. All give insights into shipboard life, the convicts, officers and crew, ports of call, discipline, injuries and deaths, and daily life in the colony. My book reflects the collective and enduring legacy of their accounts.

Many of the original published journals and accounts of the day can also be enjoyed as free e-books on Project Gutenberg (gutenberg.net.au/first-fleet.html). I particularly relied on the works of Arthur Phillip, *The Voyage of Governor Phillip to Botany Bay with an Account of the Establishment of the Colonies of Port Jackson and Norfolk Island*, London (1789) – this book includes the journals of Lieutenants Shortland, Watts and Ball and Captain Marshall; George Burnett Barton, *History of*

New South Wales from the Records Vol. 1 (1889); David Collins, *An Account of the English Colony in New South Wales*, Vol. 1, London (1798), and Vol. 2, London (1802); Daniel Southwell, *Journal and Letters of Daniel Southwell* (1893); John White, *Journal of a Voyage to New South Wales* (1790); Watkin Tench, *A Narrative of the Expedition to Botany Bay*, London (1789), and *A Complete Account of the Settlement at Port Jackson*, London (1793).

The writing of history has myriad masters. There is not always consensus. My *First Fleet* does not seek to be the definitive work on the subject. Our understanding of past events is always evolving and being refined and redefined with each published work. I consulted major historical works on the First Fleet, including the recent books of Alan Frost, as well as classics such as Robert Hughes's *The Fatal Shore* and Mollie Gillen's *The Founders of Australia: A Biographical Dictionary of the First Fleet*, which I found valuable and instructive.

Many of the proud First Fleet descendants have painstakingly created comprehensive and generous resources on the web for lovers of genealogy and history alike. The well-presented First Fleet Fellowship website (firstfleetfellowship. org.au) was of considerable assistance, as was research done by the University of Wollongong that led to a compilation of a list of convicts detailing their crimes and sentences (firstfleet.uow. edu.au/download.html).

The *Australian Dictionary of Biography*, produced by the National Centre of Biography at the Australian National University, is Australia's pre-eminent dictionary of national biography. Much of the biographic details on key individuals in this work and my other recent maritime histories were found online at adb.anu.edu.au.

The extraordinary resource of Google Earth, with its satellite images, gave me the added opportunity to check distances between destinations and points of interest and allowed me to 'visit' and appreciate some destinations remotely.

A most unexpected and auspicious moment came early in the project – on a day when I was walking through The Rocks area of Sydney Cove, surveying the scene and imaging what life must have been like back in those early days in 1788. It was a beautiful Sunday morning, and I was standing near the statue of Captain Bligh when I heard a booming male voice expounding some wonderful anecdotes of early Australian history to a small group of people. He was a tour guide, and I was quickly impressed by his presentation and his grasp of the subject. I had to meet him – and I did. His name was Brian McDonald, author of *The Landing Place of Captain Arthur Phillip at Botany Bay*, and a man with a remarkable knowledge of the early days of the settlement, thanks in no small way to having more than 7000 books on Australian history in his private library! We struck up an instant rapport, and he became an invaluable research assistant for me, particularly into the journals themselves – something for which I very much thank him.

Another big asset for the project has been my long-time personal assistant, Liz Christmas – a fabulous woman who has been with me through the thick and thin of all four maritime-history book-writing projects ... and we still have a wonderful working relationship! I thank her for her dedication to *The First Fleet*.

I also tender an enthusiastic vote of thanks to the team at HarperCollins Publishers and, more specifically, the ABC Books division. They have been a great team to work with. In particular, I must again recognise Helen Littleton, Publisher, ABC Books, whose encouragement and guidance first steered me towards writing maritime history. Most importantly, her support has been steadfast ever since. Others I must thank are HarperCollins Publishing Director Shona Martyn, senior editor Mary Rennie, editor Jon Gibbs (who smoothed out the bumps in a most impressive fashion), Paul Brunton, for his considered review of the manuscript, Matt Stanton, who delivered the original artwork for the impressive cover, Linda Brainwood, for her picture research, proofreader Pam Dunne, typesetter Graeme Jones, and the entire HCP sales team, particularly Darren, Amy and Kate.

Beyond the publishing house, I must thank the booksellers who have been wonderfully supportive of my books for many years.

Finally, there are my readers who show inspiring interest in my books. To each one of them, and the many, many people who take time to write to me with positive feedback, I say thank you. I hope you now enjoy this voyage with *The First Fleet*.

Rob Mundle, 2014

THE FIRST FLEET

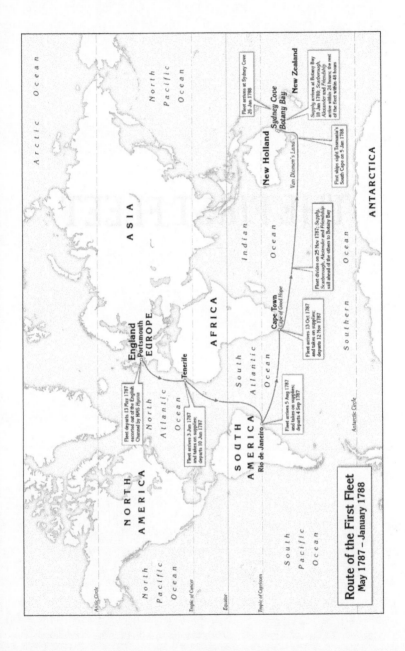

Route of the First Fleet
May 1787 – January 1788

Fleet departs 13 May 1787 escorted out of the English Channel by HMS Hyena

Fleet arrives 3 Jan 1787 and takes on supplies; departs 10 Jun 1787

Fleet arrives 5 Aug 1787 and takes on supplies; departs 4 Sep 1787

Fleet arrives 13 Oct 1787 and takes on supplies; departs 12 Nov 1787

Fleet divides on 25 Nov 1787: Supply, Scarborough, Alexander and Friendship sail ahead of the others to Botany Bay

First ships sight Tasmania's South Cape on 5 Jan 1788

Supply arrives at Botany Bay 18 Jan 1788; Scarborough, Alexander and Friendship arrive within 24 hours; the rest of the fleet within 48 hours

Fleet arrives at Sydney Cove 26 Jan 1788

England
Portsmouth
EUROPE

Tenerife

Rio de Janeiro
SOUTH AMERICA

Cape Town
Cape of Good Hope

AFRICA

ASIA

New Holland
Van Diemen's Land
Sydney Cove
Botany Bay

New Zealand

ANTARCTICA

NORTH AMERICA

Arctic Ocean

North Pacific Ocean

North Atlantic Ocean

South Atlantic Ocean

South Pacific Ocean

Indian Ocean

Southern Ocean

Arctic Circle
Tropic of Cancer
Equator
Tropic of Capricorn
Antarctic Circle

An Unprecedented Mission

The small but stout 75-foot-long, two-masted brig was rolling her way south on the face of full-bodied North Atlantic swells, and as she did, her heavy hull and deck timbers responded rhythmically by giving off subtle creaking sounds in time with the ship's motion. It was like a song of the sea.

Friendship was only a few days into a lengthy passage that had begun on 13 May 1787. She was one of eleven ships in a unique convoy making its way to a remote destination some 17,000 nautical miles away. Sailing conditions were perfect: a strong east-north-easterly wind was propelling the little armada directly down the rhumb line towards the first port of call, Tenerife, then 1200 nautical miles to the south-south-west. At 276 tons, *Friendship* was the smallest of the six transport vessels in the fleet – a fact that required the brig's twenty-man crew to sail her hard if they were to stay in contact with the larger and faster ships. They did not want to be seen as the laggards and cause delays. So, with the wind at the ideal angle, the captain, Francis Walton, had called for every possible stretch of canvas to be set and trimmed for full effect: three square sails on the foremast, two on the mizzen, the spanker, three staysails and the jib.

Before long, while standing alongside the man on the helm, Walton could look aloft with great satisfaction. All sails were billowing and drawing perfectly, and he could sense the strain on the standing rigging, braces and sheets. As a result, his proud little ship was averaging around 5 knots while cutting a swathe of pastel white across a sea that mirrored the hazy grey sky. Any time Walton cast his eye beyond the bulwarks he could see all ten of the other ships, the leaders hull-down on the horizon ahead and others in close proximity.

Apart from some of those on board still struggling to gain their sea legs, and the absence of sunshine, this was a scene that couldn't be bettered. Yet in a matter of hours the situation aboard *Friendship* became unsettled: trouble was already brewing among the scruffy tars of the lower deck. They were threatening to rebel, for reasons that were revealed by one of the ship's two junior officers, Lieutenant Ralph Clark, in his journal: 'the Seamen refused to do their duty on Account of their Provisions – the complaint was that they would have two pounds of Beef a day [instead] of having 1½ pound which is at present a half a pound a day more than we are allowed ...'

Unbeknown to Captain Walton and his officers, the basis for this mini uprising had nothing to do with the men being underfed. This disgruntled lot were objecting to the level of their rations purely because of promises they had made to others on board, when the fleet was lying at anchor on the Motherbank off Portsmouth.

Days before departure, while crammed into their dingy sleeping quarters near the ship's forepeak, more than ten of the tars had decided to implement a plan. They knew there was a prize to be won aft of the bulkhead separating their stale-aired digs from another compartment on the lower deck, and they wanted it. In sailors' jargon, it was 'baggage' – hussies – and they were there for the taking.

Using what tools they could find – some lifted from the nearby bosun's locker – the men began to carefully, and as quietly as possible, prise away from the overhead deck beam the vertical planks that formed the bulkhead.

Initially, the twenty-one women who were imprisoned in the dank, dark and unsanitary compartment wondered what was causing the unusual noises. There was a high-pitched, screeching sound as each of the fang-like heavy iron nails was gradually wrenched out from the solid oak deck beam. Soon enough, after the first plank had been pulled away, the women wondered no more.

The men needed to remove only four planks before they had a gap wide enough to squeeze through. Once inside the section beyond, they peered through the dim light, scanning the pitiful-looking women in search of a desirable prospect.

There was little or no resistance from the majority of the poor wretches, whose attire reflected their plight: tattered and filthy ankle-length woollen dresses, and little else. Certainly not 'drawers' – they wouldn't become a common form of underwear for women in Britain for another forty years.

Some of the women saw the opportunity of this invasion. Certainly, they had nothing to lose by 'entertaining' the tars. The 'return for services rendered', they calculated, would come in the form of better food, and in greater quantity.

Among the youthful, and not-so-youthful, sailors, 'Come here, lassie' was likely to have been the demand when a gap-toothed tar grabbed the unkempt hair of a chosen one. Some of the women protested on being selected. Yet they were soon seen to be disappearing through the gap in the bulkhead and out into the sailors' quarters, there to participate in the inevitable debauchery.

These easy targets aboard *Friendship* were no ordinary women. They were among the fleet's total of 775 convicts – 582 men and 193 women (the numbers are disputed among historians) – being exiled to a place virtually unknown to Europeans. It was a destination so alien that they may as well have been voyaging to a distant planet. During the preceding few weeks, the convicts had been locked aboard some of the eleven ships making up what would become known as 'the First Fleet' – the first to sail out of England bound for a foreign region

in the southern hemisphere, a large portion of which, just sixteen
years earlier, had been registered as a discovery by a European.

One could easily believe that the majority of convicts were
hardened criminals, simply because of the extreme nature of
their punishment – transportation – but that was not generally
the case. The worst of the offenders in British jails were
hanged with little hesitation. Most of the detainees aboard the
ships of the First Fleet had committed – sometimes on
numerous occasions – only petty crimes by today's standards.
Even so, the laws at the time saw them generally sentenced to
servitude of either seven years, fourteen years or life,
depending on the crime, or crimes.

In addition to being victims of Britain's extremely harsh
criminal laws, they were now facing another form of
purgatory: being consigned to a place so isolated that they
were unlikely to ever return home. For some, the prospect was
little different from the death penalty.

The man appointed by the British Government to lead the
fleet and become 'Governor and Commander in Chief of the
territory of New South Wales' was Captain Arthur Phillip, a
highly respected Royal Navy officer who, while being
recognised as a strict disciplinarian, was also a fair-minded and
practical man. He had been well briefed by the government
and the navy on the designs for the establishment of this far-
off outpost that would stand under the British flag. But not
even he could have imagined the magnitude of the trials that
would confront his expedition.

Unsurprisingly, given the lack of precedent for such an
assignment, problems had begun to arise before the First Fleet
departed from England. Aside from the debauchery aboard
Friendship, another disruptive element during their time at the
anchorage had made its presence felt on the very day the lead
ship, *Sirius*, signalled for all to hoist sail and depart –
12 May 1787. As recalled by the colony's future surgeon-
general, John White, the signal came, only for 'several of the

convoy [to be seen] not getting under way, through some irregularity in the seamen'. The ships that 'occasioned the detention' of the other vessels, White's journal continued, had not made sail for one reason: alcohol. Having no doubt smuggled the grog aboard, the crews were so drunk, they couldn't man their ships.

So, with the light breeze they'd been experiencing then on the wane, Captain Phillip had no alternative but to accept that his voyage had made a false start. The convoy was forced to remain at anchor overnight, still within sight of the Mother Bank – waiting both for a new breeze and for the drunks to sober up.

There was another, more serious, threat sweeping through one of the transport ships, *Scarborough*, although its presence would only become apparent when the flotilla was well into the Atlantic. As this vessel lay idling off Portsmouth, some of the convicts on board were developing a clandestine plan – a mutiny! Their intention was to overthrow the captain and crew once the ship was on the high seas, take charge and make good an escape to a secret destination.

At daybreak on 13 May, the signal to sail was again hoisted aboard *Sirius*. Before long the entire fleet was clear of the Mother Bank, easing its way out of the Solent and on to the waters of the English Channel by riding a favourable breeze and tide. It was an exciting time for those who had the good fortune to be on deck on any one of the eleven ships, as they watched the Isle of Wight dissolve into the distance over the stern, no doubt wondering at the same time what destiny held for them: success or failure?

For the hundreds of convicts, literally caged in their specially built claustrophobic cells below deck and suffering in conditions that were as gloomy as those in the jails from whence they came, there was no chance to view the outside world. The only way these wretched souls knew that they were departing was from hearing orders bellowed from the quarterdeck, responses from the crew, followed by the rigorous sounds associated with sails and rigging being readied. Then, after the huge cast-iron anchor had been raised to the cathead and secured, there came the change in motion of the ship – they were underway.

Once out in the Channel, the effects of the swells soon made matters increasingly worse for the majority of those in confinement. Most had never been aboard a ship, let alone at sea. So, as Captain Walton on deck of *Friendship* surveyed the six transport vessels rising and falling in time with the roll of the waves, the consequences of seasickness were adding to the already putrid stench the convicts below had to endure. The bad news for those suffering from mal de mer was that there were 17,000 nautical miles to go, and only one solution: get used to the motion, because there was no stopping it.

Any hope the tars and tarts on board *Friendship* had held that news of their impropriety days ago would not reach the ears of the officers on the quarterdeck had proved to be hopelessly fanciful. The identity of some of the female participants had become known to the ship's officers and they duly received punishment, as the puritanical Ralph Clark recorded in his journal:

> Captain [James] Meredith [the captain of the Marines]
> put the four Convict women Elizabeth Dudgeon,
> Margaret Hall, Elizabeth Pulley and Charlotte Ware
> out of Irons whom I had put in Irons on the 9 of this
> month for fighting. There was never greater whores
> living than they are, the four of them that Went
> through the Bulkhead while we lay at the Mother
> Bank. I am convinced they will not be long out of
> them [irons] … they are a disgrace to their Whole Sex,
> B[itches] that they are. I wish all the Women Were out
> of the Ship.

The penalties dispensed to the women were not harsh by the day's standards, however in this circumstance the tars, who had initiated the debauchery, escaped scot-free. Even so, the reason for the women being punished, and the real purpose behind the tars' demands for more beef, quickly filtered through the lower deck of the ship. Their appetite was carnal and not motivated by hunger – '… the men demanding more beef on a pretext that it was for them'. According to Clark, they had informed the ship's master that they would refuse 'to do their duty on Account of their Provisions'. On hearing this, Phillip sent an officer on board to hear the men's complaint, which was 'that the[y] would have two pounds of Beef a day [instead of] having 1½ pound which is at present a half a pound a day more than we are allowed'. But the tars had no argument when they were advised that seamen aboard all other transports were content with the 1½ pound ration, so they resumed their duties.

Clark's opinion of the men he was confined to a vessel with was low, but his opinion of the women was damning:

> I never met with a parcel of more discontent fellows in my life. They only want more Provisions to give it to the damned whores, the Convict Women of whom they are very fond Since they broke through the Bulk head and had connection with them – I never could have thought that there were So many abandoned wretches in England, they are ten thousand times worse than the men Convicts, and I am afraid that we will have a great deal more trouble with them …

He was right about the trouble. Not even the risk of severe punishment could stop those either side of the bulkhead from continuing to interrelate. Within days, another four convict women were found 'in the men's place'. This time the men were also caught, the ringleaders being the bosun, a sailor and the steward. All three were flogged, but the women, while harshly punished, escaped the lash, much to Clark's chagrin. '[The] four Women were to be kept in Irons all the Way,' he wrote. 'If I had been the Commander I Should have flogged the four Whores also.'

A teetotaller, Clark obviously resented the women, blaming them for encouraging the intimate liaisons with the crewmen. His journal reveals a man challenged by circumstances that were unique – as they were for all the souls upon the ships that made up this Fleet. From the day of departure through to the end of the voyage and beyond, he was a desperately homesick man who pined for his wife and young son. He kissed a small oval portrait of 'Betsey Alicia' every Sunday, and declared his undying love for her. During the journey on his third wedding anniversary, when there was no sign of a promotion coming his way, he lamented: 'All the gains on earth should never have made me leave … my dear beloved Alicia and sweet boy.'

But despite 25-year-old Clark's sanctimonious attitude, his self-righteousness was eventually eroded by the proximity of the convict women. He was as susceptible as any tar. Having repeatedly condemned both women and men aboard *Friendship* for their lasciviousness and infidelity, Clark himself formed an alliance with a twenty-year-old convict woman, Mary Branham, transported for stealing. She would bear him a daughter, which the couple named … Alicia.

Such human elements were only part of this speculative and ground-breaking venture. Before anything else, Captain Arthur Phillip's greatest challenge, and that of all the sailors, was to safely guide this small fleet of ships across a massive expanse of ocean which at times could be enraged by violent storms, and at other times mired in oily, mind-bending calms. Phillip also knew that once they were out of the Atlantic and around the Cape of Good Hope, the ships could face the supreme test – the little-travelled, always-treacherous Southern Ocean, where storms mustered in hell can deliver one giant wave holding the power to engulf an entire ship.

Botany Bay could not come soon enough …

CHAPTER 1

A Case of Ready, Fire, Aim

In London in 1789, little more than a year after the First Fleet arrived at Sydney Cove, John Stockdale published an acclaimed account of the establishment of the new colony, based on detailed reports from Governor Phillip and the journals of high-ranking officers who had accompanied him. In it Stockdale noted:

> To New South Wales England has the claim which a
> tacit consent has generally made decisive among the
> European States, that of prior discovery. The whole of
> that Eastern coast, except the very Southern point,
> having been untouched by any navigator, till it was
> explored by Captain Cook. This consideration, added
> to the more favourable accounts given of this side of the
> continent than of the other, was sufficient to decide the
> choice of the British government, in appointing a place
> for the banishment of a certain class of criminals.

The reference to 'that Eastern coast ... having been untouched by any navigator, till it was explored by Captain Cook' has been the fuel for hot debate throughout the ensuing centuries. There have been strong suggestions that three Portuguese caravels under the leadership of naval officer

Cristóvão de Mendonça sailed the east coast of New Holland between 1521 and 1524. But it was James Cook who laid claim to the coast on Wednesday, 22 August 1770. That was the day he stepped into *Endeavour*'s pinnace and was rowed ashore to a small island – Possession Island – near the tip of Cape York. Once there, as he later described the moment in his journal, he 'hoisted English Colours, and in the Name of His Majesty King George the Third took possession of the whole Eastern coast ... to this place by the Name of New Wales together with all the Bays, Harbours, Rivers, and Islands, situate upon the said Coast; after which we fired 3 Volleys of small Arms, which were answered by the like number from the Ship.'

The following year, having completed this spectacularly successful voyage of exploration, Cook and 26-year-old Joseph Banks, who led a small party of naturalists and scientific men on the voyage, delivered a mass of information to the British Government, the Royal Navy, and the Royal Society of London for Improving Natural Knowledge. Among these reports were full details of remarkable unknown lands, of new flora and fauna, much of which redefined the way even the most learned minds viewed the world in the late eighteenth century.

Cook had named the lengthy coastline that he had claimed in the name of King George III New Wales. (In his journal, 'New South Wales' is written over an erasure. The change was probably made at least two months after he made the initial entry.) The near 2500-mile tract of land was believed to be an extension of a coast that Dutch explorer Abel Tasman had stumbled across and laid claim to on behalf of the Netherlands in December 1642. It became known as Van Diemen's Land, later Tasmania, while Cook referred to his discovery as being part of New Holland.

Cook believed he had discovered a significant inlet on the coast of New Holland, and Banks would later assert that it might be suitable for a settlement, should the British

Government decide to take possession of this land. Cook named it Stingray Harbour, but, as revealed in the journal compiled by him following his return, it too went through a series of name changes. Stingray Harbour was crossed out, as was Botanist Harbour, then Botany Harbour, before the great Yorkshireman settled on Botany Bay.

Incredibly, there was no immediate surge of enthusiasm within the establishment – government or naval, at least – for a follow-up expedition to the new-found territories; no consideration was given to establishing a human presence and thereby taking the high ground for Britain in this region on the far side of the globe. The primary reason for this lack of interest was that, more than 3000 nautical miles to the west of England, the American colonies continued to be the focal point for British occupation. Since 1619, during the reign of James I, these colonies had served as a convenient dumping ground for the men and women spilling from the homeland's over-burdened jails, convicts who then provided much-needed slave labour in the new settlements. It was a highly beneficial deal for the government: as well as being able to dispose of the unwanted social surplus, the sale of convicts into slave labour in America, at £20 each, benefited England's public purse by the considerable amount of £40,000 per annum.

Not surprisingly, though, with self-belief and a national identity emerging across the thirteen American states, many of the locals were tiring of their country being a destination of convenience for England's legal system. This was reflected in the writings of two unidentified colonists during the 1750s. One wrote that 'America has been made the very common sewer and dung yard to Britain', while the other penned: 'Very surprising, one would think, that thieves, burglars, pickpockets and cutpurses, and a herd of the most flagitious banditti upon earth, should be sent as agreeable companions to us!'

Such attitudes were causing growing concern in London, and it seemed there was no stopping it. Before long, an even greater level of unrest became embedded in American society as patriots began mentioning 'independence' in less than whispered tones. By then, there was nothing the British could do to stop it: the ripple had grown into a tidal wave of discontent. A fight by the colonists for sovereignty was looming.

In a broad sense, the inevitable American War of Independence, or the American Revolutionary War, came as a consequence of an event that history records as the Boston Tea Party, in December 1773. At the time, the British Government was struggling financially and had decided that one way to ease the monetary malaise would be to have the thirteen American colonies contribute to the costs of maintaining their own defence force via taxes. One such tax emerged under the *Tea Act*, which was implemented that year.

Parliament was adamant that it had the right to impose such a tax on the importation of tea to America, but American colonists in Massachusetts' principal city soon demonstrated their disagreement, and in spectacular fashion. In a well-planned protest on 16 December, members of the Boston-based Sons of Liberty disguised themselves as American Indians and boarded a number of ships that had arrived in port carrying a cargo of tea, the import price of which included the new tax levy. Having taken control of the vessels, the Sons of Liberty entered the ships' holds and lugged the 340 chests containing the tea onto the deck, before dumping them over the bulwarks and into the harbour. The entire cargo weighed 46 tons and, according to the East India Company that shipped it, was worth £9659, 6 shillings and 4 pence – some AU$750,000 in today's currency.

The Americans had pulled the trigger, but the British Government quickly hit back where it hurt most: local commerce was stopped, and self-government in Massachusetts was abolished. The town was then placed under the control of the British Army, with General Thomas Gage as governor. The patriots realised that their only remaining option was to fight for their rights via a rebellion, which duly started in early 1775, near Boston. Their proclamation was clear: they declared themselves 'free and independent states absolved from all allegiance to, or dependence upon, the crown and parliament of Great Britain'.

Initially, it was a battle between American patriots and the British Army, which was strengthened by colonial loyalists. The conflict eventually became a world war, as support for the American colonies, through the supply of weapons and ammunition, came furtively and progressively from France, the Netherlands, Spain, and the Kingdom of Mysore in India. It was only when France became directly involved, by sending military manpower, that the tide of battle turned in favour of the Americans. The ensuing victory was officially recognised with the signing of the Treaty of Paris in September 1783, as part of the Peace of Paris.

The war had a profound impact on world history, channelling it in different directions on both sides of the Atlantic and beyond. It was a watershed moment: the victory by the patriots entitled them to become masters of their own destiny, while the loss for Britain would all too quickly create a crisis of epic proportions. Critically, the British no longer had an easily accessed foreign destination for their unwanted felons, since America had all but closed its ports to convict transport ships. Consequently, England's jails were swamped, as the nation's harsh judicial system continued to ensure that over 150 capital offences could result in the sentence of transportation.

The legislation that sanctioned transportation – to America, the West Indies and Canada – had been introduced when Britain's parliament passed its 1717 Act *For the Further Preventing of Robbery, Burglary and Other Felonies, and For the More Effectual Transportation of Felons, and Unlawful Exporters of Wool; and For the Declaring the Law upon Some Points Relating to Pirates*. It was soon better known as the *Transportation Act*, or *Piracy Act*.

Implementation had been almost immediate. On 23 April 1718, a session of the Old Bailey saw twenty-seven of fifty-one people convicted of crimes sentenced to transportation. Over the next fifty-eight years, until the defeat of the British on American soil, some 50,000 convicts were shipped across the Atlantic to serve sentences of either seven or fourteen years or life. This number represented a quarter of all British migrants into America during that century.

Until midway through the eighteenth century, the prison system in Britain had polarised into two forms. Outside the major towns, there were what could best be described as 'correction houses'. Many of these jails in the counties and shires were privately owned, but they came under the control of justices of the peace. They were the places of incarceration for felons guilty of minor crimes, such as stealing a handkerchief. The worst offenders, including those sentenced to be hanged, were accommodated in government-run institutions in the major centres. At the end of the American War of Independence, the most notorious jail of all, and the largest, was Newgate Prison in London, which became the venue for public hangings from 1783 onwards. For more than 200 years before then, executions had been carried out at Tyburn, near Marble Arch. At both locations, hangings were public spectacles, where thousands of people might gather to cheer and jeer at the proceedings. Resourceful locals built tiered timber seating and charged a fee to those wanting the best view, or, to use colloquialisms of the day, to see the convicted 'dance the Tyburn jig' or 'go up a ladder to bed'.

Before the change of venue, prisoners sentenced to be executed were transported in ox-drawn carts from Newgate to Tyburn, where, on a 'busy' day, three felons could be simultaneously hanged. An unenviable record was set on 23 June 1649 when twenty-three male and one female convict went to their deaths in a mass hanging. On 17 January 1776, an estimated 30,000 people were at the Marble Arch site to see twin brothers Daniel and Robert Perreau hanged for forgery, a crime that a vast number of Londoners believed they did not commit.

The combination of executions and transportation to foreign shores had traditionally kept England's prison population at a maintainable level. But while the powerful victory by the Americans brought one of those avenues to an abrupt dead end, it didn't stop the courts handing down sentences of transportation at a rapid rate. With nowhere to send the convicts there was a need to find at least 1000 additional places each year within the local prison system – an impossibility. In no time, the jails were filling up tight with convicts, crushed together in damp, cold, dark and disease-ridden stone dungeons. The fact that typhus was rampant caused the authorities little concern.

Building new prisons was not an option for His Majesty's government, since that would take too long and cost too much. A temporary solution came in the form of prison hulks: obsolete, decommissioned merchant and naval vessels that were converted into floating prisons. With masts and rigging removed, crude and cramped cells were built in the ships' 'tween-deck areas, some allowing a headroom of just 4 feet 6 inches. Intended as merely a stopgap measure, this solution provided the parliamentarians with time in which to find an alternative to America. Prison ships were duly legalised, initially for two years – and they would still be employed eighty years later, for what was described as 'the more severe and effectual punishment of atrocious and daring offenders'.

Confining prisoners to hulks was not really a new method of incarceration for the British. Sixteen British ships had been used on New York's East River to house prisoners captured by the British during the War of Independence. Official records confirm that more than 11,500 male and female prisoners died while being held aboard these ships during the conflict, a figure that equated to more than the entire American loss of life in all the battles during that war. What was new was the squalid presence of the hulks on the Thames around London initially, and later in other port towns, Plymouth in particular.

Meanwhile, the search for an alternative offshore destination for convicts sentenced to transportation was accelerated. A critical factor influencing the cash-strapped government was that it had thus far been more expensive to imprison convicts aboard the hulks than to simply ship them away from England, sell them into slave labour, and virtually forget them. The predicament was compounded by lawmakers who were forever increasing the number of crimes attracting the death penalty. In 1776, under what was commonly known as the Bloody Code, there were 220 crimes that carried capital punishment as a sentence – a fourfold increase in less than a century. Those sentenced to hanging had committed crimes such as pilfering goods worth more than 5 shillings, thieving from a rabbit warren, or stealing an animal. It was only when the King commuted the sentence that the convict was reprieved – to face transportation.

At the root of much of the apparent lawlessness in Britain was the Industrial Revolution. This began in England around 1760, and a decade later its influence was dramatically changing everyday life. Large factories were being built in major towns, and within them mechanical contraptions, most hissing and belching steam, were proving far more efficient than the labour-intensive methods used in cottage industries across the country. Inevitably, the opportunity for employment drew the masses towards London and other towns where the factories were located. It was like a gold rush, but the efficiencies delivered by the machines did not provide sufficient employment opportunities for the swelling masses. For the first six decades of the eighteenth century, England's population had grown at a very slow rate; in 1760 it was calculated to be around 7 million, some 740,000 of which lived in London. Ten years later, the lure of mechanisation saw tens of thousands travelling to the capital by horse, carriage or foot, but as there weren't enough jobs for everyone, the unemployed were all too often driven to crime in order to survive. Adding to this social calamity in the period following the end of the American War of Independence, 100,000 young sailors and soldiers had been discharged from service, many of whom were unable to find work.

Not to be underestimated either, at a time when law-breaking constituted the most trifling of misdemeanours, law enforcement was a far from exact science. After all, there was no police force per se in England until 1829, when the passing of Sir Robert Peel's *Metropolitan Police Act* led to the creation of a paid force. In the 1770s, policing was a hotchpotch of uncoordinated activities devoid of any real investigative capabilities. Those charged with enforcing the law were generally volunteer parish constables appointed by the village, or justices of the peace in the larger towns. Through a lack of efficiency and no real need for accurate evidence inside the courtroom, it was not unusual for someone to be found guilty on the word of someone who simply stood before the court and alleged that the accused had committed a crime.

Initially it was hoped that the logical new home for Britain's unwanted could be 'somewhere' on the Atlantic coast of Africa, where small numbers of convicts had been sent over previous years. This program proved far from successful, but, regardless, the pressure on the jails in England led to more than 700 convicts being sent to that part of the world in 1775. It would prove a disastrous exercise: the stifling African climate was unbearable and the land proved hostile to habitation by the fair-skinned English. In what was a shocking waste of human life, 334 of the 746 convicts consigned to the African settlement between that year and 1776 died, while another 271 escaped – obviously desperate to give themselves some chance of survival. No records have been found that account for the remaining 141.

That did not mean the end of the exercise. A small number continued to flow there, but by early 1785, the number of prisoners being sentenced to transportation far outweighed the number actually being sent there. Not surprisingly, parliament was awash in a sea of frustration and often the scene of uproar, such as when prominent Whig politician Edmund Burke took centre stage in the House of Commons and derided the government for its treatment of the convicts. He said: 'The merciful gallows of England would rid them of their lives in a far less dreadful manner, than the climate or the savages of Africa would take them …'

This was surely to put the cart before the horse.

The unviable situation continued until April 1785, when it was announced that a 36-member committee would be formed under the chairmanship of Francis Seymour-Conway, Lord Beauchamp, to consider all options, including two new destinations on the west coast of Africa. The decision to consider these two possibilities came under attack in a report in the *Daily Universal* newspaper, which raised alarm about the African solution, in particular in Gambia. The article stated that on one island in Gambia there were 'warlike Negroes who eat white people'.

The article had little effect. Plans were made for the sloop *Nautilus* to be sent to Das Voltas Bay, in Namibia, and a location on the Gambia River, 'in order to find out an eligible situation for the reception of the said convicts, where, from their industry, they might soon be likely to obtain means of subsistence'. The sloop returned to England in September 1785 with news the committee did not want to hear. The many parts of the coast that had been examined were found to be sandy, barren and unsuitable for the desired type of settlement.

What next? Botany Bay.

American-born James Matra was probably the strongest advocate for New South Wales as a solution to the nation's transportation crisis. He had been a midshipman aboard *Endeavour* when Cook explored the east coast of New Holland. While the ship was being guided north, the lookout perched high up the mainmast alerted the captain to what appeared to be the entrance to a large bay – a rarity over the 300 or so nautical miles they had covered so far on this uncharted shore. Cook had responded by ordering a change of course to the north-west, hoping that this would prove to be a safe anchorage.

It was 29 April 1770 (28 April ship time) when *Endeavour* entered the bay and the captain called for the best bower to be released. Simultaneously, men aloft and others on deck lowered, hauled up or furled the sails, and with that, Europeans established the first known contact with this part of the world.

The ten-gun bark lay at anchor for a week on the wide expanse of water, which the captain would eventually name Botany Bay. Much of that time was spent exploring to some degree, but not extensively. On departure, Cook described the bay as 'capacious, safe, and Commodious'. The naturalist on the voyage, Joseph Banks, and Matra (who became a lifelong friend of Banks as a consequence of this expedition), would later agree that the region offered the potential to support a foreign outpost for Britain, and might also be a suitable site for a penal settlement, should that need ever arise.

Persistent northerly winds had caused *Endeavour* to remain holed up in the bay for longer than desired. This was frustrating for Cook, as he was already under the pressure of time: he needed to sail to the north as quickly as possible in order to catch favourable weather through to Batavia, in present-day Indonesia. Once there, supplies would be replenished and much-needed maintenance work carried out on the ship.

One can only wonder what might have happened if time had allowed him to explore an inlet that was sighted soon after they sailed out of Botany Bay. Just 10 nautical miles to the north, Cook observed and named Port Jackson as *Endeavour* glided along on a gentle south-easterly breeze. Had he sent out one of the ship's boats to investigate what stood beyond the two towering sandstone edifices marking the entrance to this waterway, the party would have returned with the news that they'd just discovered one of the finest harbours known to man – and Cook would no doubt have stopped there to explore. Should that have occurred, he almost certainly would have suggested that the government move to put this harbour

under the British Jack by establishing a colony there. As fate
would have it, Port Jackson remained nothing more than one
of the hundreds of names on the charts Cook created on this
voyage. This magnificent harbour would stay unknown to the
outside world for another eighteen years.

Among his positive impressions of Botany Bay, however,
Banks is reported to have advised parliamentarians that the
climate and soil there were most suitable for a settlement,
adding that it could become self-sufficient in a very short time.
One century after the arrival of the First Fleet, Australian
barrister-at-law, and noted journalist and author, George
Burnett Barton wrote of Banks' favourable comments regarding
Botany Bay:

> ... there would be little probability of any opposition
> from the natives, as during his stay there in the year
> 1770 he saw very few, and did not think there were
> above fifty in all the neighbourhood ... he apprehended
> [the climate] was similar to that about Toulouse, in the
> south of France ... the proportion of rich soil was
> sufficient to support a very large number of people;
> there were no beasts of prey, and he did not doubt but
> our sheep and oxen, if carried there, would thrive and
> increase; there was great quantity of fish. The grass was
> long and luxuriant, and there were some eatable
> vegetables; the country was well supplied with water;
> there was abundance of timber and fuel, sufficient for
> any number of buildings which might be found
> necessary.

Nevertheless, it was Matra who truly championed the idea of
establishing a colony there. In 1783, with the full support of
Joseph Banks, he presented a powerful case to the government,
declaring that Botany Bay would be a most suitable destination
for transported convicts. Barton noted that the proposal, dated
23 August, entitled the 37-year-old to receive 'the credit of

having made the first formal proposal for the colonisation of New South Wales; and there is little doubt that, although the project he submitted to the Government ... was not adopted in its original form, the ultimate scheme carried out by the Pitt ministry was elaborated from the materials which he had put together'.

Matra's proposal was well received by the government, and both he and Banks appeared before the Beauchamp committee. When asked by the committee if he thought that a settlement at Botany Bay could proceed without further examination, Matra replied that he was so confident, he would be prepared to act in the colony as 'an officer under the Government to be the Conductor and Governor'. He added that Botany Bay was suited to be either a stand-alone British colony or a colony for convicts.

Matra's cause was well supported by Banks. He confirmed to Lord Beauchamp that of all the places they had visited aboard *Endeavour*, the eastern coast of New South Wales was the most suitable for the establishment of a colony, and on that coast, Botany Bay provided the best opportunity for a settlement.

Possibly through his association with Banks, Matra had well-established political connections, such that from 1778 to 1780 he served as secretary to the British Embassy in Constantinople (present-day Istanbul). Back home in 1783, he strengthened the merit of his suggestions by playing the Banks card: Matra made certain that all relevant Members of Parliament knew that one of their great supporters, the influential Joseph Banks, was also one of his. This sphere of influence continued with the change of government in December that year, when William Pitt the Younger became prime minister.

It was the Home Office Secretary in the Pitt government, Lord Sydney, who was given the responsibility for orchestrating the plan to settle convicts at Botany Bay, but only after it had taken a circuitous course through official channels. Sydney put the initial proposal, based on Matra's plan, to the First Lord of the Admiralty, Lord Howe – who rejected it with the words: 'The length of the navigation, subject to all the retardments of an India voyage, [does] not, I must confess, encourage me to hope for a return of the many advantages, in commerce or war, which Mr. Matra has in contemplation.'

Undeterred, Matra pressed on. Before long, he had found support from another highly regarded senior officer in the Royal Navy, Sir George Young. The latter agreed with Matra's outline, so took it upon himself to assist by rewriting the proposal using prose of a more official style, and presenting the new document direct to Lord Sydney.

The main points in this proposal were as follows:

1. The geographical position of the country placed it within easy communication with the Spanish settlements in South America on the one hand, and with China, the Spice Islands and the Cape of Good Hope on the other. In addition to the facilities for extensive trade thus disclosed, should war break out between England and Spain, English ships would have the immense advantage of a great naval station in the South Seas.

2. The variety of soil and climate within the territory would not only enable the colonists to produce almost all the products being traded among European nations at that time, but lead to 'the great probability of finding in such an immense country metals of every kind'.

3. The settlement of what Young termed this 'territory so happily situated' would establish 'a very extensive commerce', as well as 'greatly increase our shipping and number of seamen'. In addition to many other products, the New Zealand flax plant might be largely cultivated, and by that means the Royal Navy might be rendered independent of Russia for its supply of cordage and canvas.

4. Rather than the colony 'depopulate the parent State', future settlers would be principally collected from the Friendly Islands and China. The only men required from England would be a few skilled workmen, who might be drawn from the ships sent out on service.

5. The thousands of American colonists who had been loyal to the Crown in the War of Independence would find in New South Wales 'a fertile, healthy soil, far preferable to their own', where they might be established 'with a greater prospect of success than in any other place hitherto pointed out for them'.

6. The expense involved in carrying out this plan could not exceed the nominal sum of £3000, since crews of ships-of-war might be as cheaply fed and paid in the South Seas as in the British Channel.

7. The expense of transporting felons might be considerably reduced by sending them to the new territory, while the danger of their returning from it would be much less than in the case of other countries. The transportation might be cheaply carried out by means of the China ships of the East India Company, which, by altering their route after leaving the Cape of Good Hope, could land the felons on the coast of New South Wales, and then proceed to their destination.

There were other suggestions put forward for consideration. After reaching the settlement, one of the ships could be dispatched to New Caledonia, Otaheite (Tahiti), and the neighbouring islands, 'to procure a few families thence, and as many women as may serve for the men left behind'. That was a concept for the colony that did not meet with the approval of its future governor, Arthur Phillip, who suggested: 'it would answer no other purpose than that of bringing them to pine away in misery'. Joseph Banks suggested that China might also be considered as a source for new settlers, while Matra, no doubt influenced by his American heritage, supported the idea that Botany Bay could also serve as an asylum for the American colonists who had remained loyal to the Crown during the war, and had been pilloried in their homeland as a consequence. He envisioned these people forming a significant part of the foundation of the population of New South Wales. It was stated that many loyalists who had been consulted on this matter supported it, yet the anticipated migration never happened.

The government process for approving the settlement at Botany Bay was slow. It was not until 18 August 1786 that an official resolution was announced. It came in a letter from Lord Sydney to the Lords of the Treasury. The missive detailed the King's desires – as suggested to him by Prime Minister Pitt.

His Majesty … has been pleased to signify to me his royal commands that measures should immediately be pursued for sending out of his kingdom such of the convicts as are under sentence or order of transportation.

His Majesty has thought it advisable to fix upon Botany Bay, situated on the coast of New South Wales, in the latitude of about 33° south, which, according to the accounts given by the late Captain Cook, as well as the representations of persons who accompanied him during his last voyage, and who have been consulted upon the subject, is looked upon as a place likely to answer the above purposes.

I am therefore commanded to signify to your lordships His Majesty's pleasure that you do forthwith take such measures as may be necessary for providing a proper number of vessels for the conveyance of seven hundred and fifty convicts to Botany Bay, together with

> such provisions, necessaries, and implements for
> agriculture as may be necessary for their use after their
> arrival.

The announcement was well received across London, and especially by opponents of the 'sinks of iniquity' – the prison hulks on the Thames. One such voice was former Lord Mayor Richard Clark, who wrote to his friend the highly respected philosopher and social reformer Jeremy Bentham with news of the plan: 'Government has just determined to send off seven hundred convicts to New South Wales – where a fort is to be built – and that a man has been found who will take upon him the command of this rabble ...'

The historical declaration by King George III would extend well beyond those original parameters: it would see more than 163,000 convicts transported to the mainland, Van Diemen's Land and Norfolk Island over a period of eighty years. Notably absent from the declaration was any reference to the establishment of a military outpost in the region, or to the opportunities that might come through improved trade with the East. But they were surely behind it. This undertaking was also about establishing a British presence in the region, with some cheap labour.

Home Office Secretary Lord Sydney (Thomas Townshend) was given responsibility for orchestrating the plan to settle convicts at Botany Bay. He was honoured in the naming of the new penal settlement after him, as well as Sydney in Nova Scotia, Canada. Dixson Galleries, State Library of New South Wales DG214 / a5062002.

CHAPTER 2

The Spy Who Came in from the Sea

The Botany Bay decision remained controversial, among the public and in print, for decades. Even in 1861 an edition of the London-based quarterly *Meliora* carried a story headlined 'The Early Social State of New South Wales' in which a section relating to the King's pronouncement read:

> Objections were raised. Those who did not mind
> selling them [the convicts as slave labour] in America,
> were shocked at expatriating them to so wild a region
> of savages at the other side of the globe.
>   Yet what else could be done with the unhappy
> wretches, thus festering in loathsome prisons, which
> resounded with shouts of brutal vice, and the fruitless
> wailings of less-hardened ones? Botany Bay was the
> decision.

Another reason behind the plan to ship the convicts to Botany Bay was an issue that had little to do with Britain's domestic problems. It had everything to do with rivalry with the French.

Still smarting from their humiliating loss of territory – primarily Canada – to the British in the Seven Years War, the

French had hoped that by backing the Patriots in the American War of Independence, they would be able to regain some lost land and lost pride. Much to their chagrin, however, when that war ended in 1783, the United States had showed no interest in recognising any alliance with the French, or supporting their expectation for new territories to come under their control. This was an outcome that France was neither anticipating nor able to afford. Under King Louis XVI, they went into the war mired in an economic crisis and emerged from it in an even worse financial position: they had nothing tangible to show for their involvement. They could gloat about backing the side that beat their longtime adversaries, the British, but there were no spoils.

Not surprisingly, the frustrated French populous turned even more strongly against their already unpopular king. For much of Louis' reign, he had been seen as a weak man who was struggling to fulfil the role of monarch, and any support he still enjoyed was being further eroded by the antics of his high-living wife, the Austrian-born Marie Antoinette. The subsequent unrest that flowed across the nation formed much of the foundation for the French Revolution, which would erupt in 1789.

In a desperate bid to placate the people and rebuild his diminishing popularity, the French King and his subordinates formulated a strategy designed to see France achieve a greater level of influence on the shape of the emerging world, and thereby restore some semblance of national pride at home. In addition to ensuring that territories already held – such as Île de France (Mauritius) and Réunion in the Indian Ocean – were protected and developed, the first stage of the plan called for France's navy and military to exert authority over the well-travelled sea routes from Europe, around Africa and to the Far East, where India and China were the emerging centres of commerce. It also entailed taking control of important ports of call along those routes, where navy and merchant ships stopped to replenish their supplies and prepare for the next stage of their voyages to or from the Far East.

Initially, this focus took the French Navy into the South Atlantic, where they made some important gains through either military force or negotiation. They even tried to convince the Dutch that it would be in their best interests to place the most crucial port of all, Cape Town, under French control. The Dutch wanted no part of this, but France still arranged to land 600 troops there with the intention of repelling any bid that the British might make to take the port. It was a showdown that continued through the first half of the 1780s, with Britain growing increasingly wary of the French after intelligence revealed they were disguising warships as commercial vessels, with the intention of establishing a potent naval force in the waters around India. And this was despite an earlier agreement with Britain that neither side would station line-of-battle ships in India.

For the recently appointed Pitt government, concern was further heightened in 1784, as spies in France and the captains of ships sailing the trade routes confirmed the scale of King Louis' expansion. It had the potential to choke the British out of maritime trade in the region. Serious alarm was raised on 5 May when the government received a secret dispatch from the British ambassador in Paris, who advised his superiors that the French plan extended well beyond the boundaries of the existing trade routes and commercial destinations. They were planning to move into the Pacific. The ambassador had learned that the French were preparing to emulate Captain Cook's voyages of discovery to regions either undiscovered or unsettled – which included those known lands in the Pacific claimed by Great Britain. The mission had the financial backing of the French monarch, who very much admired Cook's exploits.

Soon afterwards, British spies reported that preparations for this two-ship expedition were well advanced, and that it was to be led by the highly distinguished navigator Jean-François de Galaup, Comte de Lapérouse. Other intelligence confirmed Britain's suspicions regarding its sovereignty over lands discovered by Cook: the French explorer's instructions directed him to pay particular interest to New Zealand and New Holland. Most specifically, a report reached London on 9 June 1784 that Lapérouse had been instructed to investigate the possibility of establishing a settlement in New Zealand – a base from which timber could then be gathered and shipped to France. The new French doctrine effectively meant that occupation of a land was the only way of laying a genuine claim to it. Simply raising a flag and claiming previously undiscovered lands in the name of one's monarch was no longer valid.

These developments are probably what caused Lord Beauchamp to make a veiled revelation to the parliamentary committee charged with finding a destination for the nation's convicts. Beauchamp alerted his committee members to the fact that a particular 'situation' had arisen that could well impact on the project they were discussing, but he was unable to elaborate any further at that time.

The British had to act. The only way to ensure sovereignty of unoccupied territories such as New Holland was to establish some form of settlement there as soon as possible.

It was 1 August 1785 when the two French expedition ships – Lapérouse's *Boussole*, and *Astrolabe*, which was under the command of Paul Antoine Fleuriot de Langle – executed a difficult passage out of Brest, at the western end of the Channel, and sailed off into the distance. They carried a complement of 225 officers, crew and scientists.

Little more than a year later, King George III confirmed at the opening of parliament in January 1787 that a convict colony would be established at Botany Bay. The outpost was to be founded on the official premise that the felons, male and female, 'having no Hope of returning ... would consider their own Happiness as involved in the Prosperity of the Settlement, and act accordingly'.

With the King' declaration that a little-known place 17,000 nautical miles away by sea would replace the American colonies as the destination for Britain's convicts sentenced to be transported, the government's priority was to find a well-qualified leader as soon as possible. The parliamentarians knew what they wanted: a highly qualified man from the navy or the army who could plan the project, initiate its formation, lead the fleet to the destination and, once there, successfully structure the foundation of the colony.

Lord Sydney coordinated the quest for a suitable candidate, and within a matter of days he was proposing a well-credentialled officer in the Royal Navy for the job – Captain Arthur Phillip.

Support within the government came swiftly also. And among his peers, Phillip's intellect, leadership qualities and ascendency through the ranks of the Royal Navy left little doubt that he was the man for the Botany Bay commission. Lord Howe of the Admiralty commented with some accommodating dissent: 'I cannot say the little knowledge I have of Captain Philips [sic] would have led me to select him for a service of this complicated nature. But as you are satisfied of his ability, and I conclude he will be taken under your direction …'

When Phillip received advice from the Admiralty that he was to command 'a special project' that would take him to the Southern Oceans, he was in France, possibly securing intelligence information for the government. From the moment he received his orders to return to London post haste, however, nothing else mattered.

In early October – less than eight weeks after being recalled – Phillip was home in England, and once there he headed for the Home Office, and the Admiralty at Whitehall. No doubt he strode proudly down the entrance hall attired in full naval uniform, with his tricorn hat locked under his arm, still wondering what this new commission might be and where it would take him.

He did not have to wait long to find out. On 12 October, Phillip was made aware of the directive from His Majesty: 'We, reposing especial trust and confidence in your loyalty, and experience in military affairs, do, by these presents, constitute and appoint you to be said governor of our territory called New South Wales ... from the Northern extremity of the coast called Cape York ... to the Southern extremity ... South Cape.' Of note here is the reference to South Cape. It was the name given to the southernmost point of Van Diemen's Land (Tasmania), indicating the British assumed it was part of the main landmass, an extension of the coastline charted by Cook.

One of Phillip's talents was that he was multilingual, an accomplishment derived from his German-born father, Jacob Phillip, who was a teacher 'of the languages'. His mother, Elizabeth Breach, had previously been married to a Captain John Herbert of the Royal Navy, a relative of the eleventh Earl of Pembroke. Jacob and Elizabeth welcomed Arthur into the world on 11 October 1738, in their small residence in Bread Street, London, just yards from the northern bank of the Thames and less than 2 miles to the north-east of Buckingham House.

Elizabeth had retained strong connections with the navy, which led to Arthur entering the Greenwich School for the Sons of Seamen as a twelve-year-old. Located on the opposite side of the river from the family home, the school groomed boys for life as seafarers, so, at the age of fifteen, he went to sea for the start of his maritime apprenticeship. He was assigned as a cabin boy under Captain Redhead on *Fortune*, a whaling ship that operated in the waters around Greenland, inside the Arctic Circle. It was a brutal initiation for the teenager, but this didn't deter him from wanting to pursue a career within the Royal Navy. He spent a year aboard the whaler, up until the time when friction between England and France led to the outbreak of the Seven Years War in 1756.

In going onto a war footing, the Royal Navy needed to rapidly increase its manpower, so, like thousands of others, young Arthur Phillip was drawn into its ranks. He was placed on the crew manifest of HMS *Buckingham*, a 160-foot

70-gunner, which was commanded by a relative of his, one Captain Everett. His documentation stated he was destined to learn 'the rudiments of his profession under that able officer'.

Buckingham spent a considerable amount of time on patrol in the Mediterranean, ever looking for the opportunity to intercept French ships, and Phillip witnessed first-hand some of the skirmishes that occurred. But it was not until the Siege of Havana in 1762, when he was aboard HMS *Stirling Castle*, that he experienced the real heat of battle.

Britain and Spain were then at war, and with the Cuban town of Havana being home to Spain's strongest military base and naval port, the British instituted a blockade in an attempt to confine a large part of the enemy fleet. Additionally, should the British mount a successful attack on the port, there was treasure for the taking: gold and a wealth of riches from Mexico and South America were aboard the Spanish galleons also riding at anchor in the harbour, which opened to the sea via a narrow mile-long channel.

From March 1762, the battery of British cannons established on land, and those aboard the flotilla of ships forming the blockade, pounded the Spanish stronghold for five months, until the defenders were forced to surrender on 13 August. Victory came at an enormous cost to the British, however, with around 2700 soldiers and sailors either killed, wounded, captured or having deserted during the battle. Worse still, 4708 men had died due to exhaustion as they moved the cumbersome cannons across the island's rocky terrain, or from diseases contracted via the dense swarms of mosquitoes and rat infestations on the ships. Scurvy also contributed to the death toll. For those fortunate enough to survive, there was a significant bonus: a share in 'prize money' that would amount to about £45 million today. Phillip received a lieutenant's share of the booty – £234 13 shillings and 3¾ pence. The reward for the British Government was calculated to be over 1.8 million Spanish pesos, plus treasure valued at 1 million pesos.

The commander of the British squadron, Admiral Sir George Pocock, was considered 'an excellent judge of naval accomplishment'. So it was a high honour for Arthur Phillip when the admiral promoted him to the rank of lieutenant during the campaign. While clearly a standout among his peers, the young sailor would later realise that there was considerably more to this promotion. Sir George had his eye on him for a distinctly clandestine role within the Royal Navy.

Phillip returned to England aboard *Stirling Castle* in 1763, probably around the time that the Treaty of Paris was signed, confirming the cessation of hostilities in the Seven Years War. This formal entente ensured that there was no longer any need for the British Government to maintain its military forces at battle strength, so men were retired from the service and ships decommissioned; masts, rigging and sails were removed and put into storage, while the near-bare hulls remained anchored in rivers and ports. The now 24-year-old Arthur Phillip was one of tens of thousands of navy sailors who were stood down. He was advised that he was part of the naval reserve and would receive an amount that represented half pay for a lieutenant.

Four months later, his life took a dramatic turn. He met and soon married 41-year-old Margaret Charlott Denison, the widow of an extraordinarily wealthy London merchant who had passed away just seven months after their marriage. She subsequently inherited £7.5 million from his estate − about £200 million in today's currency.

Romance aside, Phillip's bride-to-be required that he sign a premarital contract so that her wealth would remain protected. The couple wed in London on 19 July 1763, and after living for a short time in fashionable Hampton Court, on the banks of the Thames, they moved to a farming property at Lyndhurst in Hampshire's New Forest, about 100 miles by carriage to the south-west of the city. It was a lifestyle for which Arthur Phillip appeared to be the perfect fit: a gentleman farmer and squire. But the life of a true seafarer when on land can be as restless as the sea itself, and in Phillip's case, his was. The marriage was to last only six years and he was soon back in uniform and heading off to sea.

It is likely that two admirals had considerable influence on the next phase of Phillip's career – namely, Sir George Pocock and Augustus Hervey, the latter serving as Lord of the Admiralty from 1771 to 1775. Both men were aware of his seafaring skills, but bringing added bearing to their plans was his fluency in a number of languages, including German, French and Portuguese – an attribute that would make him a very valuable addition to the intelligence service. In short, Arthur Phillip became a spy.

For two years from 1772 onwards, he spent much of his time in northern France, covertly gathering details on French trade and commerce activities, as well as any important military matters, and sending all relevant information back to London. Then in 1774, the long-running aggression between Portugal and Spain saw the two Iberian nations on the brink of war once more. The Portuguese, needing all the support they could muster, looked to Britain for help. For the government and the Admiralty, this was a perfect opportunity to get members of the British intelligence service on the inside, as 'sleepers'. Phillip was a logical choice for such a mission, and he did not disappoint either side.

He arrived in Lisbon in early 1775. There, much to his surprise, he was given co-command of a ship of the line named *Nossa de Senhora Belém* – although he soon realised that appointing two captains was not unusual in the Portuguese Navy. He crossed the Atlantic to Rio de Janeiro where he became commander of the frigate *Nossa Senhora do Pilar*. One of his first assignments with this ship was to transport troops and 400 convicts from Rio to Colonia do Sacramento on the Rio de la Plata (opposite Buenos Aires). During this passage, the ship was hit by a storm so violent that Phillip had to call on some of the convicts to assist with the sailing of the ship. He was so impressed with their efforts that on arriving in Colonia he recommended to authorities that they recognise the contribution the convicts made to saving the ship by commuting their sentences. It seems obvious that Phillip's experiences in transporting convicts while in the Portuguese Navy gave him an insight into their plight, and into the slave trade.

While serving in this part of the world, Phillip was able to make extensive and detailed surveys of the coast, its ports and defences, all of which would prove to be highly beneficial to the Royal Navy. During his time in Rio de Janeiro, he also became a close associate of the Viceroy of Brazil, Luis de Almeida, a man whom Phillip impressed with his professionalism and dedication to duty.

In 1778, with Britain locked into the American War of Independence, Phillip was recalled to serve in the Royal Navy. De Almeida took time to record his impressions of his departing friend, who was 'very clean-handed; an officer of great truth and bravery'. The viceroy continued: '[Phillip] gives way to reason, and does not, before doing so, fall into those exaggerated and unbearable excesses of temper which the majority of his fellow-countrymen do ...'

When he stepped ashore in England in 1779, Phillip received the satisfying news that he was to be given his first command, HMS *Basilisk*. It was not a spectacular posting by any means, but it was a start. *Basilisk* was originally the 14-gun HMS *Grasshopper*. She took on her new name, and the new commander, after being converted to a fireship – a vessel laden with combustible materials and explosives that is set ablaze before being abandoned and allowed to drift downwind into enemy ships during battle. Although *Basilisk* did not see action, Phillip must have continued to impress, because, in November 1781, he was made post-captain of the frigate HMS *Ariadne*, where he served with a young Philip Gidley King. Months later, he was elevated even further, to the rank of captain, and given command of a 'real ship': the 64-gun line-of-battle vessel HMS *Europe* (renamed from *Europa* in 1778). He took his friend King with him.

Well aware of the captain's experiences with the Portuguese Navy in that country's war against Spain, the man who would become Lord Sydney (or more formally, the first Viscount Sydney), Thomas 'Tommy' Townshend, called Phillip to his office for a meeting to discuss and develop a strategy in 1782. At the time, Townshend was Secretary of War and in line to become leader of the House of Commons that same year. Between them, the two officers developed a plan to send a small flotilla of three ships of the line and a frigate to the Bay of Bengal, where they would lend support to the British India Squadron. As Arthur Phillip's early biographers Louis Becke and Walter Jeffery chronicled in 1897, the plan was for *Europe* and the other ships in the flotilla to undertake various engagements against the Spanish while en route to their ultimate destination. Specifically, they were to 'mount a raid on Buenos Aires and Monte Video, from there to proceed to the coasts of Chile, Peru and Mexico to maraud, and ultimately to cross the Pacific to join the British East Indian squadron for an attack on Manila, the capital of the Spanish Philippines'.

The four ships sailed on 16 January 1783, but they were barely out of the English Channel and into the Bay of Biscay when a ferocious storm – the type for which that infamous stretch of water is legendary – descended from the heavens. The wind screeched through the rigging, the few sails that were set flogged heavily and relentlessly, the ships shuddered, and the thundering sea became frighteningly powerful, surging combers. It was too much for three of the ships: they turned and ran with the storm, retreating to home waters. The one that survived the full wrath of the storm and got through was *Europe*.

Phillip pressed on for Rio de Janeiro, but while he was en route, Great Britain and Spain agreed to an armistice. Once in Rio, he befriended the new Portuguese viceroy, Dom Luís de Vasconcelos e Souza. This relationship would prove most advantageous four years later, when Phillip stopped there with the First Fleet.

The mission to the Bay of Bengal spanned almost two years, and in that time Phillip gained considerable respect from the man leading the British India Squadron, Commodore Sir Robert Kingsmill. So much so that on the return voyage to England, *Europe* was sent ahead of the fleet, carrying Kingsmill's all-important dispatches to the government and the Lords of the Admiralty.

Despite the accolades that followed his outstanding service as commander of HMS *Europe*, Phillip was again stood down from naval service, with instructions that he was returning to intelligence gathering for the government, on half pay. This led to him spending almost all of 1785 'on a holiday' in France. In truth, he was wandering the docks and streets of waterfront towns, speaking with locals in his very best French accent, observing activities, and writing regular dispatches for eager eyes back in London town. It has been suggested that he was probably in Brest when Lapérouse was preparing his ships for their voyage into the Pacific.

When Arthur Phillip's appointment as Governor of New South Wales was announced in October 1786, Lapérouse was already heading south on his way to rounding Cape Horn and entering the Pacific. From there, the Frenchman's plan was to explore the west coast of North America, before crossing the Pacific to Asia, and then heading to New Zealand and New Holland. That meant it would be more than a year before he reached the latter destination. It sounded like a long time, but for the British, it wasn't. The Botany Bay project involved building a town half a world away, and to do that they had no more than fifteen months to assemble the ships, men and equipment needed, sail halfway around the globe and confirm Britain's entitlement to the coast …

Before the French arrived.

CHAPTER 3

A Man of Letters

While Arthur Phillip fully expected to feel some level of isolation from the rest of the world in the years ahead, he was not expecting that feeling immediately after his appointment was announced. It was almost as if the British Government cut him adrift. Having declared that Botany Bay would be the site for a convict settlement, and Phillip its governor, all problems relating to the overcrowding of the nation's jails had been resolved, apparently. Those in Westminster and Whitehall could move on to other important matters, like the probable impeachment of Warren Hastings, the former Governor-General of India, for mismanagement and personal corruption.

It was also quite possible that, from the outset, the government believed that Phillip could cope: his planning ability and able leadership would bring about the desired results. It certainly appeared that way. Lord Sydney had sent instructions to the Treasury and the Admiralty outlining all that he believed was needed to prepare the project for departure, have it reach Botany Bay, see the settlement established and create a self-sufficient colony. But from the moment Phillip started to impose his own far more detailed plan and timeline, he realised the task would not be without considerable challenges. It was obvious that the government had glossed over many essential matters, as if some magical force would deliver the solutions – and Captain Arthur Phillip would be its conjuror.

Adding to the captain's woes, it was vital that his flotilla cross the Southern Ocean in that hemisphere's summer months, so as to minimise the chance of being confronted by storms of calamitous proportions. This meant that the desired time for departure was just six months away, and if that was to be achieved, then Phillip would have to treat the Botany Bay project as if it were a naval exercise. In other words, as though he had been charged with preparing a squadron of navy ships for a battle on distant shores, and the departure date was the closest thing possible to 'immediate'. Because of the urgency and the detail involved, Phillip took it upon himself not to delegate the most crucial parts of the planning process. With an eye for the finer points, he would have his own hand on everything that mattered in relation to this immense project.

His office was probably in the headquarters of the recently formed Home Office in central London, a circumstance that placed him close to many of the people with whom he needed to communicate. Even so, such a formal undertaking demanded that all important communication be done by letter – and Phillip wrote plenty of them due to the myriad issues he was facing.

Around this time, *The Times* in London published a news story outlining details of the venture. However, the article did more to confirm how little was known about the destination than to relate the facts. It contained some grossly inaccurate geographical details, regarding both the location of New South Wales and the coast on which Botany Bay was located.

> Government is now about settling a colony in New Holland, in the Indian seas, and the Commissioners of the Navy are now about advertising for 1500 ton of transport. This settlement is to be formed at Botany Bay, on the west side of the island, where Captain Cook

refreshed and staid some time on his voyage in 1770. As
he first sailed around that side of the island, he named it
New South Wales, and the two Capes at the mouth of
the river were called by the names of Banks and
Solander.

There are 680 men felons and 70 women felons to
go, and they are to be guarded by 12 marines and a
corporal in every transport, containing 150 felons.

There are several men of war and some frigates to
go, but they all come back, but one or two of each,
which are to remain there some time to assist in
establishing a garrison of 300 men intended to be left
there.

The whole equipment, army, navy, and felons, are
to be landed with two years' provisions, and all sorts of
implements for the cultivation of the earth, and
hunting and fishing, and some slight buildings are to be
run up immediately until a proper fort and town-house
are erected. This place is nearly in the same latitude
with the Cape of Good Hope, and about eight months'
voyage from England.

What wasn't mentioned was that this project was of a scale
never before attempted anywhere in the world. Yes, there had
been the settlement of Jamestown, Virginia, in 1607, and the
arrival of the Pilgrim Fathers in Plymouth, Massachusetts,
thirteen years later – key events in the foundation of what was
now known as the United States of America. But more than
150 years on, Phillip's brief was to finalise every detail for
what was effectively a small town, in a near-alien part of the
globe, with the aim of having it self-sufficient within three
years. It placed a huge demand on him, but in true Royal
Navy style, he remained stoic and undaunted.

He first documented precisely every aspect of the Botany
Bay mission, the challenge being to then create positive
solutions to each one problem raised. He was well aware of

how similar, but smaller, projects had failed, usually with an alarming death toll attached to that failure. Weighing just as heavily on his mind was the remoteness of Botany Bay. In the event of a calamity occurring, outside assistance would be a long time coming: it might take two years or more for a call to England for assistance to be received and a response delivered in the event of, say, starvation through failed crops, an outbreak of disease of epidemic proportions, or a rebellion by the convicts. He also had to accept that other, unforeseen problems might threaten the mission at any time.

The choice of ship to lead the flotilla, having been made before Phillip's arrival, served as the first broadside against his careful planning. Acting under directions from the government, the Admiralty, having decided there was insufficient time to build a flagship 'of proper class', had initiated a search for a suitable vessel within the Royal Navy fleet. This should have been a straightforward procedure, one that would cause the future governor no concern. But it wasn't like that at all.

The chosen vessel was a 110-foot, 540-ton burthen ship first named *Berwick*. Details of her origins are sketchy, but it is likely she was built in Rotherhithe (on the Thames, downstream from London) as a Baltic trader. It would have taken shipwrights and carpenters – using adzes, axes, saws, hammers and chisels – some two years to construct her hull from oak and complete the build. It was 1780 when the traditional bottle of red wine was smashed onto her topsides, her name declared, and she slid down the greased sled-like ways into the river.

The ship was purchased by the Royal Navy a year later, renamed HMS *Berwick*, and moved to Deptford Dock, where she was fitted out for battle with four 6-pounder long guns and six 18-pounder carronades. This work was completed in April 1782, and soon after she crossed the Atlantic where she played a role in the latter part of the American War of Independence. She was paid off in February 1785 and laid up at Deptford until the navy decided she would be the flagship for the First Fleet. In late 1786 she was refitted, rerigged and renamed HMS *Sirius*, after 'the bright star in ye Southern constellation of the Great Dog'.

There have been suggestions that *Sirius*'s construction was sub-standard and she was difficult to handle, but Phillip would have been in no position to question her suitability, as the ship's role in the First Fleet had already been decided when he took up his position as expedition leader. The circumstances were little different when it came to *Sirius*'s support vessel – a 28-year-old armed tender, HMS *Supply*.

It is thought that *Supply* was built in America. Up until this time, so the sources suggest, her primary purpose as a Royal Navy ship had been for the transport of materials and equipment between naval dockyards along the coast of southern England – hence her name. She was a small brig and, in the opinion of many experienced seafarers, too small for a role within Phillip's flotilla, but that theory went nowhere with the government and the naval hierarchy. This little coastal workboat would now be called on to cross wide expanses of often wild oceans on a 17,000-nautical-mile voyage.

Lieutenant Philip Gidley King, who was chosen by Philip personally as second lieutenant on the *Sirius* for the voyage to New South Wales, wrote disparagingly of both ships in his journal. These were his thoughts on *Supply*, which at 70 feet overall, would be the smallest vessel among the eleven ships in the fleet: 'The Supply, armed tender of 170 tons, 8 guns, and 50 men ... was formerly a navy transport; her size is much too small for so long a voyage, which, added to her not being able to carry any quantity of provisions, and her sailing very ill, renders her a very improper vessel for this service.'

Bad and small as she was, *Supply*'s one saving grace was that she was faster under sail than the 110-foot *Sirius*. It was because of this characteristic that she was chosen for the role of armed escort and tender. Should there be an uprising among the convicts aboard any of the transport ships, *Supply* would be able to respond quickly and put aboard marines who could retake the ship.

There was nothing the newly appointed governor could do regarding the choice of principal vessels, but he would do his utmost to ensure that the Botany Bay settlement had everything necessary to give it the best chance of survival. With quill in hand, he penned a constant stream of letters to his superiors and suppliers – in search of specific directives or answers, requesting the provision of equipment, or to report on his progress. Phillip's persistence occasionally brought the desired results, including confirmation of the supply of 'tools to enable [the convicts] to erect habitations, and also implements for agriculture'. Much more was needed, however.

One feature that the government had not considered during its earlier deliberations was the defence of the settlement. When Phillip learned that *Sirius* had been commissioned for the voyage with a total of twenty guns, he was quick to compose another letter to the Lords of the Admiralty. Dated 31 October, it requested that 'their Lordships order ten more of the six-pounders to be put on board, with the ironwork necessary for the carriages. Having the ironwork, the guns can at any time be mounted, and may, I presume, in future be of great use to us, on board or on shore, as the service may require.' The request was granted, and Phillip then had the wherewithal to establish a shore battery for defence purposes.

While the governor-elect accepted that loss of life during the voyage was inevitable, he began planning well in advance how best to ensure the health and well-being of the convicts as well as the free men and women who would be aboard his ships. The felons would contribute significantly to the success (or failure) of the settlement, after all. This was one more problem that the government left for Phillip to solve.

Arthur Phillip was the perfect choice for the job of Governor of New South Wales, and such a contention is made abundantly clear in a memo in which he outlines his initial plans, and poses additional questions. There is no addressee on the document, but it was probably written for Lord Sydney's benefit soon after Phillip took up the posting. It would almost certainly have also found its way to Evan Nepean (later Sir Evan Nepean), who, as Under Secretary of State in the Home Office, was charged with overseeing the arrangements for the First Fleet's departure and the formulation of plans for how the administration of the new colony would operate.

The memo reveals their chosen man to be one of high intelligence, professionalism, compassion and understanding. It also confirms once more his dedication to detail. The following is an abridged copy of the memo in which the first point outlines his desire to get at least one of the storeships to Botany Bay well ahead of the rest of the fleet.

> By arriving at the settlement two or three months before the transports, many and very great advantages would be gained. Huts would be ready to receive the convicts who are sick, and they would find vegetables, of which it may naturally be supposed they will stand in great need, as the scurvy must make a great ravage amongst people naturally indolent and not cleanly.
>
> Huts would be ready for the women; the stores would be properly lodged and defended from the convicts, in such manner as to prevent their making any attempt on them. The cattle and stock would be likewise properly secured, and the ground marked out for the convicts.
>
> A ship's company is landed, huts raised, and the sick provided for in a couple of days; but here the greater number are convicts, in whom no confidence can be placed, and against whom both person and provisions are to be guarded.
>
> The women in general, I should suppose, possess neither virtue nor honesty. But there may be some

[convicted] for theft who still retain some degree of virtue, and these should be permitted to keep together, and strict orders to the master of the transport be given that they are not abused and insulted by the ship's company.

At the ports we put into for water, &c., there may be some sick that may have fever of such a nature that it may be necessary for the safety of the rest to remove them out of the ship. In such a case, how am I to act?

During the passage, when light airs or calms permit it, I shall visit the transports to see that they are kept clean, and receive the allowance ordered by Government; and at these times shall endeavour to make them sensible of their situation, and that their happiness and misery is in their own hands; that those who behave well will be rewarded by being allowed to work occasionally on the small lots of land set apart for them, and which they will be put in possession of at the expiration of the time for which they are transported.

I shall think it a great point gained if I can proceed in this business without having any dispute with the natives, a few of which I shall endeavour to persuade to settle near us, and who I mean to furnish with everything that can tend to civilise them, and to give them a high opinion of their new guests; for which purpose it will be necessary to prevent the transports' crews from having any intercourse with the natives, if possible. The convicts must have none, for if they have, the arms of the natives will be very formidable in their hands, the women abused, and the natives disgusted.

The keeping of the women apart merits great consideration, and I don't know but it may be best if the most abandoned are permitted to receive the visits of the convicts in the limits allotted them at certain hours, and under certain restrictions. The rest of the women I should keep apart, and by permitting the men to be in their company when not at work they will, I should suppose, marry …

The natives may, it is probable, permit their women to marry and live with the men after a certain time, in which case I should think it necessary to punish with severity the man who used the woman ill; and I know of no punishment likely to answer the purpose of deterring others so well as exiling them to a distant spot, or to an island, where they would be obliged to work hard to gain their daily subsistence, and for which they would have the necessary tools; but no two to be together, if it could be avoided.

Rewarding and punishing the convicts must be left to the Governor; he will likely be answerable for his conduct, and death, I should think, will never be necessary. There are two crimes that would merit death – murder and sodomy; for either of these crimes I should wish to confine the criminal till an opportunity offered of delivering him as a prisoner to the natives of New Zealand, and let them eat him. The dread of this will operate much stronger than the fear of death.

Women may be brought from the Friendly and other islands, a proper place prepared to receive them, and where they will be supported for a time, and lots of land assigned to such as marry with the soldiers of the garrison.

As I would not wish convicts to lay the foundations of an Empire, I think they should ever remain separated from the garrison and other settlers that may come from Europe, and not be allowed to mix with them, even after the seven or fourteen years for which they are transported may be expired.

The laws of this country will, of course, be introduced in New South Wales, and there is one that I would wish to take place from the moment his Majesty's forces take possession of the country – that

there can be no slavery in a free land, and consequently
no slaves.

The latter point was no doubt influenced by the horrors of
slavery that Phillip observed while serving with the
Portuguese Navy in Brazil.

Phillip's letter writing to the Home Office, and sometimes
the Admiralty, became increasingly prolific as his plans
progressed. The more he advanced his planning, the more he
was confronted by questions demanding answers – vital
questions that the Home Office would have struggled to
answer because of the unprecedented nature of the venture. In
one memo to Whitehall he was adamant about what should
happen if the waterway was found to be an unsuitable location
for the settlement: '[The decision] must be left to me if I find it
[not] a proper place, to go to a port a few leagues to the
northward, where there appears to be a good harbour and
several islands. As the natives are very expert in setting fire to
the grass, the having an island to secure our stock would be a
great advantage, and there is none in or off Botany Bay.'

It is highly probable that the 'good harbour' Phillip was
referring to was Broken Bay (25 nautical miles north of Botany
Bay) and not Port Jackson, which Captain Cook had described
as appearing to offer a 'safe anchorage', with no islands to be
seen. Broken Bay, however, has Lion Island standing as a very
conspicuous edifice in its midst. The reference to natives
burning the grass came from an experience that Cook and his
men faced when repairing *Endeavour* on the banks of the river
in Cooktown. Aborigines had set fire to grass alongside the
ship in an act of retaliation after the Englishmen did not share
with them any turtle they had caught.

The reply that came to Phillip's question regarding the
siting of the settlement was curt and to the point.

There can be no objection to your establishing any part
of the territory or islands upon the coast of New South

Wales, in the neighbourhood of Botany Bay, which you
may consider as more advantageously situated for the
principal settlement; but at the same time you must
understand that you are not allowed to delay the
disembarkation … upon your arrival on the coast, upon
the pretence of searching after a more eligible place
than Botany Bay.

He was also reminded by the government that the security of
the convicts was paramount. This settlement was to be a place
of confinement for the transportees in this fleet and those that
followed.

It is our royal will and pleasure that you do not on any
account allow craft of any sort to be built for the use of
private individuals which might enable them to effect
such intercourse [escape to foreign ports], and that you
do prevent [those aboard] any vessels which may at any
time hereafter arrive at the said settlement from …
having communication with any of the inhabitants
residing within your Government, without first
receiving especial permission from you for that
purpose …

From the available correspondence written during the months
preceding the voyage, there is ample evidence to suggest that
the Home Office and the Admiralty respected Phillip's
perceptiveness. On many occasions, his requests elicited only
cursory comment: while he was following protocol, his
superiors were confident in his judgement, so often didn't
bother replying in the affirmative. Consequently, Phillip got
on with the job as he saw fit.

One letter he was most pleased to receive came from
Lord Sydney. It confirmed that his salary would be an
impressive £1000 net per annum, plus an allowance of 5
shillings a day to pay for a secretary. During earlier

deliberations regarding salary, Phillip had suggested he might also receive 'table money' – a gratuity – for his services as governor. The answer to that request was blunt: 'With regard to the compensation you solicit by way of table money, I am to inform you that no allowance whatever of that sort can be granted to you ...'

The overall plan for the colony was growing in detail daily, but all the effort would be worthless if the governor did not have the right ships at his disposal to transport all and sundry to Botany Bay. The naval vessels, *Sirius* (captained by John Hunter) and *Supply* (by Henry Lidgbird Ball) had been acquired. An additional nine others were required: three storeships to carry livestock, materials and equipment, and six vessels to transport the convicts. The 245 marines and their families would be spread across the fleet.

The storeships were easily found; they were chartered from the large fleet of British merchant vessels that plied local and international trade routes. It was a different scenario when it came to the convict transports, however. They did not exist in the desired form – essentially floating dungeons that could sail the 17,000-nautical-mile passage to Botany Bay. The only solution was to find suitable ships in the merchant fleet and convert them, in the most basic form, for human cargo.

There are no known drawings of the accommodation plans for these six convict ships, but it is known that life 'tween decks was little better than the transportees had experienced in prisons on land or on the prison hulks. Headroom was of no consequence (4 feet 5 inches in some places aboard *Scarborough*). The areas below decks normally assigned to cargo were divided up into cells with the placement of temporary bulkheads and iron grilles. Some cells were so small that four men, some of whom wore chains or irons, could barely lie on the floor to sleep, and the toilets were buckets. For security reasons, portholes, hatchways and any other means of viewing the outside world were covered, which meant it was almost as dark by day as it was by night ... and fresh air was virtually nonexistent, especially for those in the cells most distant from the companionways leading to the deck. Wind scoops were fitted to these companionways to catch what they could of any breeze wafting across the ship. When there was no breeze, no fresh air circulated. It would be even worse when the ships sailed in storms. The hatches had to be battened down in those conditions, and this caused the already fetid air below deck to become virtually unbreathable.

Philip Gidley King explained the fit-out of the convict transports:

> The transports are fitted up for the Convicts the same as for carrying troops; except the security, which consists of very strong & thick Bulkheads, filled with nails & run across from side to side in the 'tween decks abaft the Mainmast with ... holes to fire [through] between decks in case of irregularities. The hatches are well secured down by cross bars, bolts & locks & are likewise nailed down from deck to deck with oak stanchions. There is also a barricado [barricade] of plank about 3 Feet high, armed with pointed prongs of Iron on the upper deck, abaft the Mainmast, to prevent any connection between the Marines & Ship's Company, with the Convicts. Sentinels are placed at the different Hatchways & a guard always under arms on the Quarter deck of each Transport in order to prevent any improper behaviour of the Convicts, as well as to guard against any surprise.

The selection of the ships was influenced by their suitability for conversion and capacity for carrying convicts – 775 in all. The half-dozen transports were as follows:

- *Alexander*, 452 tons (under the command of Captain Duncan Sinclair)

- *Charlotte*, 335 tons (Captain Thomas Gilbert)
- *Friendship*, 278 tons (Captain Francis Walton)
- *Lady Penrhyn*, 338 tons (Captain William Cropton Sever)
- *Prince of Wales*, 350 tons (Captain John Mason)
- *Scarborough*, 430 tons (Captain John Marshall)

The storeships were to carry 'provisions and stores for two years; including instruments of husbandry, clothing for the troops and convicts, and other necessaries'. By the time of departure, the extensive cargo manifest would detail more than 170 items, each one important to the founding of the colony: forges and fowls, harpoons and hammocks, carts and cows, bulls and bricks, tents and turkeys, crockery and camp kettles, hoes and handkerchiefs, ropes and rice, panes of glass – and a piano. It was noted that the bricks and glass were for the construction of a governor's residence, and that almost all the animals and birds would be purchased in Cape Town.

As a precaution in case a ship were lost during the voyage, no vessel was to carry the entire consignment of any one item of cargo destined for the colony, or for use during the voyage. As King reasoned: 'an accident happening to one Ship would not have those disagreeable consequences, which must be the case, if ye whole of one Species of Stores was onboard each Ship …'

The three storeships were:

- *Borrowdale*, 272 tons (Captain Houston Reed)
- *Fishburn*, 378 tons (under Captain Robert Brown)
- *Golden Grove*, 331 tons (Captain William Sharp)

These vessels and all but *Prince of Wales* among the transports were docked at Deptford in south-east London by September 1786, so that refits and general preparations could be undertaken. *Prince of Wales* was later added to the fleet, with the approval of the Treasury, when it was decided to increase the number of women convicts from 70, first to 150, then to 180.

This was done to create a better balance between the sexes in the colony, and the prerequisite for the additional women was for them to be young and healthy, able to cope with the rigours of the voyage, and able to assist with the establishment of the settlement. *Prince of Wales*, which had been launched only five months earlier, was considered ideal for the task.

Phillip's original schedule for departure was frustrated on many occasions, often by a slow bureaucratic process, but his biggest bugbear was the delays that occurred at Deptford – and all too frequently in docks across England. News of these delays made it into print. One newspaper reported that 'orders had come for the men to work double tides to get those ships out of dock which are to sail to Botany Bay'. Compounding these and other problems, winter was making its march towards England. That could only slow progress even more.

During December, the Navy Board calculated that it would take six weeks to load the convicts onto the transports, but the process ultimately took three times longer. It would be a similar story regarding the loading of the equipment and supplies needed for the long voyage to the far-off land. It seems that the reason for this was that the procedures lacked the desired level of coordination, however, the blame did not lie with Phillip.

Beyond the government and the navy, there were two key participants in Phillip's plan-making: the pompous William Richards Jnr, and Duncan Campbell. Richards, a contractor to the Royal Navy, was the successful tenderer for the job of arranging the charter of the fleet's transports and storeships, and of provisioning them. In what was a logical decision, some of the vessels he secured were from the East India Company fleet. It was a move designed to save money: the charter would not be for a passage from England to England via Botany Bay, but instead, to Botany Bay only. Having arrived there and disembarked their convicts and unloaded supplies, the ships would be free to sail to China, where they could take on a cargo of tea and carry it back to England. Lieutenant King explained the financial arrangements: 'The terms of the Contract with the Owners of the Transports are, for the *Alexander, Prince of Wales & Friendship*, 10 Shillings a Ton per month, until they return to Deptford after the Voyage is performed; for the *Lady Penrhyn, Scarborough & Charlotte*, Twelve Shillings a Ton per Month, until they are cleared at the place they are destined for [China] …'

Campbell was the overseer of the prison hulks on the Thames. It was his task to list the names of those prisoners aboard his ships who were to be transported, and to arrange for delivery to their respective vessels. It is quite possible that he did Phillip no favours; that he had at the top of his list the worst troublemakers and the slackers who refused to work as ordered on shore-side projects. In fact, the structure of the convict manifest would later prove to be ill-conceived. Much to Phillip's frustration, no particular consideration had been given to good or bad behaviour, nor to any skills a convict had that might assist with the development of the colony – like those of carpenters, farmers and fishermen.

If there was some encouraging news as the year drew to a close, it was that work on *Sirius* and *Supply* had been completed at Deptford. On 10 December, the two ships worked the tide downstream to Long Reach, where guns, gunpowder and stores were loaded. They remained there until 30 January, waiting for *Alexander* and *Lady Penrhyn* to arrive after the two transports had embarked convicts upriver at Gallions Reach.

In line with Phillip's directive that the entire fleet be anchored in the Solent, between Portsmouth and the Isle of Wight, by 16 March 1787, the four ships then sailed in company to the Downs, at the mouth of the Thames. While at anchor there, they were 'detained by very violent & constant hard gales of Wind' for two weeks. When the weather turned favourable, the convoy sailed for three days to the Mother Bank in the Solent, arriving on 22 February – well in advance of the date Phillip had set.

CHAPTER 4

The Shackle Draggers

It's safe to say that every convict destined for the penal colony in Botany Bay had a remarkable story to tell, some more colourful or unfortunate than others. There were those who still had the word 'Africa' alongside their names, to signify the place where they were to serve their term of seven or fourteen years. But now, with the African option cancelled, everything related to Botany Bay.

Some prisoners had spent three years or more housed in unimaginably horrid conditions, before being herded onto wagons or small boats and transported to whichever of the six ships was taking them to the far side of the world. The mortality rate on England's hulks was nothing short of appalling: it was estimated that as many as one-third of those in confinement died while being held on board. Between August 1776 and April 1778, almost 25 per cent of the prisoners aboard the hulks *Justitiar* and *Censor* died from typhus. These deaths were due mainly to what was called 'jail fever' – a form of typhus that was spread rapidly through the ships by rats. Making matters worse was that the sick were not segregated from the healthy, making it easy for the disease to run rife through the ships.

One of the more notable convicts to be transported to New South Wales was James Hardy Vaux, who was exiled there from England on no less than three separate occasions, the first time in 1801. He became an author of note, and in doing so told of the misery experienced aboard the hulks.

> There were confined in this floating dungeon nearly 600 men, most of them double ironed; and the reader may conceive the horrible effects arising from the continual rattling of chains, the filth and vermin naturally produced by such a crowd of miserable inhabitants, the oaths and execrations constantly heard among them …
>
> On arriving on board we were all immediately stripped and washed in two large tubs of water, then, after putting on each a suit of coarse slop clothing, we were ironed and sent below; our clothes being taken from us …

Vaux went on to say that, because of the utter desperation of their plight, it was not unusual for a convict to 'rob his best benefactor, or even a messmate, of any article worth one halfpenny'.

The grime-laden inmates slept in extremely cramped conditions and the most troublesome were forced to wear fetters at night. A report in *The Scots Magazine* in 1777 revealed the squalid life the men faced, saying that the prisoners 'have fetters on each leg, with a chain between that ties variously, some round their middle, others upright to the throat'. Sometimes, to eliminate any chance of escape by the worst offenders, men were chained together in pairs using the heaviest fetters. Any attempt by a prisoner to remove the chains and shackles would lead to savage floggings with the cat-o'-nine-tails, and being sent to solitary confinement in a minuscule cell referred to as 'the black hole'.

More often than not, officers aboard the hulks pocketed the money that the government allocated for inmates' clothing – a linen shirt, brown jacket and a pair of breeches.

As a result, many of the convicts were in tattered rags and had no shoes. It was only those given clothing by family or friends, during extremely rare visits, that were half-decently clad. Personal hygiene was virtually unknown, bathing occurring only on the rarest of occasions.

As for food, the monotonous menu was kept to the absolute basics when it came to nourishment: ox cheek, boiled or made into soup, peas and either a mouldy biscuit or equally unpalatable piece of bread. The water they drank, drawn from the river, was often contaminated and, consequently, the cause of illness. The one consolation: 2 pints of beer per man, on four days of each week.

It is quite likely that none of the male and female convicts of the First Fleet knew of their fate until the final weeks or months before departure. Their destination became 'known' to them only when guards arrived at their cells and said they were being moved 'elsewhere', or when they were actually put aboard the ships, a process that got underway from late January onwards. The fact is, none of them would have heard of Botany Bay, or known where on earth it was.

If anyone had caught whispers about what was planned, it would have been the men crammed into the prison hulks on the Thames. Word might easily have filtered through that a fleet of ships was being assembled up at Deptford to exile those destined for transportation – perhaps as the prisoners went about their daily ritual of hard labour – usually dredging up large rocks from the riverbed and heaving them into boats, then putting them ashore, so that bold stone dock walls and the like could be built on the banks of the Thames.

The cross-section of vagabonds, vagrants and half-decent individuals among the First Fleet transportees was quite remarkable. But not to Arthur Phillip, who, well before departure, read what skills each man or woman offered, and became greatly concerned. There was nothing he could do about it but register his disapproval when presenting a final report to Lord Sydney and others.

Ninety per cent of the malefactors had been convicted of theft. No matter the magnitude of the offence, a verdict of guilty generally carried the same sentence: death. In most cases, though, the worth of the stolen goods was undervalued by a considerable amount in the hope that the sentence would be commuted to transportation.

Such was the case for Ann Forbes, aged nineteen, and seventeen-year-old Lydia Munro. Spinsters of no given occupation, the pair were found guilty of being prigs (thieves), having stolen 10 yards of printed cotton valued at 20 shillings. A note scrawled across the top of their court papers said simply: 'Guilty, No Chattels, To be Hanged.' However, word soon reached them in Southgate Prison that their death sentences had been commuted. Both women were to be transported – Ann for seven years, Lydia for fourteen – but they didn't know where.

There were no concessions or considerations for age. Robert Abel was just fifteen years old when he was convicted of 'assault and highway robbery' after attacking and stealing from labourer William Rough, at night, while armed with a pistol. It was alleged that he and his accomplice, William Rellions, stole 5 shillings and 1 penny. In court, the victim was adamant that the two accused were his assailants, yet Rellions claimed that Abel was not involved. The young lad told the court, 'I know no more of the robbery than the child unborn', but he was unable to provide a character reference, saying: 'I have nobody living but a brother, and he is just come home from sea ...' Both were sentenced to death. On 15 November 1784, two days before they were due to be hanged, Abel was saved from the gallows because of doubt as to his guilt. Even so, the judge considering the case stated that Abel had 'connected himself with thieves and pickpockets', and as his Honour did 'not wish him to be turned loose upon the public', transportation for seven years would be very much in the young man's interests. This meant that, unlike all other convicts, Abel was transported to Botany Bay despite not being convicted of committing any crime.

With more than 750 male and female convicts, representing a broad demographic of eighteenth-century English society, it was inevitable that some would emerge via infamy and become characters of note in the early history of Australia. One such person was a woman named Mary Bryant – née Braund, Broad or Brand, depending on various sources. In this era, the spelling of surnames was often erratic: it could be phonetic according to accent, just poorly spelled, or deliberately altered to avoid additional convictions accumulating against the name. Whether the Braunds, the Broads or the Brands, Mary's family eked out a living from fishing at Fowey, in Cornwall, but their headstrong daughter soon decided that such a confined life was not for her. Aged in her teens, Mary headed for Plymouth where, unable to find work, she took to petty thievery – in official terms, 'highway robbery' – for which, on 20 March 1786, she was convicted at the Exeter Assizes and sentenced to seven years' transportation. Soon after arriving in New South Wales, Mary married a fellow prisoner, William Bryant, who had been aboard *Charlotte*, as had Mary. Three years later, the Bryants, along with their children (one of whom was born on board *Charlotte*) and six other convicts, made a remarkably bold escape from the colony, one so spectacular that it became the stuff of legend.

Another convict to earn a place in Australian folklore was John Caesar, who, because of his black Madagascan parentage, became popularly known as 'Black Caesar'. He was a man of imposing and powerful build, and in the early stages of the colony he was recognised as a diligent and conscientious labourer. Nonetheless, a year after arriving with the First Fleet, he was tried for theft and subsequently convicted to a life term (fourteen years) in New South Wales. With nothing to lose, he made numerous, often daring, escapes – always armed, for the purposes of robbery and to prevent arrest. In late 1795, with a group comprising escaped convicts and other vagabonds backing him, Black Caesar claimed the dubious honour of being recognised as the first bushranger in the land.

*

It was a long and uncomfortable wait aboard the transport ships – four months for the earliest arrivals, through the bitter cold of an English winter – as interminable delays plagued preparations onshore. One consideration that Richards was trying to implement was the supply of hammocks, instead of having four individuals crammed into one large berth.

Friendship and *Charlotte* were sent to Plymouth to accept their guests of the government – men and women – who had been held there aboard the hulk *Dunkirk*. The order for their embarkation, along with a detachment of marines to guard over them, was received from the Secretary of State's office in London on 7 March, together with a directive to immediately thereafter join the other ships in the expedition at the Mother Bank.

The remaining convict-carrying ships went to Portsmouth to have their respective quotas of prisoners put aboard. All six transports were allocated a detachment of marines for the voyage, their number being in proportion to either the number of convicts on board or the threat their charges might pose to the security of the ship.

Those 210-odd convicts destined to join the transports in Portsmouth were removed from the hulks at Woolwich, on the Thames, during the last week of February 1787 and put onto a convoy of thirty open horse-drawn wagons. *The Times* reported that the convoy was 'under proper guard'. The prisoners struggled when they came ashore from the hulks, their chains and shackles rattling and ringing, dragging behind them as they slowly made their way across the dirty dockside area towards their assigned wagons. It was a considerable exercise, since their belongings – meagre as they were – and the provisions for their three-day road trip to Portsmouth also had to be loaded. Once the shackle draggers were crammed into the wagons, each one was chained in place to prevent escape.

The convoy then rolled down the rutted and rocky road leading away from Woolwich and towards the English countryside, the guards on each wagon sitting high so they could watch over their consignment of felons. Adding to the misery for these poorly clad wretches was that their bodies had to absorb every bump in the rugged road, while the cold bit into their bones.

The organisers were confident that the security they had in place was ample for the ride to Portsmouth, but the people of that Hampshire town obviously didn't agree. With hundreds of the country's least-wanted criminals due to be trundled along the main cobblestone thoroughfare, some shopkeepers boarded up their premises, while many residents cleared the streets and hid in their homes. As an added precaution, it was reported, soldiers lined the route through town and the road leading down to the shingle beach. Once there, the convicts were loaded aboard longboats and launches, before being rowed to the transports lying at anchor off the port.

Details contained in a bill for transporting one wagon-load of convicts tell more of the story:

> Bread, cheese and beer and other articles for 20
> convicts on the road £2/4/6
> Expenses attending and guarding said convicts from
> Woolwich to Cumberland Fort [Portsmouth] £8/-/-
> Horse hire for 6 days £3/-/-
> Wagons £13/3/3

The arrival of these prisoners in Portsmouth heralded another setback, however. Duncan Campbell, who was responsible for supervising the conversion of *Scarborough*'s below-decks area into prison cells, had failed to do his job. The ship's master, John Marshall, discovered that the entire convict holding area was so inadequate that the felons would've been able to break out with virtually no effort. In addition, there was no captain's cabin for Marshall to sleep in! So, all convict accommodation below deck had to be ripped out and rebuilt, as carpenters constructed a captain's cabin on the quarterdeck. Meanwhile, Marshall organised for the prisoners to be held aboard the 44-gun fifth-rate HMS *Gorgon* in Portsmouth.

A different problem surfaced among women convicts generally. It was realised when they were taken from the prisons, particularly in rural areas, that many were so drunk from cheap gin secured within the prison compounds, they were on the verge of being deranged. More critically, though, the increase in the number of women scheduled for transportation contributed significantly to the departure date being continually pushed deeper into the year.

From the start of boarding, during the worst of winter, Phillip recognised that the female convicts were already in a 'deplorable condition'. In a letter to Lord Sydney, he wrote: 'The situation in which the magistrates send the women on board ... stamps them with infamy – almost naked and so very filthy, that nothing but clothing them could have prevented them from perishing.'

His immediate solution was to take crew-issue clothing already put aboard *Sirius* and give it to the women. With there then being more than 100 additional female convicts in the fleet, it was imperative that new clothing be ordered for them, but here again, circumstances were beyond Phillip's control. Red tape and production delays would result in much of the order not being delivered before the ships sailed. By then, all he could do to ease the problem was source additional clothing from the sailors' slops store aboard *Sirius* and from anywhere else.

The women's issue, for those fortunate enough to receive it, was to last them for more than two years. It included the following items: four white shifts, one grey jacket, one white jacket, two checked jackets, one woollen jacket, two canvas petticoats, two linsey woolsey petticoats, one serge petticoat, three handkerchiefs, two caps, four pairs of stockings and

three pairs of shoes. By comparison, the clothing supplied by
the government to male convicts comprised: two jackets,
four woollen drawers, one hat, three shirts, four pairs of
worsted stockings, three frocks, three trousers and three pairs
of shoes.

The challenges that Phillip faced seemed to grow in
inverse proportion to time remaining before departure. With
there being little more he could do with regard to planning
and preparation, he was looking more towards the voyage, and
the need to ensure that as many people as possible survived
what could well be a very arduous, nine-month passage. On
12 March, after the Navy Board had advised him that no
changes could be made to the victualling of Royal Marines
personnel during the voyage, he wrote to Lord Sydney in
protest. Every one of the eleven ships would be severely
crowded, and that combined with a poor diet, would almost
certainly lead to a considerably greater loss of life. In particular,
the very limited supply of flour was most concerning, as he
informed Sydney.

> It is to prevent my character as an officer from being
> called in question, should the consequences I fear be
> realised that I once more trouble your Lordship on this
> subject. This must be fatal to many, and the more so as
> no anti-scorbutics are allowed on board the transports
> for either Marine or convict; in fact, my Lord, the
> garrison and convicts are sent to the extremity of the
> globe as they would be sent to America – [only] a six
> weeks passage.

In a bid to minimise the chance of disease impacting on all
members of the flotilla, Phillip requested of Lord Sydney that
any new prisoners be 'washed and cloathed' before leaving jails
or hulks. He confirmed that some fevers had broken out
among the convicts already aboard *Lady Penrhyn*. He also
reminded His Lordship:

> ... there is a necessity for doing something for the
> young man who is on board that ship as surgeon, or I
> fear that we shall lose him, and then a hundred women
> will be left without any assistance, several of them with
> child. Let me repeat my desires that orders immediately
> may be given to increase the convict allowance of
> bread; 16lb of bread for 42 days is very little ...

As was too often the case, Phillip's request was ignored.

Over the months leading up to the fleet's departure, there had been considerable speculation in the press regarding what the death toll among the convicts would be during such a long passage. Their accommodation, diet and the weather were expected to deliver a heavy toll. Some predicted an inordinate number of fatalities – 80 per cent – while others were more conservative.

John White, the man who had been appointed to the challenging position of 'Surgeon-General for the First Fleet, and the Settlement in New South Wales', took up his position on 5 March 1787, as he revealed on the opening page of his new journal.

> I this day left London, charged with dispatches from the
> Secretary of State's office, and from the Admiralty,
> relative to the embarkation of that part of the marines
> and convicts intended for Botany Bay; and on the
> evening of the seventh, after travelling two days of the
> most incessant rain I ever remember, arrived at
> Plymouth, where the *Charlotte* and *Friendship* transports
> were in readiness to receive them.
>
>   ... The weather being moderate ... the convicts
> were put on board the transports, and placed in the
> different apartments allotted for them; all secured in
> irons, except the women. When this duty was
> completed, and the wind now freshening ... we

proceeded to Spithead, where we arrived the
seventeenth, and anchored on the Mother Bank, among
the rest of the transports and victuallers intended for the
same expedition, under the conduct of his Majesty's
ship the *Sirius*.

As soon as was practicable after arriving at the Mother Bank,
White visited the four other transport ships and was 'surprised
to find the convicts on board them so very healthy'. However,
while aboard *Alexander*, he had an unexpected confrontation
with a 'medical gentleman from Portsmouth' whom he did not
know. White recalled: 'He scarcely gave me time to get upon
the quarter-deck before he thus addressed me – "I am very glad
you are arrived, Sir; for your people have got a malignant
disease among them of a most dangerous kind; and it will be
necessary, for their preservation, to get them immediately re-
landed!"'

White hastily headed below deck to see these people whom
he was told were destined for their deathbeds. When he
returned to the deck, the other man said with a superior note of
importunity: 'I suppose you are now convinced of the
dangerous disease that prevails among these people, and of the
necessity of having them landed, in order to get rid of it.' To
this, White replied tersely that there was 'not the least
appearance of malignity in the disease under which the convicts
laboured, but that it wholly proceeded from the cold; and was
nearly similar to a complaint then prevalent, even among the
better sort of people, in and about Portsmouth'.

The doctor continued to insist that the men should be
landed for medical treatment onshore. That was enough for
White.

I could no longer keep my temper; and I freely told
him, 'that the idea of landing them was as improper as
it was absurd'. And, in order to make him perfectly
easy on that head, I assured him that when any disease

rendered it necessary to call in medical aid, he might
rest satisfied I would not trouble him … but [would]
apply to some of the surgeons of his Majesty's ships in
Portsmouth harbour, or at Spithead, most of whom I
had the pleasure of knowing, and on whose medical
knowledge I was certain I could depend.

White added: 'This peremptory declaration had the desired
effect. The gentleman took his leave, to my great
satisfaction …' It is distinctly possible that the convicts were
feigning illness in the hope of being transferred ashore, thus
avoiding departure with the fleet.

By midway through spring, the eleven ships of varying shapes
and sizes were anchored on the well-sheltered Mother Bank in
the Solent, just to the north-west of Ryde on the Isle of Wight.
It was then a frustrating waiting game for all, particularly for
those convicts who had been in irons aboard ship for more
than twelve weeks. There was still no definite date for
departure. The actual time would be decided by how long it
took for Captain Phillip to receive his final documentation
from the Admiralty and the government.

It was a pitiful existence for the convicts while the ships
lay at anchor. After a period of time, it was decided that
prisoners would be allowed to go on deck in small numbers,
for brief periods, so they could enjoy some respite, but every
man had to be properly secured in irons 'tween decks at night.
The masters of these transport vessels had already agreed to a
penalty of £40 for any prisoner who might escape.

One of Phillip's later dispatches revealed that the time at
the Mother Bank provided an opportunity to outline his rules
for the voyage.

This necessary interval was very usefully employed, in
making the convicts fully sensible of the nature of their
situation; in pointing out to them the advantages they

would derive from good conduct, and the certainty of severe and immediate punishment in case of turbulence or mutiny. Useful regulations were at the same time established for the effectual governing of these people; and such measures were taken as could not fail to render abortive any plan they might be desperate enough to form for resisting authority, seizing any of the transports, or effecting, at any favourable period, an escape. We have, however, the testimony of those who commanded, that their behaviour, while the ships remained in port, was regular, humble, and in all respects, suitable to their situation: such as could excite neither suspicion nor alarm, nor require the exertion of any kind of severity.

Captain-Lieutenant Watkin Tench of the Royal Marines, who wrote two books giving valuable insight into the voyage to Botany Bay and the embryonic stages of settlement, was stationed aboard the transport ship *Charlotte*. His recollection is of a more clearly defined message to the convicts: 'an opportunity was taken, immediately on their being embarked, to convince them, in the most pointed terms, that any attempt on their side, either to contest the command, or to force their escape, should be punished with instant death …'.

Having entered into an arrangement with London publisher Debrett's, Tench commenced writing the first of his acclaimed journals when *Charlotte* was being prepared for the voyage. While at the Mother Bank, he noted, the prisoners seemed quite happy with their existence, but they had concerns regarding the unlikelihood of ever returning to English shores.

In this period … the ships were universally healthy, and the prisoners in high spirits. Few complaints or lamentations were to be heard among them, and an ardent wish for the hour of departure seemed generally to prevail … happily, the behaviour of the convicts [was] in general humble, submissive, and regular … but

their constant language was, an apprehension of the
[impossibility] of returning home, the dread of a sickly
passage, and the fearful prospect of a distant and
barbarous country ...

There were two convicts aboard *Alexander* who had every
reason to rejoice while at the anchorage. They were advised by
the ship's captain that they had received a full pardon and
would therefore remain in England.

The 'universal' health that Tench wrote of was no doubt
reflective of Phillip's efforts. On the First Fleet, a sailor's basic
allocation each week consisted of the following:

Ship's biscuits (bread) – 7 lbs
Salted pork – 2 lbs
Salted beef – 4 lbs
Peas – 2 lbs
Oatmeal – 3 lbs
Butter – 6 ozs
Cheese – ¾ lb
Vinegar – ½ pint
Water – 3 quarts per day
Beer and wine was allocated to the sick for remedial
purposes

Determined to minimise the inevitable death toll on the
voyage, Phillip had implemented the best possible diet for
everyone, convicts included. The evidence of this is in the fact
that the weekly food allocation for sailors and marines was
only one-third more than that for the male convicts, while the
women and children received a slightly different menu.
Whenever the fleet was in port, every effort would be made to
supply fresh food.

By the first week of April, Arthur Phillip knew that all
that could be done had been done: everything was in readiness
for his fleet to sail, as best could be. He would have been to

the Home Office and formally accepted his final orders from King George III, as drafted by Nepean and approved by Lord Sydney. The whereabouts of the 4100-word document, if it exists, is unknown to this day, but it's believed to have recognised his commission and provided a more detailed outline of what was expected of him as Captain-General of the Fleet, and Governor of New South Wales. The latter territory, in an amendment dated 25 April 1787, was defined as including 'all the islands adjacent in the Pacific Ocean' and westward to the longitude of 135 degrees.

The draft of this document was highly detailed and dealt with every consideration relating to the establishment of the colony. Among these were the following guidelines concerning the native population and respect for religion:

> You are to endeavour by every possible means to open an Intercourse with the savages ... and to conciliate their affections, enjoining all Our Subjects to live in amity and kindness with them. And if any of Our Subjects shall wantonly destroy them, or give them any unnecessary Interruption in the exercise of their several occupations, it is our Will and Pleasure that you do cause such offenders to be brought to punishment according to the degree of the Offence.
>
> And it is further Our Royal Will and Pleasure that you do by all proper methods enforce a due observance of Religion and good order among all the inhabitants of the new Settlement ... that you do cause the Laws against Blasphemy, Profaneness, adultery, Fornication, Poligamy, Incest, Profanation of the Lord's Day, swearing and Drunkenness to be rigorously executed and that you do take due care for the punishment of the aforementioned Vices ...

Having read the document, Phillip carefully packed it into his leather trunk, along with the clothing and personal items he deemed necessary for him to successfully execute his role for an indefinite period. The 48-year-old was then ready to depart his London abode and take a carriage ride of more than 75 miles through villages, across green farmlands, hills and gently sloping dales to Portsmouth. As the miles passed, his mind would have been full of anticipation, wondering about the life that lay ahead for him in a very different world.

This image gives a sense of the activity and squalor around the convict hulks. Most of the inmates had committed petty crimes by today's standards, but heavy sentences were applied. *A view near Woolwich in Kent, shewing the employment of the convicts from the hulks* (circa 1790–1800). NLA nla.pic-an23672354.

CHAPTER 5

A Slow Start

Phillip arranged with the naval authorities at Portsmouth to be transferred from the port to his ship, which was then at anchor about 7 miles away across the Solent, in company with the rest of the fleet. His mode of transport that day, 11 May, would have been an open navy launch about 23 feet in overall length, manned by four oarsmen and possibly fitted with a small rig. The outbound trip most likely took between two and three hours.

Once alongside *Sirius*, he clambered up the accommodation ladder and onto the deck. There, he was formally greeted by the ship's master, Captain John Hunter, who, like Phillip, was in full Royal Navy uniform. Simultaneously, Phillip's pennant was hoisted to the top of the mainmast so that all ships were aware that the commodore of the fleet had arrived.

No doubt Phillip would have walked the deck to see what improvements had been made to a ship since refitting began. He would have been pleased with much of what he saw. Over £2500 had been spent refurbishing the hull and making changes above deck – the three masts, the yards, sails and rigging, all of it was new. Other refinements, such as the refit below decks, cost an additional £4500. This included four new boats: a launch and three cutters. All things considered, he could now only hope that the performance of his upgraded vessel would match her pleasing appearance.

With all ships present and ready to sail, the commodore was keen to get underway the moment the weather suited their chosen course out of the Solent. But he was soon to learn from Hunter that the weather was not their immediate problem. The judge advocate for the colony, David Collins, later reported on the episode:

> The sailors on the transports refused to proceed to sea unless they should be paid their wages up to the time of their departure, alleging as a ground for their refusal that they were in want of many articles necessary for so long a voyage. The custom of their employ, however, [was] against a demand which yet appeared reasonable. Captain Phillip directed the different masters to put such of their people as refused to proceed with them to sea on board the *Hyaena* frigate [the fleet's temporary escort], and to receive an equal number of her seamen, who should afterwards be re-exchanged at sea, her captain being directed to accompany the fleet to a certain distance.

Phillip's threat had the desired effect. The problem was soon resolved.

Unlike the crews of the transport ships, the navy crewmen aboard *Sirius* and *Supply* had no reason to complain as they were paid their wages two months in advance. And, while Phillip had laid down the law in no uncertain fashion, Philip Gidley King sympathised with the sailors.

> I think the Seamen had a little reason on their side. They had been in employ upwards of seven Months, during which time they had received no pay except their River pay & one Month's advance. The great length of the voyage rendered it necessary that they

should have more Money, to furnish themselves with
such necessaries as were really indispensable. But it
became the Master's interest to withhold their pay
from them, that they might be obliged to purchase
those necessaries from them on ye course of the
Voyage at a very exorbitant rate; however our sailing,
obliged some of them to return to their Duty, others
compromised with the Masters, and ye *Fishburn* lost 5
men who never returned.

The missing hands from *Fishburn* were immediately replaced
by five men from HMS *Hyaena*, a 24-gun post ship that would
accompany the fleet for the first 300 miles or so.

Sometime that day, Phillip went to his cabin to write what
would be his final communication prior to departure. It was
addressed to his good friend and supporter Evan Nepean, and
read in part: 'Once more I take my leave of you, fully sensible
of the trouble you have had in this business, for which at
present I can only thank you; but at a future period, when this
country feels the advantages that are to be drawn from our
intended settlement, you will enjoy a satisfaction that will, I
am sure, make you ample amends ...' Since it was vital for the
safety and security of the fleet that all vessels remained in visual
contact, Phillip also took the time to establish an understanding
with the various ships' masters regarding the signals that would
be used both day and night to ensure there was no separation.

Phillip's weather eye had him confident that the fleet
would be sailing shortly after sunrise on 12 May. His faith
appeared justified because, when the eight bell chimes rang out
from all the ships at 4 am – accompanied by the familiar call
from each quarterdeck, 'Eight bells and all is well' – there was
every reason to believe that the wind and tide would soon be
suitable for weighing anchor. The bells marked the changeover
from graveyard watch to morning watch – and within a very
short time, Phillip and Hunter had met on deck and concurred
that it was right to signal the fleet to prepare for sea.

Although the breeze was only light, it was from the south-south-east, a direction that made it ideal for sailing their preferred course: 20 nautical miles to the west through the Solent, past the Needles, and out into the English Channel. However, this planned departure came unstuck shortly after the flag had gone aloft on *Sirius* for all ships to weigh anchor and follow her lead. As the flagship and some other vessels moved off from the Mother Bank, the commodore could only look back and wonder why a few of his ships had failed to get underway. Later in the day, he would be advised that the bulk of the crewmen on those ships were so inebriated that it had not been possible to get them sailing.

Coincidentally, while Phillip and others were struggling to understand why all the ships were not joining the flotilla, the wind died down to a wisp. There was no alternative: *Sirius* sent out the signal to drop anchor.

The following day's attempt to commence the voyage was successful.

For the second time, the decks of all ships had come to life before sunrise. It was a crisp Sunday morning, and Phillip having been woken once again to the sound of the eight bells at four o'clock, climbed out of his cot and changed from his nightshirt into his uniform in readiness for the big day. After stepping from his small sleeping quarters adjacent to the great cabin, he would have then made his way up the companionway ladder to the quarterdeck to observe the weather and the preparations that were already underway. When he looked aft and aloft he was pleased to note that the large Jack was flying proudly from the peak of the mizzen gaff in response to a fresh morning breeze.

This was definitely the day to sail.

Having endured the worst of an English winter aboard ship, the crews were equally eager to be underway and sailing towards the warmth of the subtropical weather that was only weeks away. While they worked on rigging and preparing their ships, their tasks became easier as the approach of sunrise brought increasing light to the new day. A short distance away, smoke seen wisping from the chimneys of cottages in the tiny village of Ryde, on the Isle of Wight, also confirmed the presence of an easterly breeze.

The sun rose just after 5 am, and as departure time approached so the activity on all ships accelerated. Windlasses could be heard clattering as the anchors were raised from the seabed, while, at the same time, small teams of men were calling in unison, and repetitiously, 'haul away', each time they locked their leather-like hands around halyards and lines and heaved on them. As they did, heavy hand-stitched canvas sails were seen to unfurl from the masts and yards like huge buds bursting into flower. There was a heavy thumping sound as each untamed stretch of canvas flogged in the morning breeze … until they were contained by the sheets, then billowed forth in the light of the morning sun.

While standing near the man on the wheel, just forward of *Sirius*'s mizzenmast, Phillip could look out and see the ten other ships in his fleet also getting underway. It was an impressive and satisfying scene, one that he had long envisioned. His mission, which had cost the British Government £84,000 thus far, was finally on the move – launched into the near unknown full of hope, confidence and determination.

Still, there had to be an air of uncertainty for almost everyone associated with this endeavour. The marines and their wives standing on the decks of their respective ships that morning, absorbing the views of the lush green countryside one last time, knew they would be absent from English shores for at least three years, and it might be longer. It was little different for Phillip's officers. No one could mentally grasp what to expect, save what they could glean from a few morsels of information that had filtered through from the voyage of Cook. Only time would provide the answers. The crews of the transports and storeships were the only ones who did have some certainty as to their future: they would be heading back to England after delivering their cargoes, human and otherwise, to Botany Bay.

As the ships began to glide west through the Solent on the run of a favourable tide, there would have been early risers on the Isle of Wight, and the English mainland just 2 miles to the north, looking out and wondering as to where this small armada might be headed. Soon though, the ships were only specks in the distance, their sails still highlighted by the sun.

Later that day, Watkin Tench wrote of the historic departure:

> Before six o'clock the whole fleet were under sail; and, the weather being fine and wind easterly, proceeded through the Needles with a fresh leading breeze ...
> By ten o'clock we had got clear of the Isle of Wight, at which time, having very little pleasure in conversing with my own thoughts, I strolled down among the convicts, to observe their sentiments at this juncture ...

This was an emotionally charged time for everyone on board, but especially those secured in their dark, dungeon-like environment below deck. The realisation that they were all now sailing towards a future where nothing was even remotely familiar, was a powerful one. Not that the convicts could see outside, but England was fast becoming a hazy image on the distant horizon, astern. In his description, Tench noted that the females were not manacled and, with some level of compassion, he observed of the reaction among the transportees: 'the pang of being severed, perhaps for ever, from their native land, could not be wholly suppressed; in general, marks of distress were more perceptible among the men than the women; for I recollect to have seen but one of those affected on the occasion, "Some natural tears she dropped, but wiped them soon."'

A few hours after the fleet had cleared the Needles, two of the transport ships gave cause for concern. They were embarrassingly slow, so much so that they were destined to hold up the flotilla's progress to a considerable degree. *Charlotte* fell sufficiently far behind that she had to be towed by *Hyaena* twice during the first forty-eight hours, simply to keep her in contact with the other ships. *Lady Penrhyn* was the second laggard.

To ensure that visual contact was maintained across the flotilla, Phillip frequently had to order the other vessels to shorten sail and slow their pace. At night, all ships were required to reduce sail, so that there was a constant speed across the fleet. As lead ship, *Sirius* would have a bright lantern burning at her main topmast, to make her as visible as possible in the darkness.

On 15 May, Phillip signalled all ships to pass within hailing distance of *Sirius* so that their masters could report any problems at this early stage of the passage. He was surprised to learn from John Mason aboard *Prince of Wales* that the man destined to be the colony's provost-marshal had been left behind. Thomas Gilbert, *Charlotte*'s captain, reported that the same had happened with his third mate.

The fleet was still in sight of England's south coast when it was confronted by a change in the weather, and while the seas were not considered to be rough, they were bad enough for the landlubbers to realise how uncomfortable this environment might become. The first 200 nautical miles from the Isle of Wight to the rugged French island of Ushant, at the southern entrance to the English Channel, took three days to cover and gave the uninitiated a broad taste of life at sea. They were all struggling to adapt to the perpetual motion, and because of this, seasickness was endemic across the fleet.

It's possible that even Arthur Phillip succumbed to mal de mer. His vulnerability to this malaise, which can affect the most seasoned sailors, was confirmed in an anonymous reference to him that was written some years later: 'Well I remember his little figure, smothered up in his brown camlet cloak lined with green baize, his face shrivelled, and this aquiline nose, under a large cocked hat, gathered up in a heap, his chin between his knees, sitting under the lee of the mainmast, his sharp and powerful voice exclaiming, "I cannot bear this, I am as sick as a dog!"' At the time, Phillip was aboard a small navy boat that was being pitched about by stormy seas off Plymouth.

Life became more tolerable for everyone once the fleet cleared Ushant's uninviting rocky shoreline. At that point, the ships changed direction so that they were sailing downwind, surging along with the waves. As each swell approached from astern, the ships would be lifted before receiving a powerful nudge forward.

The planned course from there would eventually lead to the first scheduled stop – Tenerife, 1300 nautical miles to the south. On each of the eleven ships, this change of course also brought a call from the quarterdeck to re-trim the yards and sails: the end of the yards extending out to windward had to be hauled aft, the jibs eased, and the spanker, or mizzen, eased out. So, while some of the crew on watch on the larboard (port) side eased out the braces and sheets on that side, men on the starboard side hauled away on the windward braces and sheets. With each call of 'Haul away!', the pulley blocks screeched in unison as the braces were pulled in, while simultaneously, the crewmen at the belaying pins near the mast would take up the slack and secure the line. This was a continuous action until the sails were set at the optimum angle for the course and wind direction.

It was then far more pleasant sailing, even for the convicts in their dark and gloomy quarters. They sensed things were better, simply because the motion of the ships had gone from being turbulent to tolerable. For now.

No one aboard *Sirius* had previously sailed the ship on the open sea, so inherent traits, such as sea-kindliness, manoeuvrability and speed, were unknown. The passage down the English Channel towards the Atlantic Ocean revealed little because everyone was familiarising themselves with their new environment. It was not long after *Sirius* had rounded Ushant, and held a course that would lead the fleet well out into the Atlantic on the face of a fresh easterly wind and rising swell, that the first concerns emerged. The ship was definitely slow, and her heavy displacement – due to the amount of equipment and stores she was carrying – plus the hull shape aft, made her near impossible to steer. In designers' parlance, *Sirius* had 'large buttocks': a full shape aft that impacted the effectiveness of the rudder and the water flow around the hull. This meant that for much of the time, she had a mind of her own, in that it was difficult to sense which way she would want to turn when running with the waves. Because of this unpredictability, each timoneer struggled to anticipate the direction in which the helm should be turned so that an appropriate correction to her course could be made. And even when he was successful, *Sirius* was always slow to respond. Only time at the wheel could provide the expertise needed to keep her on course.

Apart from that, everything appeared to be going smoothly during the first eight days at sea. Phillip therefore had a signal hoisted to advise the captain of *Hyaena*, Michael de Courcy, that he was happy for the escort to leave the fleet and return to England. *Hyaena*'s presence among the flotilla had been initiated by the Royal Navy as a precaution against a possible attack by the French, and the commodore had also hoped to compile a lengthy report for de Courcy to take back to the Home Office. As recorded in Phillip's journal, the weather put paid to this last idea.

> As we are now nearly one hundred leagues clear of the Channel, the *Hyaena* leaves us this evening to return to Plymouth, but the sea runs too high to send [officers] on board the different transports to get any particular account of the state of the convicts … At present our motion is such that I find it very difficult to sit at table; but the weather is good, and tho' the *Charlotte* and *Lady Penrhyn* sail very badly, clearing the Channel is one

great point gained, and with which I look on all our
difficulty as ended ...

Rather than a detailed report, Phillip could send only brief
notes back to his superiors in England. At the same time, all
crewmen in the flotilla had been given the opportunity to
send letters home with *Hyaena*. These had been transferred
by each ship's boat to *Sirius* days earlier, before the seas
turned foul, then rowed across to *Hyaena* aboard the
flagship's launch.

On the day of the escort's departure, the launch also took
news to Captain de Courcy that the five members of his crew
who had filled in aboard *Fishburn* had chosen to stay and
continue on the voyage. All ships lay-to while the transfer was
being executed, after which, King affirmed, 'at 5 in the
Evening the *Hyaena* saluted us with three cheers, which was
returned, when she bore up & parted company ...'.

That same afternoon, Phillip diarised how he had been
confronted by a quite serious distraction, which a convict
aboard *Scarborough* had brought to the attention of that ship's
captain, John Marshall, as well as the commanding officer of the
marines. It was a revelation that, had it not surfaced at the time,
might have brought dire consequences for the entire mission.
The governor-elect recorded: 'I have received a report from the
officers on board the *Scarborough* respecting the convicts, who, it
is said, have formed a scheme for taking possession of the ship. I
have ordered the [two] ringleaders on board the *Sirius* ...'

This was Phillip's first chance to be seen exerting his full
authority over the expedition, and he had no hesitation in
doing so. Once aboard the *Sirius*, both prisoners were tied
hand and foot, probably to the mainmast, and flogged two-
dozen times by the bosun's mate, with no mercy being shown.
They were then transferred to *Prince of Wales*, where they
would remain.

With the emergence of this plot to mutiny, it would have
been understandable if Phillip had ordered a more strict watch

over all the convicts throughout the fleet. Instead, he appears to have applied a degree of reverse psychology, by easing one of the regulations regarding prisoner security to ensure they were treated more humanely. According to Tench, each transport ship was hailed from *Sirius* and the captain advised that 'where they judged it proper, they were at liberty to release the convicts from the fetters in which they had been hitherto confined'. This applied only to the men, as no women were held in irons – unless they were being punished for an offence committed on board.

Collins, the future judge advocate, noted that this considerate act was to generally make life easier for the male transportees. As a result, he wrote, these convicts 'might have it more in their power to strip their clothes off at night when they went to rest, be also more at their ease during the day, and have the further advantage of being able to wash and keep themselves clean'.

Tench was similarly full of praise for the commodore's move. Being a commander of marines, he also lauded Phillip for his decision to employ marines to oversee the convicts on the voyage, reasoning: 'Had [army troops] been sent out, sea-sickness would have incapacitated half the men from performing the duties immediately and indispensably necessary; whereas the marines, from being accustomed to serve on board ship, accommodated themselves with ease to every exigency, and surmounted every difficulty ...'

It was not until nearly two centuries after the First Fleet arrived in Botany Bay that the world of maritime history became aware of one of the most interesting perspectives of the expedition – an account, written truly from 'the inside', of the passage to New South Wales, as well as the early days of the settlement. It has become known as *The Nagle Journal*: 161 folio pages that were hand-written by one Jacob Nagle, forty years after the events described, from the diaries he kept during the voyage. The journal lay dormant until 1982, when it was unearthed by John C. Dann, director of the Clements Library at the University of Michigan.

What sets this document apart from others relating to the First Fleet is that it was written by a salt-of-the-sea sailor who was capable of giving his impressions of the adventure accurately, honestly and using the colourful prose of the day.

Nagle was born in Pennsylvania in 1761 and later fought alongside his father in the War of Independence. He was captured by the British and, like many other Americans, eventually opted to change sides: he joined the Royal Navy. One of six Americans who were members of the crew of *Sirius*, Nagle volunteered for the mission while serving aboard HMS *Ganges*.

He was a lithe, fit and energetic individual who boasted that he was able to beat much bigger men in a stoush and could climb to the top of any mast in a mid-ocean gale. He proved his prowess as an oarsman while aboard *Ganges* when she was on guard station in the Solent. 'Having but little to do, laying as a guard ship,' he writes, 'I belonged to a fast pulling pinnace, and the officers would send us to the Isle of Wight and smuggle gin and brandy, as the customs house boats could never come up with us before we could reach the ship.' This reputation led to him being assigned to the crew of Phillip's barge. Later in life, when he retired to America, Nagle was possibly the only man on earth who could claim to having met three of the world's great men of the era: naval hero Lord Nelson and the founding fathers of two nations, George Washington and Arthur Phillip. On the flip-side, he survived hand-to-hand combat during battle, bar-room brawls, shipwrecks and heinous storms.

Although his persona reflected a man who was as tough as teak, Nagle was also a person of compassion and understanding. Interestingly, he was the one individual to note an incident of brutality aboard *Sirius* when she was about halfway to Tenerife.

It occurred when the third lieutenant took it upon himself to have the bosun's mate flog the men of two watches because they weren't on deck at the same time, which was what he expected of them. The offending crewmen were lined up for punishment, but as soon as the lash was wielded, the attendant cries of pain and shouts of objection caused Captain Hunter to rush up to the deck, to discover the cause of the commotion. He was aghast to see his sailors being flogged and called for an immediate halt. The captain then learned from the men of the watch that, as a result of this officer, they were on the verge of revolt; if this was the way they were to be treated on the voyage, the tars told him, they would rather jump overboard there and then.

When Phillip was subsequently informed of the ruckus, he ordered every officer aboard *Sirius* to appear in his cabin. Nagle's account continues:

> [The governor] told them all if he knew any officer to
> strike a man on board he would [punish] him
> immediately. He said, 'Those men [the tars] are all we
> have to depend upon, and if we abuse those men that
> we have to trust [then] the convicts will rise and
> massacre us all. Those men are our support. We have a
> long and severe station to go through in settling this
> colony, and we cannot expect to return in less than five
> years. This ship and her crew is to protect and support
> the country, and if they are ill-treated by their own
> officers, what support can you expect of them? They
> will be all dead, before the voyage is half out, and who
> [then] is to bring us back again?'

Phillip then hurried up the companionway ladder and strode to the quarterdeck, where he ordered all hands to appear before him. After severely reprimanding the lieutenant who had initiated the flogging, he left the entire crew in no doubt as to how he expected the ship to be run. The recent episode was clearly in violation of such requirements – and he would deal with any officer who took it upon himself to maltreat the tars. He then retired to his cabin.

For Arthur Phillip, there was far more to this voyage than the arduous passage to Botany Bay. On 25 May the commodore directed Lieutenant John Shortland, of *Alexander*, to visit some of the transports by launch and prepare a list of the trades and occupations of all the convicts on board. This would allow him to more easily and effectively allocate manpower to the most essential tasks after arriving at Botany Bay. It was just one example of how he was constantly working on plans for the settlement once the fleet arrived.

CHAPTER 6

Around the High

The fleet's first taste of a true Atlantic storm came during the final week of May. It brought, in Phillip's description, 'exceedingly fresh' winds and 'a heavy rolling sea', each wave of which was capped with turbulent white foam. This blow lasted for four days and, fortunately, came from the north, thus allowing the ships to run with it and make good speed direct towards Madeira, which was in line with Tenerife.

As a safety precaution, Phillip signalled for the fast-sailing *Supply* to cram on all possible sail and extend her lead over the fleet while on the lookout for land. She was to be ahead by 6 nautical miles during daylight hours and 2 nautical miles at night. Just twenty-four hours later, *Supply*'s ensign was seen to be hoisted – the signal that land had been sighted. It was part of the Desertas Islands, a barren ridge of rocks located 15 nautical miles to the south-east of Madeira. There was now another 250 nautical miles to be sailed due south to Tenerife.

By this time, a strong north-easterly breeze saw the fleet romping along under full sail towards its first, eagerly anticipated stopover. The beneficial conditions were destined not to last, however, as David Collins recorded.

> Our strong trade wind appeared to have here spent its force, and we were baffled (as frequently happens in the

vicinity of islands) by light airs or calms. With these
and contrary winds our patience was exercised until the
evening of the 2nd of June, when a favourable breeze
sprang up, which continued during that night. At six
the next morning the island of Teneriffe was seen right
ahead ...

The lookout on the mainmast of *Supply* was no doubt the first person to sight land, but from a distance of 15 leagues, it was a very blurred outline. The weather was 'thick & hazy', to such an extent that Mount Teide, the island's snow-capped, 12,200-foot volcanic peak, was barely distinguishable.

It was early evening when the convoy approached the anchorage in Santa Cruz Bay, on Tenerife's eastern shore. As the ships progressed into the bay, Phillip called for the traditional salute to the settlement and its governor. Thirteen booming blasts from *Sirius*'s cannons then echoed across the waterway, which brought an identical response from the island's shore battery.

By seven o'clock, the leadsman on each ship – the burly crewman standing in the chains, swinging the lead – had advised his quarterdeck that the depth was a suitable 15 fathoms. With that, the massive iron anchor was released from its cathead, accompanied by a mighty thumping sound as the bower broke the surface of the water. Beforehand, each of the vessels had launched a boat with which to carry out an important safety measure. The ocean floor was known to be very rocky, so this safeguard involved attaching the bower cables to large wooden casks, thereby having the thick hemp ropes suspended above the seabed and prevented from dragging across the sharp rocks and ultimately becoming chafed through.

The following morning, Captain Phillip went ashore to meet the governor of the Canaries, Marquis de Brancifort, pass pleasantries and arrange for his ships to take on water and wine (the last of which had not been put aboard in any quantity before departure from England) and to purchase what fresh produce might be available. The presence of a Spanish packet in the bay gave Phillip the opportunity to write a communiqué to Lord Sydney. This vessel was due to sail for Europe within days, and her captain agreed to have the commodore's letter delivered to London as soon as possible.

Sitting at the table in his cabin at the stern of the ship – where windows filled the entire transom, along with the quarter galleries on each side, providing ample light – Phillip took up his finely sharpened quill, dipped its tip in the inkwell, and began to write a lengthy update for His Lordship. In it he expressed considerable concern about one particular matter: he had just learned that the marines had next to no ammunition at their disposal. What little they possessed was certainly not enough to last the anticipated two years before a second fleet of supply ships was expected to arrive at Botany Bay. The finger of blame for this oversight should have been pointed directly at Major Robert Ross, who had been appointed lieutenant governor of the colony as well as Royal Marines commander across the fleet. Phillip stopped short of making any accusations, however, writing: 'I understood that they [the marines] would be furnished with ammunition, but, since we sailed, find that they were only supplied with what was necessary for immediate service while in port; and we have neither musket balls nor paper for musket cartridges; nor have we any armourer's tools …' This was the start of a fractious relationship Phillip would have with Ross in the years ahead.

Naturally, he requested that ammunition be sent with the next fleet sailing to Botany Bay. As things transpired, he would be able to solve the immediate problem by procuring 10,000 musket balls at their next port of call, Rio de Janeiro.

Phillip also advised Sydney on the condition and behaviour of the transportees. 'In general the convicts have behaved well,' he reported. 'I saw them all yesterday for the first time [since leaving England]. They are quiet and contented, tho' there are amongst them some complete villains …'

The expedition leader was pleased to report that all his ships had come through this first stage virtually unscathed. The only damage of note had been aboard *Friendship*, whose topgallant mast broke during a squall before her sails could be hauled up and furled, and the storeship *Golden Grove*, where a similar incident occurred. These breakages were replaced by the ships' carpenters in a very short time. *Golden Grove* would have the same mast break three times before the First Fleet cleared the Atlantic.

While anchored in the bay, the ships were forever surrounded by so-called 'bum boats', all manned by locals wanting to trade a wide variety of produce and goods with the sailors and marines. On one of the transports, this led to some quick-thinking seamen supplying metal spoons to a 'coiner' among the convicts, whose talents were sufficient to create imitation English shillings and sixpences from the spoons, as counterfeit currency that the tars then used for their purchases. This fraudulent activity was quickly exposed, however, and with predictable results. The sailors paid a price – their grog supply was stopped – while the coiner was flogged.

The fleet's principal surgeon, John White, visited all eleven ships soon after arrival in Tenerife, to check on the health of crew and convicts alike. His report back to the commodore confirmed that in the three weeks since leaving the Mother Bank, fifteen adults and one child had died, and eighty-one were on the sick list – figures that apparently caused no great alarm.

There was one noteworthy incident while the flotilla lay at anchor in Santa Cruz Bay. A convict, John Power, was working on deck aboard *Alexander* when he noticed one of the ship's boats lying unattended near her stern, and immediately recognised it as a means of escape. He deftly climbed over the side and down a rope to the boat without being noticed, before rowing towards a newly arrived Dutch East India ship, his hope being that the crew would take him on board and sail him away to England or some foreign port. Denied asylum by

the Dutch sailors, Power then rowed out to a distant shore
with the intention of hiding there until the convict fleet had
departed for Rio.

By this point, a boatload of marines from *Alexander* had
been dispatched ashore to search for him. After they had
located the boat drifting close to shore at the southern end of
the island, they landed there and found Power hiding among
the rocks – dazed, bleeding and exhausted. He had injured
himself after tumbling down the steep coastal escarpment he'd
been attempting to scale. Power was returned to his ship,
where he received a thorough flogging and was put in the
heaviest of irons.

Another event showed how treacherous an anchoring place
the ultra-rocky seabed could be, despite the precautions taken
through the use of floating casks. Nagle recorded the episode in
his journal: 'One of the transports parted their cable and drifted
to sea having no sails bent [attached to the yards so they could be
set]. The Governor sent us in the barge to help her in. She was
full of women. We bent her sails and brought her to anchor ...'

By 10 June, the replenishment of the fleet with water and other
necessities was completed as well as could be. But with there
being a severe shortage of fresh produce on Tenerife, Phillip
decided to sail to the Cape Verde Islands, around 800 nautical
miles to the south-south-west, in the hope that the required
produce could be procured there. So, that morning,
preparation for departure was called for, as explained by King:
'the Signal was made for every Person to repair onboard their
respective Ships, & unmoored; the next Morning at daylight
we weighed with a light air at NNW which lasted long
enough to give us an offing, when it fell Calm ...'.

For the next three days, the wind wafted in from almost
every point of the compass, making for very slow progress on
a flat and glassy sea. Then, when they were 50 miles to the
south – and the volcanic peak of Mount Teide could still be
seen to the north – another taste of the much-needed north-

east trade wind arrived on the scene. This caused considerable activity on deck as the then bosoming sails were trimmed to best suit the refreshing 20-knot wind. The breeze also brought relief for the convicts held below decks on the transports, who had been surviving in stifling conditions.

It was Phillip's intention to anchor for a day in the reasonably protected bay at Porto Praia, on Cape Verde Island, the largest of ten islands making up the archipelago. Porto Praia, he believed, would provide the best opportunity to secure what was needed for the eight-week passage to Rio de Janeiro. As recalled by Collins, however, the vagaries of the weather spoiled that idea.

> At noon we were ranging along the south side of [the island], with the signal flying for the convoy to prepare to anchor; but at the moment of our opening Praya-bay ... the fleet was suddenly taken aback [the wind blew from the opposite direction and the sails went inside out], and immediately after baffled by light airs. We could however [then] perceive ... that the wind blew directly in upon the shore, which would have rendered our riding there extremely hazardous ... it was probable that our coming to an anchor might not have been effected without some accident happening to the convoy ...

In short, the safety of the ships was under threat. Lieutenant King explained: 'A great Swell was running, & had we persevered in endeavouring to get into the Bay, it was more than probable that some one or more of the Ships might have been disabled ... which would at these Islands have been irreparable. Many of the transports were not more than half a mile from the reef ...'

Every ship needed to achieve offing as quickly as possible to avoid the hazards of what was a foreboding lee shore. Phillip led the way, ordering that the anchoring signal flying from

Sirius's rig be lowered to the deck immediately so that the fleet would recognise that plans to anchor had been abandoned. To escape the danger confronting them, each crew then had to work their utmost to ensure their ship clawed its way back out to sea. It wasn't an easy task, as each erratic wisp of wind had to be harnessed by the sails. Every skill the sailing master had learned over his years at sea was being called on: he shouted orders for every manoeuvre, willing the tars to ease, or haul away, on the braces and sheets in quick response to every puff. Officers on the quarterdeck watched for the tell-tale signs of catspaws heading their way – light breezes that ruffle small areas of the otherwise near-smooth sea surface – calling their approach so that the men trimming the yards and sails were prepared to make changes as quickly as possible.

It was a painstakingly slow exit from the bay, but all the ships emerged unscathed. With that achieved, Phillip had no alternative but to abort his plan to obtain fresh produce on the island. He later wrote in a document that this decision was 'of much disappointment to many individuals on board, who, as is natural in long voyages, were eager on every occasion to enjoy the refreshments of the shore'. The next 'intended station' was Rio, more than 2500 nautical miles away to the south-west, on the opposite side of the Atlantic. This meant that the rationing of food and water would be a distinct possibility.

After Rio, the ultimate destination on this stage of the voyage was Cape Town, where the fleet would be prepared for the potentially dangerous passage across the Southern Ocean. Here, the ships would also take on board all the remaining equipment, general supplies and livestock essential to the successful establishment of the planned settlement at Botany Bay.

The direct route from the Cape Verde Islands to Cape Town was 3700 nautical miles, whereas to reach there via Rio de Janeiro added another 2000 nautical miles. While it might appear to be an illogical track, the more circuitous route was in fact the fastest way to get there. The reason for this was a weather phenomenon, the South Atlantic High, an enormous high-pressure system that plagues the waters extending well wide of the coast of Africa. It is like a huge vacuum where, through thermal activity, frustrating and sometimes mind-bending calms almost shackle a ship to the sea. By sailing across the Atlantic to Rio de Janeiro, however, ships coming out of Europe stay to the north of the high, so are able to maintain a considerably faster speed because they remain, for the most part, in fair winds. The same goes for the subsequent looping course they take from Rio: deep into the southern waters of the Atlantic before turning east towards Cape Town. It's a course that sees them skirt the lower edge of the high.

Once well clear of Porto Praia, the crews were relieved to have a refreshing north-easterly trade wind come to their aid; a perfect angle across the starboard aft quarter that let them sail a comfortable course to the south-west, towards the Equator. All ships were making good speed – except *Lady Penrhyn*. Once again, she struggled to keep pace, no matter how much sail was crammed onto her three masts. It was as if she was hobbled. Nevertheless, in keeping with Phillip's demand that visual contact be maintained at all times, and to the frustration of the other ships' crews, sail was reduced across the fleet so that the slow *Lady* could catch up.

In the first week of July 1787, the flotilla was closing on 'the Line' – the Equator – and with that came the legendary doldrums, where, as the name suggests, the wind stagnates. In this region, the tropical heat causes the air to rise and create a vast, vacuous area of little or no wind.

Scottish-born Ralph Clark, the puritanical lieutenant aboard *Friendship*, noted 'the sun exceedingly hot' – an understandable comment from someone used to far cooler temperatures year round. In his detailed journal of the voyage, he also compared the daily distances sailed, as recorded in the ship's log, to reveal that the impressive 174 three weeks before had now plummeted to a miserly 43. The latter figure equated to an average speed of less than 2 knots for the day. *Friendship* was barely making headway, lolling around on a gentle swell, the limp sails slatting laboriously with each surge.

It was a challenging time for her crew, who were helpless in the situation: no wind, no progress. They could have walked faster, and making matters worse was the steamy atmosphere: punishingly high temperatures and high humidity during the daylight hours, which, as Clark wrote, 'produce considerable annoyance'. At least, they were in fresh air, unlike the convicts in their dark confines below deck. With next to no ventilation 'tween decks, there was no respite from the oppressive heat for the transportees. It was the closest thing to hell imaginable, and not surprisingly many couldn't cope, either fainting or convulsing in fits.

Crewmen on the forenoon and afternoon watches struggled to find shade anywhere on deck. Conversations, even on the quarterdeck, were somewhat hushed, because there was no noise that had to be shouted over. Only the occasional banging of the yardarms on the masts, and the screeching sound of the sheaves in the pulleys.

Now and then, by day and night, massive thunderheads would roll in from the horizon, bringing with them vivid and jagged bolts of lightning, accompanied by long, booming rolls of thunder, and heavy downpours of rain that peppered those on deck like musket shot. More often than not, these thunderstorms were accompanied by intense and fierce squalls, which could shred sails, or worse still, splinter masts and spars and send them crashing down to the deck or over the side. Consequently, the doldrums demanded constant and interminable vigilance from all on deck.

These conditions sapped everyone's energy, and dehydration became a concern. Yet water remained a highly valuable commodity and had to be allocated sparingly. Clark's account continues:

> When the *Sirius* hoist a Blue flag with a Yellow Cross at
> the Main Top Gallant Masthead the officers Seamen

> Marines and Convicts are to go on allowance of water
> — Three pints for the Twenty four hours, one half to
> be served in the Morning and the remainder in the
> afternoon — A Lieutenant of Marines with a Sergeant
> or Corporal and two of the Convicts always to be
> present when the Water is Served ...

Almost everything about sailing through this tropical convergence zone was exasperating – particularly when the navigator aboard *Sirius* calculated that the convoy had drifted backwards by 10 nautical miles during one 24-hour period. Throughout the voyage, and especially for the period spent idling in the doldrums, Clark's candid journal-writing would provide a valuable picture of shipboard life on the First Fleet. The following is a sample from just a few days, reflecting the author's desperation at the circumstances, as well as his predilection for using the long dashes that were the style of the time.

> I wish to God that the wind would come fair otherwise
> we shall make a long passage and the Ship will get very
> Sickly — Very heavy Squalls of wind and rain all day,
> all the Ships in company — wish in Christ that the
> wind would come fair — a great number of fish about
> the Ship — Mr. Laurance the first mate caught three
> Dolphins and one Bonito with the grains [harpoons]
> — gentle Breeze and pleasant Weather — Very little
> wind all day and that from the Southward the worst
> wind that can blow for Us — little wind today, Log 47
> miles — last night one of the Marines wives was
> brought to Bed of a fine Boy — departed this life
> Patrick Delany Convict which has been expected ever
> Since he came aboard — caught a large Shark today —
> [Marines commander] Capt Meredith ordered one of
> the Corporals to flog with a rope Elizabeth Dudgeon
> for being impertinent to Capt Meredith — the

> Corporal did not play with her but laid it home which I
> was very glad to see — then [the captain] ordered her to
> be tied to the pump — caught a very large Shark one
> Bonito, 2 Dolphin with the hook and one very large
> Dolphin with the grains — thank God for the fish as it
> is a very good fresh meal and Made into chowder eats
> most Excellent — I wish we may get Some fish Every
> day which will Save our Stock as it begins to grow low
> having now only 5 fowls and one Small pig belonging
> to the Mess — caught a large She Shark this morning
> with 37 Young ones in her …

Clark also noted that sometimes when the ships were becalmed, the time was put to good use. On these occasions, boats were hoisted out so that some of the tars could scrub the area along the waterline, removing the weed and molluscs that had taken up residence there. The presence of this natural build-up reduced each ship's speed, especially in light winds.

It was 14 July when the eleven vessels crossed the Line and entered the southern hemisphere, the point where the North Star begins to fade in the northern sky as the Southern Cross emerges in the south. The passage through the doldrums had been tedious, but as they neared the Equator, Phillip and those aboard *Sirius* learned that they had actually been quite fortunate. Close to the Line, they crossed tacks with a small English vessel, the 40-ton *Remembrance*, which had sailed from London and was bound for the Falkland Islands, deep in the South Atlantic. Her master advised that for the previous three weeks, headwinds and near calms had forced his vessel backwards and forwards across the Equator no less than seventeen times.

In keeping with maritime tradition, there was jocularity and unrestrained fun aboard all ships when King Neptune and his 'Queen' (sometimes bearded) appeared on deck in ridiculous garb, to welcome all newcomers to the south side of the Equator. As was customary, the two nautical royals also proclaimed what punishments should be dealt these first-timers – usually a dunking over the side, or being sluiced in a tub containing vile liquid ingredients. The hijinks aboard *Lady Penrhyn* must've been exceptional. With no one apparently manning the helm or keeping a lookout, she almost collided with *Charlotte*. Only shouts from the crew of *Charlotte* alerted the men in time for them to avoid an impact.

When normality returned to the fleet, Phillip had a white pennant hoisted on the ensign staff, signifying that all other vessels should pass close to the flagship's stern, so their navigators could check the longitude calculated by *Sirius*'s Captain Hunter, Lieutenant William Dawes and Lieutenant William Bradley when the convoy crossed the Equator. The figure was written on a large board mounted at the taffrail. This would enable all the navigators to have identical positions on their charts so, in the event of a ship becoming separated from the flotilla, her captain could set a course for Rio. The precaution of synchronising navigation plots was undertaken a number of other times during the voyage.

The southern hemisphere welcomed Phillip's fleet with perfect sailing conditions – a brisk south-easterly trade wind that enabled all to sail fast and almost directly down the rhumb line towards Rio de Janeiro. Every ship, that is, apart from the habitual laggard of the pack. 'All the fleet in company – the *Lady Penrhyn* a good way astern,' wrote Clark. 'She sails very bad for She was up with the fleet last night.' *Sirius* then signalled the remainder of the flotilla, with the usual instruction to reduce sail, so that the struggling *Lady* could again make up the lost ground.

Two weeks after crossing the Equator, the fleet continued to make excellent speed in the direction of Rio. With the wind now coming from further aft, the ships were able to cram on more sail and continue to steer a direct course for the Brazilian port. Soon though, the wind strength increased and with that came rising seas, which also greatly assisted progress.

'Hard squalls with heavy rain, but thank God it comes from abaft the beam,' Clark reported. 'I know that we will be in Rio in a few days.'

But the weather had plenty more to offer, necessitating Phillip to have a blue flag hauled to the top of *Sirius*'s main topgallant mast: the signal for the fleet to sail in close company, for fear that visual contact might otherwise be lost. By then the weather had begun to deteriorate and the ships soon had walls of white water sweeping across their decks as the waves broke over them. On *Friendship*, one wave was so powerful that it smashed to splinters the convicts' caboose (their cooking facility on deck), washing much of it overboard. In addition, tired canvas sails couldn't cope and were exploding under the pressure from the wind, while *Golden Grove* had another fore-topgallant mast bend alarmingly then fracture and shatter into pieces. The size and power of these waves caused a heavy rolling motion for every ship, no matter her size. It was so severe that it was almost impossible for anyone to sleep.

After a few days, this blow, like all others, began to abate and some level of normality was restored. Even the more rebellious women prisoners were soon back to their vitriolic best aboard *Friendship*, as Clark related:

Elizabeth Barber one of the Convict Women abused the Doctor in a most terrible manner and [accused him of trying to have sex with her] … called him all the names that She could think of … After dinner Capt. Meredith enquired into the matter … She was very much in liquor [probably supplied by the tars] and was ordered [into] a pair of leg irons. When she [was] getting them on She began to abuse Capt. Meredith in a much worse manner than She had done the doctor. She called him everything but a Gentle man and Said She was no more a Whore than his wife. The Capt. ordered her hands tied behind her back and to be gagged to prevent her from

> making noise. She was certain that she Should See us all
> thrown overboard before we got to Botany Bay. I wish
> to God She Was out of the Ship. I would rather have a
> hundred more men than to have a Single Woman ...

Barber, aged twenty-seven, had originally been sentenced to
death for assault and robbery, before having that sentence
commuted to transportation for seven years. From the time
she was embarked aboard *Friendship*, she gained a reputation
for her vile tongue, and for being one prisoner everyone tried
to avoid. Barber wasn't alone when it came to foul language or
fighting, Clark's account continuing: 'Capt Meredith put
Elizabeth Barber and Elizabeth Thackery in irons together and
Elizabeth Dudgeon and Elizabeth Pulley [in irons] together –
the damned whores the moment that they got below fell a
fighting amongst one another and Capt Meredith ordered the
Sergeant not to part them but to let them fight it out ...'

From the moment that his ship departed from England,
Clark had pined for his wife, Alicia, and his young son, often
questioning his decision to join the fleet. He had served with
the Royal Marines during the American War of Independence;
then, like so many others, he took this opportunity within the
Royal Navy in the hope that it might improve his chances for
promotion in the service. Clark received some solace for his
loneliness when his captain aboard *Friendship*, Francis Walton,
gave him a puppy just before the ship crossed the Equator. 'I
have called it Efford after the dear Sweet place [in Devon]
where first I came acquainted with my Alicia my Virtuous
Wife,' he wrote in his journal.

Sadly, Efford's time aboard the ship was brief: 'Lost my
dog Efford overboard I am apt to think that he was thrown
overboard by the first mate ... if I was certain I would make
some of the men give him a good thrashing ... I am sorry that
I lost him poor dog for he began to be very fond of me ...'

There were more tragic incidents on this stretch to Rio
de Janeiro – two fatalities and a close call. A sailor aboard

Alexander was lost overboard and could not be recovered, while on *Prince of Wales* a female convict, allowed on deck for exercise, died twenty-four hours after being crushed by one of the ship's boats which, during rough seas, had broken free of its mountings. A seaman sailing with *Scarborough* had a close call, escaping death when he fell from the main topgallant yard and crashed to the deck. Somehow his fall must have been cushioned on the way down, as Nagle's journal revealed that he 'fractured his head and broke his arm all to pieces, but the Surgeon says that he will do very well'.

On 2 August, after calculating sun and star sights, and applying timing from a Kendall clock (the device used to determine longitude), the navigator aboard *Sirius* advised the commodore that land should be in sight within twenty-four hours. Phillip then signalled Lieutenant Henry Ball, the captain aboard *Supply*, to proceed ahead of the fleet and keep a lookout. From that moment, officers on watch on the flagship's quarterdeck used their telescopes regularly to look ahead for any signal, and it came that afternoon: *Supply*'s ensign was hoisted to the top of its staff. They had sighted the coast of Brazil fine off the port bow and low on the horizon.

As is often the case in these waters, the wind began to fade as the fleet closed on land, so much so that it was virtually calm late in the day. Realising that they would have to wait at least another twenty-four hours before being able to enter the harbour at Rio de Janeiro in daylight, Hunter had the leadsman aboard *Sirius* heave the lead and advise him of the depth. On hearing a favourable report, Phillip, as commander of the squadron, then called for the Dutch Jack to be broken out at the masthead of the mizzen – the daytime signal for the fleet to bring-to and anchor for the night.

The calms persisted, however, and it was not until three days later – 5 August – that the ships were able to enter the port. At eight-thirty that evening, two large lanterns were lit on *Sirius*'s aft deck for all to see, and two cannon shots fired, signalling that the fleet was to yet again anchor for the night.

The following morning, as the rising sun slowly brought colour and definition to what had been an inky-black night, those on deck aboard the eleven ships were greeted with a majestic sight: a wide bay where the town of Rio de Janeiro was located, and a backdrop of spectacularly high, rocky mountains dotted with extensive canopies of rich green trees. Phillip, having spent considerable time in Rio during his time with the Portuguese Navy in the 1770s, described it as one of the finest harbours in the world, and 'capacious enough to contain more ships than ever assembled at one station'. It was also explained that Rio de Janeiro, which translates to mean 'January River', was given its name because Portuguese explorer Gonçalo Coelho dicovered it on 1 January 1502. At the time Coelho believed they were anchored at the mouth of a major river, when it was, in fact, a large bay – now Guanabara Bay – into which a number of small rivers flowed.

Before the First Fleet's passage to Rio was officially complete, the ships had to sail a short distance deeper into the bay where they would anchor off the town's waterfront. Fortunately, the tell-tale signs of a sea breeze arrived late that morning, bringing life to the flags and pennants that had lain limply all night. By 2.30 pm, the call came to weigh anchor and get under sail.

When the convoy was abeam of the town's fort, Phillip ordered a thirteen-gun salute to be fired in honour of Rio's governor and the residents, a gesture that was duly mirrored by the shore battery. Ironically, it was as if these cannon-blasts blew holes in the wind, because an oily calm descended on the bay almost simultaneously. The boats therefore had to be hauled out so that all eleven ships could be towed the rest of the way. At 5.30 pm, a flag was attached to the halyard leading to *Sirius*'s mizzen peak and sent aloft – the signal for the fleet to come to anchor at that location, 1 nautical mile from the shore.

The next few weeks would be consumed by repair work, replenishment of supplies and some level of rest, but no real respite for the convicts, except that the constant rolling motion of a ship on the open sea had been stilled. The fleet was almost a third of the way into the planned voyage, with at least 10,000 nautical miles to go before reaching Botany Bay.

CHAPTER 7

Noah's Ark

As early as was practicable the morning after their arrival, Phillip directed that one of his officers be taken ashore by boat so that he could call on the Portuguese viceroy, Dom Luís de Vasconcelos e Souza. In keeping with official protocol, Phillip's emissary was obliged to seek permission for the fleet to be in Rio de Janeiro. This approval came without hesitation, as the viceroy remembered having met Phillip four years earlier and was well aware of his distinguished service with the Portuguese Navy.

An invitation for the commodore to come ashore for an audience with Vasconcelos was relayed back to Phillip, who accepted immediately. At 11 am, the two men met in convivial circumstances at the viceroy's palace in the Royal Square, adjacent to the waterfront. During their discussion, Phillip's host consented to the officers of the British fleet being permitted to come ashore without restraint, a privilege not normally granted to visitors. The sailors would not be granted such liberties, however, because of their tendency to abuse hospitality, especially when drunk. The tars would have to be escorted while ashore.

Vasconcelos had advised the senior officers in his garrison that Phillip should be accorded the same level of respect and honour that he received in his role as viceroy. Phillip wished to decline such privileges, but Vasconcelos was insistent. The surgeon aboard *Lady Penrhyn*, Arthur Bowes Smyth, recalled one example of how Phillip's presence was officially recognised: 'At night the town was most beautifully illuminated & the Tops of the Churches & several Monasteries also, in honour of the Commodore who had some years ago been employed with much credit in the Portuguese Service ...'

Back on the water, small boats manned by 'some black men' came off the beach to welcome the visitors by 'hoving oranges on board'. The scene on the decks was that of a treasure hunt, as tars scampered in every direction trying to catch or pick up a prize – the oranges being their first taste of fresh fruit in months. There was an interesting activity in the great cabin the following day that similarly led to the procurement of fresh food while at anchor: officers were catching fish out of the quarter windows and hauling them on board. No doubt this took place when the commodore wasn't present, for he spent a considerable amount of time at his table, deep in thought, writing letters to Lord Sydney and Nepean regarding the progress of the fleet, the condition of the convicts and other relevant matters. These dispatches would be delivered aboard *Diana*, an English whaling ship that was heading home after having her 'leaky hull' repaired in Rio.

Apart from the convicts, everyone associated with the fleet spent time onshore, enjoying a town and countryside that Smyth described as being 'beautiful in the extreme, indeed so much so, that I find myself inadequate to the task of doing it justice by any description I could give it'. But he also wrote of a dark side to life in Rio: 'Saw many black Slaves being led about the streets to be sold ... This afternoon a Snow from the Coast of Guinea moored very near us, with a cargo of some hundreds of black Slaves for the Slave market at Rio. At daylight in the morning I was awoke with their singing, as is their custom previous to their being sold or Executed. They were all naked ...'

The master of each ship in the fleet was charged with the task of purchasing all the fresh supplies required for the passage to Cape Town, which was likely to see them at sea for at least six weeks. The locals advised that there were two grand market days held in town each week, and they proved to be an Aladdin's Cave of remarkable tropical and more familiar produce, including yams, lettuces, beans, pumpkins, watermelons, bananas, guavas, oranges, pineapples and mangoes, as well as a wide array of fresh meat. For Smyth, the prawns he purchased were 'the largest I ever saw. Some of them when extended were near a foot in length, & their bodies as big as my finger …'

This provisioning for the voyage was found to be surprisingly inexpensive: three-pence and 3 farthings per head, excluding the cost of each man's 20-ounce daily meat allowance. Beef was priced at almost two-pence a pound, and hogs, turkeys and ducks were readily available. Additionally, many seeds and plants that were expected to 'flourish on the coast of New South Wales' were bought in Rio, including coffee, indigo (a tropical pea) and cotton. As a precaution against the failure of an early wheat crop in the new colony, 100 sacks of cassava (a type of flour that originated in Africa) were put aboard the storeships.

One thing in short supply was wine, but that caused little concern. Rum was plentiful and cheap – so much so that Phillip bought as much of the stuff as possible. He wrote in a dispatch to Nepean: 'One hundred and fifteen pipes [bottles] of rum has been purchased for the use of the garrison, when landed, and for the use of the detachment at this port.' It was a purchase that would cause considerable trouble in the early days of the settlement of New South Wales, as rum became the principal bartering medium in a colony bereft of currency.

On a professional front, John White, being the fleet's surgeon-general, acquainted himself with the military surgeon in town, Senhor Ildefonse, who had studied in England. According to White's account, he left a lasting impression on his Portuguese colleague.

> I prevailed on the surgeon who was about to amputate
> a limb to allow me to take it off according to Allenson's
> method. During the operation I could plainly see that

> he and his pupils did not seem much pleased with it,
> and he afterwards told me it was impossible it could
> ever [heal]. A very short space of time, however, made
> them of a different opinion; and in eighteen days after I
> had the satisfaction to leave the patient with his stump
> nearly cicatrized, to the no small joy of the surgeon ...

While the crews got down to repairs and maintenance work on their respective vessels, the officers were more able to take in the sights and colour of this colonial outpost, set across the bay from Sugarloaf Mountain and in the shadow of the imposing peak of Corcovado, south-west of the town. Apart from the stunning scenery, superbly coloured butterflies filled the air like none of the visitors had seen before.

Phillip spent a considerable amount of time ashore during the fleet's four weeks in Rio. Embarrassed by the formal attention afforded him by the viceroy's guards each time he landed, he almost always had his launch take him to the opposite side of the bay in an effort to outwit the ever-vigilant sentinels. On spotting the commodore's craft depart *Sirius* and head towards the steps at the far end of town, the uniformed guards would run, huffing and puffing, along the road that curved along the waterfront, in an effort to be there before the launch arrived. Only then could they fulfil Vasconcelos's directive to 'attend the steps at the landing of the barge' and form a guard-of-honour to mark the commodore's arrival.

For the tars, seasoned sailors that most of them were, their shore leave was usually motivated by the hope of meeting some of the local women. It was a near impossible mission. The attractive young ladies of Rio were high fruit on the tree, the men of the town consistently discouraging them from fraternising with the visitors. Even Phillip noted this, writing: 'It must be known however, that our people did not find the ladies so indulgent as some voyagers have represented them.'

Yet the sometimes wayward and adventurous Jacob Nagle was not one to be deterred from having an enjoyable experience – and in this setting, it almost brought about his end. The episode took place after he had rowed Phillip from *Sirius* to the town's waterfront one day.

No One was Permitted to land without a permit or a Soldier with him. We had a Sargent to Attend us as protection that no One should Molest us, but he Would not walk about the town with us as our curiosity led us to see it. He, finding we had money, wished to sit in the Punch houses [drinking] all day. We acquainted the Governor [with this] and were then permitted to go where we pleased without any Guard, though they were Ordered to protect us wherever we should be insulted.

One Evening Two of us got into a grog Shop … and a Very handsome Young woman being there who was very familiar With me & Asked me home with her. I accepted the offer and had walked one square, arm-in-arm, and my comrade following me, [when] up came a Portuguese with a great cloak on [who] pushed me away from her, but I would not let go of my Hold. He drew back & drew his Sword & was Raising his Sword Over his head to Cut me Over the head. At that Instant a Soldier turned the corner drew his Sword & guarded the Blow he was going to Make at me, & another Soldier Behind him Abused him and threatened to cut him down for meddling with me – but the fellow begged their pardons & said I had taken his Wife from him …

Nagle then took the soldiers to a grog shop where he 'treated them for Saving my Life'. He and his comrade ended the evening 'pretty well seized over' – so drunk in fact that they were not present at the dock when Phillip was ready to be transported back to the ship. With the launch gone, there was no way for the pair to get back to *Sirius* that night, so they dossed down in the market place and fell into a comatose state of sleep. When they awoke, the two sailors discovered that they had been deftly robbed of their caps, the kerchiefs tied around their necks, and all the money they'd had. Nagle continued the story: 'In the Morning Mr King Came on Shore & took us on board with him then enquired of the Governor what was to be done with us, expecting we would be Ordered into Irons. [The Governor] was glad to hear we were Alive & desired King to send me to my hammock to Sleep as I would be wanted in the barge at 9 o'clock ...'

In fact, it was Smyth who was one of the few visitors to enjoy friendly contact with the local women. It occurred during the town's celebration of the birthday of José Francisco Xavier, the hereditary Prince of Brazil, a social engagement that saw the women dressed up in silks and gay colours. Judging by Smyth's description, it also appears to have been his first taste of traditional flamenco dancing. 'Ladies danced to a Violin played by a Negro Slave & made Mr Watts & me dance with them,' he recalled, adding: 'their dancing consists of little else than footing, turning round & snapping their fingers to the Music ...'.

Rio de Janeiro had a population of 40,000 at this time, about 10,000 of whom were slaves. David Collins observed a facet of local life that was most intriguing to the men of the First Fleet, that 'Ladies or gentlemen were never seen on foot in the streets during the day.' Instead, they were transported across town in private horse-drawn carriages or carried in gaudily decorated sedan chairs.

The visitors were also surprised by the highly visible role that religion played in the community. Collins noted: 'To a stranger nothing could appear more remarkable than the innumerable religious processions which were to be seen at all hours in this town. At the close of every day an image of the Virgin was borne in procession through the principal streets. At a corner of almost every street in the town, we observed a small altar ...'

While in port, the below-decks area of each ship was treated with disinfectant to rid it of the bugs and insects that had made life uncomfortable while sailing from Tenerife. Extensive checking of the hulls, rigs and equipment led to all the transports striking their yards and topmasts so that they could be inspected for damage, especially for stress cracks in the timber. The fleet's sailmakers were sent to a small island nearby where they could make repairs to the sails. Some of the equipment that would be used to set up the settlement in Botany Bay was landed on the same island and aired.

As for the transportees, Collins explained that as well as undergoing a general health check, each convict was well cared for.

> During their stay in this port of refreshment, the
> convicts were each served daily with a pound of rice
> and a pound and half of fresh meat (beef), together
> with a suitable portion of vegetables. Great numbers of
> oranges were at different times distributed among
> them, and every possible care was taken to refresh and
> put them into a state of health and condition to resist
> the attacks of scurvy, should it make its appearance in
> the long passage over the ocean which was yet between
> them and New South Wales. The Reverend Mr
> Johnson gave also his full share of attention to their
> welfare, performing divine service on board two of the
> transports every Sunday of their stay in port ...

Early on during the Rio stopover, Phillip was another to visit each transport ship and address the convicts – primarily to establish that they would face the most severe punishment for any unruly behaviour. He also assured them that, should they 'redeem their characters', their life would be a lot better once Botany Bay was reached.

As the departure date neared, Ralph Clark's prejudice towards the female prisoners aboard *Friendship* resurfaced:

> Lieut Long [Phillip's adjutant] had been on board with
> an order to discharge the following Women to the
> *Charlotte* Viz Susannah Gough, Hannah Green,
> Frances Hart, Eliz Harvey, Mary Watkins and Ann
> Beazley — the Six Very best Women we have in the
> Ship — and to receive Six of the Worst from the
> *Charlotte* which I don't think is right and I don't know
> what I shall do now as well as the rest of us for they
> are the only Women that can wash [themselves]
> amongst them …

Shortly before the fleet set sail, a Portuguese soldier was found aboard *Sirius* — a stowaway. When brought before the commodore, the man begged to be taken to Botany Bay, but Phillip refused, eager not to jeopardise his good relations with the town and its viceroy. He showed the man some consideration, however: when issuing the order to have the stowaway returned to shore, he directed his men to 'land him at some spot where he can get back to barracks without his absence being discovered'.

Smyth reported a similar situation that occurred not long after the fleet had cruised into Rio.

> In this place we met with a young man of the name of
> Dagnell who came from Coventry [and arrived here
> aboard an] East Indiaman & deserted about 11 months
> since at this place. We found him very useful being a
> complete master of the Portuguese language. He
> seemed very desirous of leaving Rio & once applied
> for leave to attend me as a Servant to Botany Bay &
> elsewhere; but for prudential reasons I declined,
> especially as no individual is suffered to leave this
> place clandestinely …

As it turned out, rather than take on newcomers, Phillip reduced the number of people in the fleet at this time. He decided to repatriate three men to England due to illness, one of whom was the sailing master aboard *Sirius*.

On 4 September, almost a month to the day after the fleet arrived in Rio de Janeiro, a flag signal hoisted high in *Sirius*'s rig stirred in a moderate offshore breeze. Its colours confirmed for the other ships' masters that it was time to weigh anchor and put back to sea. Every ship's deck was soon a hive of activity. While the sailing masters orchestrated every task, tars were aloft, fully absorbed in unfurling sails and having them ready to be hauled down and sheeted home.

Aboard each vessel, in preparation for retrieving the ship's anchor, heavy wooden bars were inserted into either the horizontal windlass near the bow or the vertical capstan mounted on the deck amidships. Then, when the call came to haul away and begin the slow process of raising the cast-iron bower – a weight of 3 tons or more – as many as forty crewmen would man the bars and rotate the mechanism, accompanied by the monotonous clacking sound of the heavy ratchet pawls.

As the thick, tarred-hemp bower cable came on deck, men sent below would carefully coil it into the well-ventilated cable locker, in order to have the rope dry as quickly as possible, and so reduce the chance of the timber bulkheads becoming damp and open to rot. Once the anchor on each ship had arrived at the cathead and was safely secured in its sea-going position, then the master called for the square sails to be hauled down and the jibs hoisted.

Eventually, all eleven vessels were gliding near-silently across the smooth waters of the bay – a small armada, heading for the open sea. *Sirius* led the way, and as she sailed past the naval fort near the entrance to the port, a 21-gun salute thundered forth at even intervals from the cannons situated there, farewelling Phillip and the British fleet. The governor-designate of New South Wales responded by having the same number of guns fired from his ship.

*

The flotilla received a land breeze that was perfect for propelling it away from the Brazilian coast on its south-easterly course towards Cape Town, more than 3000 nautical miles distant. Over the subsequent days, the placid conditions were similarly welcome, as everyone reacquainted themselves with the incessant motion of a ship at sea. By 7 September, however, they were experiencing their first storm: heavy squalls of rain, thunder and lightning, which lasted for the next week.

The seas became increasingly large and powerful as the storm raged, so those who were prone to seasickness had no choice but to surrender to it. This was bad enough for the men who could make it onto the deck before being ill, but for the convicts locked inside their quarters on the transport ships, the stench of vomit turned a nightmarish experience into hell. Making matters worse was that, with the heavy wash from the waves cascading across any available surface, the ships' deck hatches had to be battened down to prevent water from pouring below. The air was virtually unbreathable for the convicts.

Remarkably though, in the middle of the storm, there came a small level of joy. The ship's log of *Charlotte* recorded: 'on the evening of the 8th, between the hours of three and four, Mary Braund, a convict was delivered a fine girl ...'.

Mother Nature did eventually show some mercy. On 14 September, the storm abated as quickly as it had developed, and a calm descended on the fleet. But the motion did not end there. With no life in their sails, the ships were now rolling around on the leftover sea like drunken sailors staggering along a dock. This would not be the last time the fleet endured a hammering in the South Atlantic, nor the worst example.

When the wind returned, it came from the desired direction – aft of abeam. Crews were kept alert, however, since any heavy shower of rain was usually accompanied by squalls capable of causing severe damage to rig and sails. The men had to be ready to reef or haul up the square sails and lower the jibs at a moment's notice.

On 19 September, a concerned Clark recorded an observation he had made from the deck of *Friendship*: '*Charlotte* hove all aback today – I hope that nobody has fallen overboard ...' White would elaborate soon afterwards:

> William Brown, a very well-behaved convict, in
> bringing some clothing from the bowsprit end, where
> he had hung them to dry, fell overboard. As soon as the
> alarm was given of a man being overboard, the ship
> was instantly hove to, and a boat hoisted out, but to no
> purpose ... notwithstanding every exertion, the poor
> fellow sunk before either the *Supply* or our boat could
> reach him. The people on the forecastle, who saw him
> fall, say that the ship [which was doing 6 knots] went
> directly over him, which, as she had quick way through,
> the water, must make it impossible for him to keep on
> the surface long enough to be taken up, after having
> received the stroke from so heavy a body ...

The unfortunate incident at least ensured that, with *Charlotte* hove-to, delays caused by the traditional back-of-pack *Lady Penrhyn* were kept to a minimum that day. Phillip and his officers aboard *Sirius* were forever scanning the horizon with their telescopes, keeping a watchful eye on the entire flotilla, and almost every time they looked, it was the same transport vessel struggling to stay in touch. As on the previous leg of the voyage, Phillip had the continually frustrating experience of calling for his ships to reduce speed, to give the sluggish *Lady Penrhyn* an opportunity to catch up.

Another message passed on to all vessels concerned the need for the ships' captains to be more prudent with their lantern lights at night, lest they be interpreted as a signal from *Sirius* or *Supply*. The request was that curtains be drawn in the aft cabins after sunset.

*

Sunday, 23 September heralded the start of a storm that would be recognised as the worst that the First Fleet had endured since departing from Portsmouth, more than four months earlier. Lieutenant Clark recorded:

> It blows very hard, much harder than it has Since we
> have Been at Sea — the Sea broke over us Several
> Times today although it blows so hard the wind is
> fair [from astern] which is one good thing —
> battened the hatches down of the Marines and
> convict women, the Sea Breaking over the Ship — it
> blowed very hard all night and the Ship rolled her
> Gunwale under Several times and a great deal of
> water went between decks and washed the marines
> out of their beds and the Convict Women [were]
> rolling about — it now Blows very hard and a great
> deal of hail falls as it did last night ...

This tempest lasted less than three days, although fatigue and seasickness made it feel as if it were a lot longer. Yet, within hours of the storm passing, that level of misery was forgotten as the fleet began to record its best ever 24-hour runs. Clark commented once more: 'Since yesterday — and having no more than our two top Sails close furled — went in the 24 hours 183 miles — not bad going — I like our little bark very much — would not change for any one in the fleet ...'

At the same time, Clark was sad to note that Captain Meredith's dog, Shot, was lost overboard, becoming the fifth canine to be lost that way since leaving England. 'We have been very unlucky with our dogs,' he added.

About a week before Cape Town came into view, Clark's disapproval of his female charges aboard *Friendship* emerged once more. 'Two of the convict Women that went through the Bulkhead to the Seamen on 3 July last have informed the doctor that they are with child,' the lieutenant wrote. 'I hope the commodore will make the two Seamen that are the Fathers of

the children marry them and make them stay at Botany Bay …'
Clark needn't have worried. For each of the women, Sarah
McCormack and Elizabeth Pulley, it would prove to be a false
alarm.

On 4 October, Phillip received the disconcerting news
from Thomas Gilbert, the master of *Charlotte*, that thirty of his
contingent of convicts – about a third of those aboard the
ship – were ill, some so seriously that they were close to death.
In most cases, dysentery and scurvy were to blame. For the
afflicted, the unfortunate reality was that all that could be
done to ease their suffering was to get to Cape Town as soon
as possible. Before proper treatment became available to them
there, the ship's doctor would do what he could to remedy
their malaise.

After thirty days of what had, so far, been a mostly wet,
wild, cold and miserable passage across the South Atlantic,
everyone in the fleet, from the commodore to the lowliest
convict, was relieved to know that they were closing on Cape
Town. The Dutch outpost offered much-needed respite, and
the promise of early spring on a new continent. Arthur Phillip
had every right to be pleased that his convoy had got this far
with little in the way of serious incident. Fate ensured that
there was one last drama, however, a week out from the Cape.

It concerned the crew of the transport *Alexander*, captained
by Duncan Sinclair, some of whom had demonstrated a
rebellious attitude while in Rio. As Smyth penned in his
journal, the situation had since escalated into an uprising.

> This day about 10 a.m. the *Supply* Brig spoke us &
> informed us that there was bad work on board the
> *Alexander* so much so that Captain Ball apprehended
> there would be some hanged as soon as we arrived at
> the Cape – we had not the particulars as Capt. Ball was
> not very near us when he spoke us but we apprehend it
> to be a Mutiny amongst the Ships Company &
> Convicts. [Apparently they were] declaring they would

do as they pleased for Captain Sinclair, who they said
had no power over them, & who indeed appeared to
have lost all Authority over his people – for what
reason I am at a loss to guess, but I apprehend from his
not exerting a proper Spirit amongst them …

The four accused were transferred to *Sirius*, charged with
having entered into a conspiracy to release some of the
prisoners while the ship was in Cape Town. It was claimed
they had provided the convicts with implements that would
enable them to break out of their cells.

Once informed of the plot, Phillip had the accused chained
on deck and severely flogged. The four were then ordered to
remain aboard *Sirius* until the fleet reached Cape Town.

With the majestic and bold plateau of Cape Town's Table
Mountain well in sight on the morning of 13 October, Phillip
put the swift-sailing *Supply* to good use. At the commodore's
behest, Captain Ball intercepted the slower ships at the rear of
the fleet and advised them on the course into the bay, and how
to approach the anchorage off the town. *Sirius* then led the
flotilla into port, and once anchored, Phillip had an officer go
ashore and carry out the usual protocol – advising the governor
of the arrival of the ships, where they were heading after Cape
Town, and the name of the fleet commander. Phillip was
subsequently advised that the Dutch governor welcomed the
fleet and 'politely promised us every assistance in his power'.

With the opening formalities thus completed, Phillip
initiated the traditional response to the welcome: he rose early
the next day so that 'at sun-rise the *Sirius* saluted the garrison
with thirteen guns, which were returned by an equal number
from the [town's] fort'. Later that morning, Phillip, along with
his principal navy officers and commanders, proceeded to their
host's official residence, where they were introduced to
Cornelis Jacob van de Graaff, 'the governor, for the Dutch
East India Company, of this place and its dependencies'.

Meanwhile, there was considerable activity across the fleet that morning. As a necessary precaution while at anchor off Cape Town, the yards and topmasts on all vessels were struck. This time-consuming measure reduced windage aloft and thus minimised the chance of a ship dragging its anchor and being blown either onshore or out of Table Bay – a not altogether unusual occurrence when the notoriously violent south-easterly wind howled across the Cape. Phillip's notes reveal his concerns about the bay, stating that by definition Cape Town could not be called a port, 'being by no means a station of security; it is exposed to all the violence of winds which set into it from the sea, and is far from sufficiently secured from those which blow from the land'. Four weeks after arrival there, he would write of his relief that 'our fleet ... lay perfectly unmolested as long as it was necessary for it to remain in this station'. Apart from the threat that came from this exposed anchorage, Phillip was anxious to be back at sea as soon as practicable: he wanted to ensure that the fleet crossed the Southern Ocean at the height of the southern hemisphere summer, and he was forever mindful of the possibility that the French or others might arrive in Botany Bay before him.

Once the yards and rigging were lowered and the decks cleared, carpenters aboard *Sirius* and some of the transports started building stalls to accommodate the cattle and horses that were to be purchased in the port for the benefit of the new settlement.

To this day, the overall panorama of Cape Town is one of spectacular beauty, in which an arc of high hills and mountains form an amphitheatre beyond the town. However, in 1787, the finer visual detail around the waterfront caused Smyth some uneasiness. It was nothing short of gruesome.

> The face of the Country appears beautiful. The Town is
> backed by very lofty Mountains many of which are
> covered with verdure. The Town is pretty large &

appears to have many exceeding good houses in it.
There are many Gallows & other implements of
punishment erected along shore and in the front of the
Town. There were also Wheels for breaking Felons
upon, several of which were at this time occupied by the
mangled Bodies of the unhappy wretches who suffered
upon them: their right hands were cut off & fixed by a
large nail to the side of the Wheel, the Wheel itself
elevated upon a post about 9 or 10 feet high, upon
which the body lies to perish.

Early one morning, not long after the fleet had arrived,
crewmen on one of the transports looked over the side of their
ship and were surprised to see a man in the water. After
helping him aboard, they learned that he was a member of the
Swiss mercenary troop Régiment de Meuron, which provided
support for the Dutch East India Company in Cape Town –
and he wanted to desert and be taken to New South Wales.
On being advised of the man's request, Phillip declined, citing
the agreement he had with Governor van de Graaff, whereby
deserters had to be 'given up'. Before the soldier was sent back
ashore, however, Phillip secured the guarantee of a pardon for
him from his regiment.

Soon after this incident, Collins wrote of the expedition
having had its own deserters.

It had been always imagined, that the police of the
Cape-town was so well regulated as to render it next to
impossible for any man to escape … This, however, did
not appear to be the case; for very shortly after our
arrival four seamen belonging to a ship of our fleet
deserted from her; and although rewards were offered
for apprehending them, and every effort made that was
likely to insure success, two only were retaken before
our departure …

There is no mention of what punishment was dealt to those who were captured.

At one o'clock in the morning on Monday, 29 October, tragedy visited *Friendship* while she was lying at anchor. After a heavy night of drinking with fellow sailors, the second mate, Patrick Vallance, disappeared over the side in the darkness. Clark explained the circumstances: 'He fell overboard from the head of the Ship where he had gone to ease himself and was drowned for although three men Jumped overboard after him they could not Save him for he Soon after Sunk and has not been Seen Since — he was drunk they Say when he fell ...'

As part of the preparation for the daunting stretch across the Southern Ocean, Phillip allowed his officers the opportunity of spending nights ashore, away from the claustrophobic and impersonal environment on board ship. The majority took up this chance and stayed in one of the town's numerous guesthouses. For many of the men, the highlight of their break was a visit to the wineries for which the region was famous. The temptation to overindulge was very real, as Collins acknowledged: 'A stranger should not visit more than one of them in a day, for almost every cask has some peculiarity to recommend it and its contents must be tasted ...'

While the convicts were not permitted to leave the ships, Phillip insisted that they have the best diet possible, to ensure optimal health over the final stage of the journey. Their daily allowance included 1½ pounds of soft bread, 1 pound of beef or mutton (¾ pound for each child of a convict), plus a generous serving of fresh vegetables. The commodore was gratified to learn that of the thirty convicts aboard *Charlotte* who had been seriously ill, only three died and the rest had recovered. It was with understandable pride therefore that, as the time for departure approached, Phillip would write: 'we had the satisfaction to see the prisoners all were of the appearance of perfect health ...'.

A flag flying from Signal Hill, indicating that a ship of sail was approaching the Cape, was a cause of delight for the officers, marines and sailors. The captain of the approaching vessel, which was sailing under the Danish flag and on a return voyage to Europe, agreed to carry mail back to his home port; from there, he would ensure that it reached its ultimate destination. Collins described the reaction among some members of the fleet: 'By this ship every officer gladly embraced the last opportunity of communicating with their friends and connections, until they should be enabled to renew their correspondence from the new world to which they were now bound ...' For Phillip, of course, it was the route by which he could send final dispatches to Lord Sydney and Nepean.

In the week before the fleet sailed from Cape Town, most of the equipment, produce and livestock that had been purchased was put aboard the ships. This prompted Phillip to record: 'the ships, having on board not less than five hundred animals of different kinds, but chiefly poultry, put on an appearance which naturally enough excited the idea of Noah's ark ...'.

The animals being carried included a bull and one bull calf, several cows, one stallion, three mares and three colts, plus a considerable number of rams, ewes, goats, boars and breeding sows. Unbeknown to Phillip, these ungulates would be the first hard-hoofed animals to be introduced to the continent: all native animals were soft-pawed.

Among the array of poultry were geese, while the variety of plants was considerable: coffee, cocoa, banana plants, cottonseed, oranges, lemons, quinces, prickly pear, fig trees, bamboo, sugar cane, apples, pears, strawberries, oak and myrtle seeds. Additional supplies of rice, wheat, barley and corn were also procured, in case the supplies brought from England turned out to have been damaged during the voyage. Corn and hay were loaded as fodder for the animals, along with flour, wine and spirits for use at the colony. Most importantly, across the fleet, every water cask was filled to the brim.

With so much livestock to be accommodated on the ships, Phillip decided to transfer the twenty-four female convicts aboard *Friendship* over to *Charlotte* and have their quarters converted into pens for some of the sheep. No one was happier with this development than Ralph Clark. On hearing that they were to depart he wrote: 'I think we will find [the sheep] much more agreeable shipmates than [the women] were ...'

The navigators on the ships were required to double-check the accuracy of their instruments so that the chances of being off-course while traversing the Southern Ocean – should their ship become separated from the fleet – were minimised. As part of this exercise, Captain Hunter pinpointed *Sirius*'s current position on his chart, a latitude which by coincidence was identical to that of Botany Bay.

In the final days before departure, a vessel flying American colours sailed into Table Bay, having completed a 140-day passage from Boston en route to the East Indies. Watkin Tench, after meeting the captain of the ship, made some interesting notes.

> The master, who appeared to be a man of some information, on being told the destination of our fleet, gave it as his opinion, that if a reception could be secured, emigrations would take place to New South Wales, not only from the old continent, but the new one, where the spirit of adventure and thirst for novelty were excessive ...

On 10 November, almost a month after arriving in Cape Town, the signal for the fleet to prepare to put to sea was attached to a halyard aboard *Sirius* and hoisted into the rig. Phillip's plan was for them to sail early the following day, but when that time came, an onshore wind rendered it an impossibility. The fleet was forced to remain at anchor for another twenty-four hours.

It was ten minutes before two o'clock in the afternoon when the heavily laden ships were finally under sail, heading off from Cape Town in what appeared to be a building breeze. As they did, all aboard were steeling themselves for what lay ahead at sea: there were 6000 nautical miles to be covered before their ultimate destination, and all but 650 of those miles were across a barbarous and bitingly cold stretch of ocean. As sobering a reality as this was, many found themselves contemplating a threat that was more abstract, regarding challenges that defied physical description. The colony's judge advocate, David Collins, was among them.

It was natural to indulge at this moment a melancholy reflection which obtruded itself upon the mind. The land behind us was the abode of a civilized people; that before us was the residence of savages. When, if ever, we might again enjoy the commerce of the world, was doubtful and uncertain. The refreshments and the pleasures of which we had so liberally partaken at the Cape, were to be exchanged for coarse fare and hard labour at New South Wales. All communication with families and friends now cut off, we were leaving the world behind us, to enter on a state unknown; and, as if it had been necessary to imprint this idea more strongly on our minds, and to render the sensation still more poignant, at the close of the evening we spoke [to] a ship from London. The metropolis of our native country, its pleasures, its wealth, and its consequence, thus accidentally presented to the mind, failed not to afford a most striking contrast with the object now principally in our view.

CHAPTER 8

A Sea But Little Known

While the fleet gained offing from the shore on 12 November, tell-tale clouds signalled that a strengthening south-east wind was sweeping over the top of Table Mountain and would soon be descending onto the waters of Table Bay. When that happened, the crews were alerted to the speed of its approach by the rapid appearance of white caps, which grew in size until the sea surface was churned into a mass of white – a maritime snowfield. The tars had already jumped into action, responding to the sharp and precise orders being barked out by officers on the quarterdecks, as the first line of attack from the squall raced their way. Sails had to be taken in, reefed or lowered as quickly as possible to minimise the chance of damage occurring aloft.

In almost any other situation, the increase in speed associated with the squall would have been welcomed, but not at this point. A wind from the south-east was the worst possible development for these cumbrous ships: it forced them in the opposite direction from their desired course, which was 30 nautical miles south to the Cape of Good Hope. Once at the Cape, so the plan went, it was another 80 nautical miles, to the east-south-east, to the southernmost point of the African continent – Cape Agulhas – where the north–south longitude defines the border between the Atlantic and Indian oceans.

From there, they would venture into a region that James Callam, the surgeon aboard *Supply*, would appropriately describe as 'a sea but little known'.

On the 32-point compass typically used in that era, each navigator could see that the course being steered away from Cape Town was north-by-west, which meant they would soon be in the unsatisfactory position of leaving Robben Island, some 6 miles north of the port, to larboard. Inevitably, the time came to wear ship and change course, which Phillip signalled via a pennant flown on *Sirius*. Ever so slowly, each ship carried out a turning manoeuvre by which the wind went from being on the vessel's starboard quarter to the larboard quarter, then before long, forward of abeam. Among the teams of sailors executing the move, those manning the starboard lines eased away the sheets and braces, while crewmen on the other side hauled away and sheeted them home on the belaying pins mounted on the rack at the mast. Simultaneously, the mizzen swung across with a thundering thump as the wind went from filling one side of the sail to the other.

With the fleet now heading towards the southern latitudes, the challenge for the helmsman was to sail his ship as close as possible to the direction of the south-easterly wind while still keeping the sails drawing. It was a losing course, though, one that took them well west of south for close to a week. On board *Charlotte*, Tench would note with some frustration: '[The] south-east wind … continued to blow until the 19th of the month; when we were in the latitude of 37 deg 40 min south, and longitude 11 deg 30 min east, so that our distance from Botany Bay had increased nearly an hundred leagues [300 nautical miles] since leaving the Cape …' By then, they would be 400 nautical miles south-west of the Cape of Good Hope, and more distance was being lost by the day.

It was tough going. The ships laboriously ploughed onwards, their bows rising into each approaching South Atlantic swell and diving into the trough beyond amid a heavy surge of white water. At least there was some reward for all on deck. For much of the time after departing from Cape Town, the fleet was escorted by huge pods of whales making their way north from the Southern Ocean to the warmer tropical waters, where they would calve and breed.

Aboard *Friendship*, Clark related that a more liberal approach to security surrounding the transportees had a downside. One of the convicts, John Bennett, had stolen provisions allocated to other prisoners and hidden the lot in the longboat. Clark's account continued: 'This Young Rascal had come on deck about 10 o'clock to make water and had while the sentinel's back was turned Slipped into the long boat where he had eat So much that he could not Stir and fell aSleep until about 2 oClock in the morning when he was found there ...' Bennett's punishment was to have both legs put in irons. 'Mark my words,' Clark added, 'that we will not have been at Botany above Six months before this Young Villain Bennett comes to the Gallows.' He was correct!

Such predictions were dependent on the ships reaching New South Wales as soon as possible, if there was any hope of minimising the chance of life-threatening circumstances for the fleet – humans and livestock alike. On the morning of 15 November, Phillip sent the signal aloft for all ships to tack – for each ship to turn its bow through the eye of the wind so the sails are set on the opposite side. It was a desperate move, and not surprisingly, there was no quantitative gain to the east. Instead, each new morning brought added frustration.

In the few days since departure, the commander's life had become a ritual. He would rise as dawn's first hue flushed the eastern night sky, put on his uniform and make his way up the companionway ladder to the quarterdeck, where his officers acknowledged his arrival. He would check the ship's course on the compass before walking across to the weather side where, in solitude, he began to scan the slowly brightening sky, searching for evidence of a change in the weather that might come in their favour. But it was not to be seen.

The commodore continued to muster his thoughts and play out every possible alternative available to him. On 16 November, he made a proclamation that he would be, in Watkin Tench's words, 'shifting his pennant from the *Sirius* to the *Supply*, and proceeding on his voyage without waiting for the rest of the fleet'. *Lady Penrhyn*'s surgeon, Arthur Smyth, provided the detail:

> On the 16th, Captain Phillip signified his intention of proceeding forward in the *Supply*, with the view of arriving in New South Wales so long before the principal part of the fleet, as to be able to fix on a clear and proper place for the settlement. Lieutenant Shortland was at the same time informed, that he was to quit the fleet with the *Alexander*, taking on with him the *Scarborough* and *Friendship* transports. These three ships had on board the greater part of the male convicts, whom Captain Phillip had sanguine hopes of employing to much advantage, before the *Sirius*, with that part of the fleet which was to remain under Captain Hunter's direction, should arrive upon the coast. This separation, the first that had occurred, did not take place until the 25th, on which day Captain Phillip went on board the *Supply*, taking with him, from the *Sirius*, Lieutenants King and Dawes, with the time-keeper. On the same day Major Ross, with the adjutant and quarter-master of the detachment, went into the *Scarborough*, in order to co-operate with Captain Phillip in his intention of preparing, as far as time might allow, for the reception of the rest of the convoy …

In other words, Phillip planned to have the four fastest ships arrive at Botany Bay sufficiently far ahead of the others so that all necessary buildings could be erected by the time the main portion of the fleet arrived. To achieve this, there had to be a transfer of some men, primarily convicts, and equipment between ships: all experienced sawyers, carpenters, blacksmiths, gardeners and others who could benefit the plan had to be part of the newly created vanguard. In addition, the marine battalion aboard *Sirius* was to be transferred to *Scarborough*, so that it would be on hand to defend the new settlers should any form of attack be made by the indigenous population.

In the nine days between decision and division, the convoy was hit by a gale and pelting rain – a brutal blow from Mother Nature that provided a taste for the uninitiated as to why the Southern Ocean had a reputation for being so treacherous. A punishing westerly burst onto the scene in darkness and caused sails to be shortened on all ships in a trice. Conditions became so rough that, for the first time, the nimble but diminutive *Supply* could not keep pace with the others. Even when she had the barest amount of sail set, her minimal overall length and the size of the seas combined to make the former coastal workboat near uncontrollable, to the point where she was continually on the verge of being knocked down and thrown onto her beam ends.

Before long, the helmsmen were battling to hold course as enormously powerful swells urged the ships forward, sometimes at the surprising speed of 8 knots. These swells were unlike anything previously seen on the passage – liquid hummocks that had generated their size and force over thousands of miles. For such angry emissaries of Poseidon, the only obstruction on their way around the globe was Cape Horn and the southern tip of South America.

By 25 November the fleet was 80 leagues east of the Cape of Good Hope. The gale had abated by then, and the sea state was sufficiently smooth for Phillip's plan to be put into action. The fleet moved into close formation and lay-to so that boats could be hoisted out from the transports, and the movement of men and equipment begun. By late morning the task had been completed.

Soon afterwards, *Supply* was leading her convoy away from the others under full sail, heading towards the wide open horizon while riding a steady north-westerly wind and sailing a course to the south-east. An hour later, all the small boats belonging to the remaining transports – *Lady Penrhyn*, *Charlotte* and *Prince of Wales* – had been hoisted in and they too were under sail, following in the wake of *Sirius*, which continued to be under the command of Captain Hunter. The course that had been plotted for all ships would see them sail east along the 40th parallel – the edge of the Roaring Forties.

On board *Sirius*, Philip Gidley King had spent much time considering the commodore's plan. It led to him penning his own views:

> The governor flatters himself that he shall arrive at a
> place of our destination [Botany Bay] a fortnight before
> the transports in which time he will be able to make
> his observations on the place whether it is a proper Spot
> for the Settlement or not & in the latter case he will
> then have time to Examine Port Stephens before the
> arrival of the Transports on the Coast; Should Botany
> Bay answer our expectations he may have time to erect
> a Log Store house for the reception of the Provisions
> which will hasten the departure of the Store Ships &
> Transports …

It is curious to note that King refers to Port Stephens, 90 nautical miles north of Botany Bay, as the only alternative, when Phillip actually had another possibility to first consider. It was Port Jackson, which like Broken Bay, had been sighted and noted with interest by Captain Cook in 1770.

Within twenty-four hours of the fleet separating, the ships in the trailing flotilla were hull-down on the western horizon – barely visible specks from the aft decks of the transports that had moved ahead with *Supply*. Phillip was no longer waiting for anyone, however; his new command would sail towards Botany Bay as fast as possible, leaving in his wake the three larger vessels, and get there first. For Hunter aboard *Sirius*, the instructions were clear: he should continue to ensure that the storeships and remaining transports stayed in visual contact at all times, which meant keeping to a speed dictated by the leisurely *Lady Penrhyn*.

After a couple of days, the ever observant Clark was explaining in his diary how fresh food, particularly meat, was transferred between ships mid-ocean. In his description, *Scarborough* came into close quarters with *Friendship* and hailed her to trail a long line astern; *Scarborough* then sailed in the other vessel's wake while crewmen at the bow picked up the line, attached a quarter of a slaughtered sheep to it, and threw it back into the water so that the mutton could be hauled aboard *Friendship*. Clark added that he was looking forward to 'cutting a few slices from it for I am Quite Sick of Salt Beef and Salt Pork but I must make the best of it. I have nothing else in the Mess. I never lived So poor Since I was born.'

With Lieutenant Ball pressing her hard, *Supply* was soon showing the way by a considerable margin. For Phillip, this achievement confirmed that he had made the right decision, even though the wind remained unreliable in strength and direction. But after enjoying an impressive downwind run since leaving the bulk of the fleet, *Supply*'s progress was suddenly slowed when the wind went light and towards the east without notice. It meant that the ship could no longer hold the desired course towards Van Diemen's Land.

A day later, there was cause for optimism – and then some degree of concern. While the wind remained what Clark termed 'as foul against us as it can blow', the sighting of small sooty brown-coloured seabirds, known as Mother Carey's Chickens, left any sailor who had previously ventured into the Southern Ocean convinced that a westerly wind was on its way. Possibly storm force. The prediction was based partly on experience and partly on superstition, the latter being something that most seafarers feared and respected. In the eighteenth century, the prevailing wisdom held that these flighty, surface-skimming birds were an omen that rough weather was approaching, since they carried the souls of sailors who had perished in storms across cruel and dangerous seas. Mother Carey was a mythical figure who, it was suggested by some, was the wife of the dreaded Davy Jones – the sailor's devil. Today, Mother Carey's Chickens are also known as storm petrels.

Clark's diary for the following day, 28 November, left no room for doubt that the legend surrounding Mother Carey's Chickens had some merit. 'It blows So hard that I cannot Sit to write – it blow much harder Yesterday than it has Since I have left England,' he contended. 'I was exceedingly Sea Sick much more So than Since I have been in the Ship. The Ship rolled her sides under water and the Sea broke over us almost every moment ...'

Hunter described the toll these storm conditions took on the animals, in particular the cattle, aboard *Sirius*. 'The rolling and labouring of our ship exceedingly distressed the cattle, which were now in a very weak state, and the great quantities of water which we shipped during the gale, very much aggravated their distress. The poor animals were frequently thrown with much violence off their legs and exceedingly bruised by their falls.'

Remarkably, despite the enormity of the storm and the seas, and the fact that the ships were semi-submerged time and time again, all the vessels survived virtually unscathed. When the worst of the weather had passed, Mother Nature changed her mood in a matter of hours, the sea state going from one extreme to another. The next day delivered glassy calm waters that mirrored the cloudless blue sky. The only suggestion of what had been was a long leftover swell that caused the ships to roll uncomfortably (and there was no sign of Mother Carey's Chickens). At night, such windless and clear conditions brought a spectacular, celestial bonus. The Milky Way cut a magnificent silver-grey swathe across the heavens like a subtle smear, stars twinkled brightly, and the Southern Cross took pride of place in the tranquil setting.

At eleven o'clock the following evening, there was cause for alarm aboard *Supply*. Lieutenant King reported: 'The men on the lookout forward called out "rocks under our bows", on which the helm was put a-lee and instead of rocks, were presented with the view of 2 very large Whales, & so close to the Vessel that I could have stepped from the Gunwale on either of their backs. The Vessel was felt going over their tails by those below …'

A similar situation arose one morning a few days later. The master of *Supply*, Henry Ball, was on the quarterdeck when he shouted a warning to the crewman at the wheel that he could see white water breaking on rocks just off the larboard bow. Every man on watch then searched intently for the perceived danger, but the burst of white water that came into sight was the consequence of a spectacular attack on a whale by a thresher shark, around 20 feet in length. King's observation of the fight reads: 'As ye Whale swims along the Thresher watches when the Whale is going to Spout, at the time he throws himself out of the Water and falls with the greatest force on the Whale's head or shoulders. The Whale defends himself by endeavouring to strike the Thresher with his tail.'

This break from the cruellest that the Southern Ocean had to offer – howling winds and violent breaking seas – would prove to be brief. On 4 December, Clark detailed yet another horror storm.

> It blow … very hard in the night much harder than Since it has done Since we have been from England. Several heavy seas broke over us in the night … a very great sea running … this is a nasty dirty day. Exceedingly cold. What must it be [like] in the winter if it is so cold now [in] the middle of Summer. I have hardly found it So cold in England at this time of the Year as it is here at present …

The clothing the sailors wore did little to protect them from the raw cold and stinging rain, which had its origins in the icy Antarctic region to the south. Woollen breeches, leather shoes, woollen vests and jackets were no match for nature's fearsome force when it was at its worst. On another day in early December, when the ship was experiencing 'Fresh Gales accompanied with Squalls of Wind & Rain', the elements simply proved too much for those on deck, as King reported: 'The wind shifted suddenly to the south-by-east & south-south-east with rain which made it so very cold that Many of the people were affected so much by it that some were obliged to quit their duty, particularly the man at the Helm, John Breedon, who was affected with a kind of Stupor ...'

Moving around on the pitching and heaving deck was difficult at all times, but the dangers that came when men had to go hand over hand up the ratlines, no matter the weather, were now far greater. The tars' dedication to duty in such extreme conditions did not go unnoticed by teetotaller Clark. 'Gave the Seamen a bottle of Rum,' he wrote at this time, 'for they are very wet and cold and a Glass won't do them any harm.'

By 11 December, the leading ships were 500 nautical miles to the north of the Kerguelen Islands, which confirmed that they had covered 2500 nautical miles since clearing the southern tip of Africa. This meant that they had 3200 nautical miles to go before reaching their major turning point, Van Diemen's Land.

Nine days later, thanks to consistent winds of varying strengths from the western sector, the convoy was at the halfway point between Cape Town and Botany Bay. Understandably, every man, woman and child aboard the four ships hoped that the worst of the weather was now behind them. But the brutal cold returned with a vengeance that same day, as Clark recorded: 'It hailed and Snowed today it being So cold that I have been obliged to put on a flannel Waistcoat and [in] place of one pair of stockings two pair – and obliged to keep on my great coat constantly all day …'

The cycle of Southern Ocean tempests and speed-sapping calms continued as the scattering of flotillas pushed ever onwards across the vast plains of ocean to the east. Whenever the most extreme conditions descended on one of the transports – bringing waves that swept the deck and sent torrents of water cascading below – the fittest of the male convicts were ordered to man the pumps on deck so that the bilge could be emptied. Among the forward group of ships, the severity and the sheer relentlessness of the climate led to Christmas Day 1787 passing almost unnoticed. One of the few references to the day came from Clark, whose entry for 26 December simply noted: 'Several of the Marines got much in Liquor Yesterday …'

The fate of the livestock was still cause for great concern. The sheep, in particular, were dying from exposure to the volatile conditions. Just occasionally, there was reason for celebration when a ewe gave birth.

This was tough going for even the most rugged seaman. In the worst of the weather, it was not possible to light the fires in the brick-walled galley stoves so hot food could be prepared. The only option then for the men was to eat uncooked whatever rations they had left.

Phillip continued to push the small *Supply* as hard as he dared. Under his instructions, the maximum amount of sail was carried in the conditions that prevailed, to ensure he arrived in Botany Bay as far ahead as possible of the remainder of the fleet. King wrote about life aboard the sturdy little ship, while she was pressed across the Southern Ocean and nearing Van Diemen's Land:

> Had very strong Gales of Wind from ye SW to NW
> with a very heavy Sea running which keeps this vessel
> almost constantly under water & renders the Situation

of every one onboard of her, truly uncomfortable —
The Squalls during this time were very violent &
great quantities of rain, Sleet, & large hail stones, &
when the Wind is to the Southward the Cold is as
extreme here as in England at this time of ye Year,
altho' it is the height of Summer here. [On 2 January]
in the Morning ... had very heavy Gales & a
Tumbling sea from ye NNW which obliged us for the
first time since we left England to furl the Topsails.
The Brig labours very much & Ships a great quantity
of Water.

Phillip, already concerned about *Supply*'s seaworthiness in
rough weather, now wrote that he considered her to sail 'very
indifferently', and was 'hardly a safe conveyance'.

By 4 January 1788, *Supply*'s increasingly distant convoy of
transport ships — *Friendship*, *Scarborough* and *Alexander* — were
closing on the southern cape of Van Diemen's Land. As a
precautionary measure, to eliminate any chance of their being
wrecked on an unseen coast in miserable darkness, the signal
hoisted into *Scarborough*'s rig called for all three vessels to cease
sailing and bring-to for the night. Once again, the weather
was foul: an icy and rain-laden wind howling in from the
west, and heavy seas.

From the moment first light arrived, eager eyes were
transfixed to the east and north, looking for a first glimpse of
Van Diemen's Land. It came late that morning when the
lookout at the masthead aboard *Friendship* shouted to those on
deck that he could see a shadowy outline of the coast to the
north — their first sighting of what would become the new
homeland for so many members of this flotilla. It was a most
exciting moment, one laden with anticipation for all.

Watkin Tench would note his first impressions on seeing
the land from the deck of *Charlotte*, when she arrived later
with the rearguard ships.

In running along shore, we cast many an anxious eye
towards the land, on which so much of our future
destiny depended. Our distance, joined to the haziness
of the atmosphere, prevented us, however, from being
able to discover much. With our best glasses we could
see nothing but hills of a moderate height, cloathed
with trees, to which some little patches of white
sandstone gave the appearance of covered with snow.
Many fires were observed on the hills in the evening.

Still, there was a fair way to go to Botany Bay – around
750 nautical miles. This was a fact that caused Clark some
concern.

I wish to God that we were at Anchor at Botany Bay as
well for myself as for the Poor Sheep on Board. They
have hardly hay Sufficient to keep life in them if we
Should be obliged to Stay out much longer — they
must all die and we be obliged to Eat our Provision
without cooking it as there will be no firing in the
Ship — the wood has been out these 3 weeks past and
they Say there is not a weeks coals in the Ship ...

The lieutenant suggested that had they 'not had Such fair
winds as we have been Blest with', they could well have
starved.

In a letter home, *Supply*'s surgeon, James Callam, would
provide a tidy summary of the wind patterns endured on this
passage across the bottom of the world. He told his brother,
Alexander, in England:

... in general we had a fair wind, with a heavy rolling
Sea from the Southward – if at any time foul, its
duration was short – when it blows from the Northwest
quarter, it is generally warm, and if it does not
commence with thick weather and rain, it is sure to

terminate so after a day or two's duration, when it shifts
to the South-west quarter, accompanied with a heavy
Sea, and piercing Cold from the vast track of Ocean and
Ice surrounding the South Pole, where it proceeds
from …

While *Supply* was pushed east as fast as possible, the remainder
of the fleet was making unexpectedly good time while
bringing up the rear. This was due to their experiencing
strong and favourable winds for much of the time after *Supply*
was seen to go hull-down over the horizon ahead of them.
Such was their speed that the governor was destined for a
surprise not long after he reached Botany Bay.

For those on board almost every ship, it seemed that the
sighting of land also brought the end of the worst of the
weather. The wind generally went very light and turned
towards the east-north-east as the vessels rounded the southern
tip of Van Diemen's Land. Nevertheless, there was still some
severe punishment to come, as Jacob Nagle described when
Sirius was off the east coast and heading north. The ship was
knocked down to the point where a massive wave of green and
white water poured over the leeward bulwark, nearly bringing
about the American's demise.

We were struck with a sudden white squall in the
middle of the day which laid us down upon our beam
ends. Taking in sail, she righted. The main topmast sail
being hauled down, I ran up to pass a gasket [lashing]
around the sail. I jumped on [the sail] to ride it down.
The wind blew so powerful it blew me off like a
feather, but catching one of the lashings of the foresail
that blew out, it brought me upright, and I fell with my
backside on the bitthead without being hurt. The
officers seeing me fall, from the quarterdeck, came
running forward, expecting I was killed, but
recovering myself, I ran up the lee rigging and furled

the sail. Every ship in the fleet received some damage
in that squall ...

Like Christmas, the start of the New Year had come and gone
with little recognition, crews being simply too engrossed in
combating the dangerous conditions. Now, though, there was
a positive side to the endeavour as the wind continued to blow
from astern with considerable force for much of the time, and
they were covering an impressive number of nautical miles,
around 170, each day. This meant that by about the end of the
first week in January, all eleven of the ships had cleared the
bottom of Van Diemen's Land and taken up a new course
where the layline was initially to the north-east, to the tip of
Tasman Peninsula; from there, the plan was to follow a course
to the north and towards Botany Bay, which was then less than
600 nautical miles away.

While that distance sounded minor relative to the 17,000-
plus nautical miles already covered since leaving England, the
ships were far from being home safe. The east coast of New
Holland promised more testing times for the newcomers to this
part of the world. All too often on their final stretch, what
would later be recognised as a summer sea breeze – a north-
easterly – made its presence felt with gusts up to 30 knots and
nasty short seas. Worse still, it was a punishing headwind,
which resulted in the fleet clawing its way north in painfully
small increments. Instead of this being a powerful and
stimulating downwind run where the bow wave was a surging
mass of white water, each ship was pitching over the crests and
corkscrewing awkwardly in the troughs while battling its way
to windward. For crewmen off watch and in search of much-
needed rest, it was practically impossible to sleep, since the lack
of rhythm to the ship's motion meant that hammocks were
continually banging into each other.

Mild relief came when the wind tended to fade at night,
or when a brief change in the wind pattern moved in from
the south, but it was still tough going. And adding to the mix

some evenings were thunderstorms: vibrant and saw-toothed bolts of lightning, roaring and rolling claps of thunder, heavy rain and wind squalls where sail and rig damage was inevitable.

Because tacking in these conditions was difficult and time consuming, the most expedient way to get north was to sail deep into the Tasman Sea, out to the east, then tack and sail back towards a specific point on the coast to the south of Botany Bay. This was the method adopted by most of the masters, yet it provided only a partial solution. Some of the ships' logs would reveal how, once a vessel had reached the coast and the typically calm night-time conditions set in, the south-flowing current skirting the coastline would cause an overnight loss of around 15 nautical miles to the south.

Supply remained ahead of the fleet, but no one on board knew by how far. The only certainty was that the lookout at the top of her mainmast was unable to see any ship on the southern horizon. *Supply*'s course towards the coast on 18 January was from the south-east, and when it was gauged that she was 3 nautical miles offshore, Phillip called for the course to be changed so that they paralleled the coastline.

Dominating the shore were the bold and spectacular light-coloured sandstone cliffs that, in Cook's 1770 description, resembled chalk. King was quick to supply a description of his own.

> The Shore along here is steep & a surf beating on it.
> The hills are clothed with a verdant Wood with many
> beautiful slopes, at the Same time a very high Chalk
> cliff which rose perpendicularly from the Sea bore
> NWbN [north-west-by-north] This Chalk Cliff is
> mentioned by Capt. Cook in his first voyage ... the
> Northernmost of which is just at ye Commencement of
> the Land which forms Botany Bay ...

This was an exciting time for everyone. *Supply*, the lead ship in this historic convoy, was now only 15 nautical miles south of the target. The scene and the sense of anticipation raised pulses and generated wonder for all on deck.

The face of the modern world was about to change – the first pioneering steps towards European settlement of this unknown land were about to be taken. The enormity of the moment, and the hopes embedded in the hearts of those who had worked so hard to be there, were reflected in a note written by Watkin Tench, reading: 'To us it was a great, an important day, though I hope the foundation, not the fall, of an empire will be dated from it.'

CHAPTER 9

Bay of Disappointment – Harbour of Splendour

When the man at the wheel responded to an order from the quarterdeck to follow a course that would take *Supply* through the entrance to Botany Bay, every man from the governor to the youngest tar would have been on deck. It was Friday, 18 January 1788, and all aboard were eager for a first glimpse of the destination that had taken them 250 days to reach. No doubt Phillip would have stolen a last look towards the southern horizon, wondering how far astern the remainder of the fleet might be, and if everyone was safe.

Simultaneously, Aborigines on the northern side of the entrance provided some intrigue for those on deck. Although barely visible in the distance, they were definitely there, and waving … But was it a form of welcome or a sign of aggression?

As *Supply* glided into the bay, with the large red British ensign flying proudly from the peak of her mizzen gaff, she was aided by a flood tide and the surge of an ocean swell coming from astern. And with each wave, more of the wide expanse of this waterway, together with the low land beyond its shores, opened up to view. As significant a moment as it was, the crew could not yet relax: the ship had to be slowed and readied for anchoring at her final destination, which called for the sails to be furled sequentially. The square sails were duly hauled up then lashed to the yards by bare-footed men high up on the yards, while on deck, others took down and made fast the fore-and-aft sails – the staysails, jibs and mizzen. The last remaining sail, probably a jib, would have come down just prior to the 175-ton brig reaching the location where Phillip had chosen to anchor, her momentum being sufficient to carry her to that point. Once there, the bosun relayed an order from back aft: release the line holding the best bower and let it fall.

Phillip had directed that *Supply* be anchored on the northern side of the bay, close to the entrance, for two good reasons. Cook had indicated the presence there of a welcome stream of fresh water, and the ship would be visible to the remainder of the fleet when they were on approach to Botany Bay from the south.

Where exactly it was that Phillip anchored, and subsequently went ashore, has been the cause of debate for centuries. It is now generally accepted that *Supply*'s bower hit the bottom in 8½ fathoms in what became known as Yarra Bay, about 2 nautical miles north-west of the entrance. Opinions continue to differ, however, over the issue of where Arthur Phillip first set foot on Australian soil. In 1952, historian Charles H. Bertie calculated that Phillip had landed on the beach at Yarra Bay, and a year later a monument was erected in the bay proclaiming as much:

> In this vicinity, about 3pm on 18th January 1788,
> Governor Phillip first set foot on Australian soil.
> He was seeking fresh water. On his approach,
> a group of natives,
> who had watched him land, withdrew into the bush.
> Later that afternoon, some of them directed him to a
> stream nearby

Today, though, with the discovery of previously unknown material, and the benefit of more precise calculations, there is a firm belief that Phillip stepped ashore at picturesque Congwong Bay, 1 nautical mile east of Yarra Bay. One of the staunchest supporters of this theory is historian, Brian McDonald, author of *The Landing Place of Captain Arthur Phillip at Botany Bay*. McDonald concludes that the governor directed his men to row around a small headland and into Congwong Bay after Aborigines had repelled their approach to shore at Frenchmans Bay, the inlet immediately to the east of Yarra Bay. McDonald is adamant that had Bertie and all adherents to the latter's theory had the same information available to them, they would've come to the same conclusion.

With there being a pressing need to find water for the approaching fleet, not to mention a fair degree of enthusiasm for setting foot on land, the ship's boats were hoisted out within thirty minutes of dropping anchor. Through the eyes of surgeon James Callam, the following is what took place that afternoon, starting with their arrival at Botany Bay.

> On the *Supply*'s entering the Bay, the alarmed Natives run along the Beach, shouting and hallowing, seizing their wretched Canoes, and carrying them to the Woods – together with their Fishing-tackle and Children; we brought up pretty close to the North Shore, open to the Sea – to be seen by the Fleet, which we daily expected. Seven of them came opposite to the Ship, brandishing their implements of War, such as Spears of an amazing length, armed with Fish-bone, Lances, Clubs, etc., etc. throwing their bodies in threatening Postures, called out in harsh notes, Warraw! Warraw! Warraw!
>
> After dinner, his Excellency Governor Phillip, with Lieutenants Ball and King, Lieutenant Dawes of the Marines, myself included, rowed towards them in two Boats. As we approached, one or two of them seemed to retreat a little, but the others continued to threaten us, as if they meant to dispute our landing, we rowed along

shore and landed a little way from them, and walked round a great part of the Bay, looking for water, without any molestation ... near Sun-set we embarked in the Boats, and rowed towards the place where we left them, opposite the Ship, having found no water, we endeavoured to make them understand by every means what we wanted, which they at last did, and on our laying down our arms, conducted us to a delightful rivulet of Spring Water, which emptied itself in the Bay close by us – here we partook of the pleasing Stream, drank Success to the Colony, and the Speedy arrival of the Fleet.

They still watched our different motions with much seeming attention. The Governor held out several Trinkets, such as Glass Beads, & at last an old Man was prevailed upon to accept of some, and then all the others on the accidental discharge of a Musket, they all left us.

In the continuation of Callam's account, early the next day, some of the men were hauling the ship's seine net in the bay, whereupon the natives returned and 'received Fish, after which, they daily grew more familiar'. The surgeon added: 'They were anxious to know (being entirely naked themselves) whether we were Men or Women ... they pointed to where their Women were full of mirth, but would not permit them to approach us ...'

Early that first morning, Phillip was out on deck, in uniform, eager to commence his exploration of the bay and the search for a source of fresh water that could support the settlement. All officers, sailors and marines due to accompany the governor were also on deck, watching the boats being hauled out while listening to the unfamiliar songs and cries of unseen birdlife on the shore. Once the oarsmen were in position, the exploration party clambered down the side of the ship and into the boats. Governor Phillip then took his seat in the stern sheets of his launch, following which the call would have come to release the painter and 'toss oars'.

The boats headed in a north-westerly direction, to investigate a river that Cook had positioned on his inaccurately proportioned chart of Botany Bay. Today it is known, appropriately enough, as Cooks River. Phillip's choice to go there first was based on Cook having described it as a 'fine freshwater stream' featuring 'fine meadows' along its banks. Phillip soon realised otherwise: there was no sign of a freshwater stream. Their search took them about 6 miles up this tributary before they turned back towards Botany Bay. Callam later noted: 'numbers of Natives [were] Fishing in their Canoes, while others were employed dressing [scaling and gutting] them on its Banks; they retired on our approach, Howling and Crying. Here we first observed them to have Dogs ... they are of the Wolf kind, with long shaggy Hair ...'

The newcomers had seen their first Australian wild dogs – dingoes.

It was about midday when the exploration party arrived back at the bay. Once there, Phillip directed that the boats head for the mouth of another river known to exist in the south-west corner – now called the Georges River. They landed at what they perceived to be its mouth, in order to have a midday meal. The party then walked along the shore to where, according to Callam's report, they observed 'the Native's miserable Huts, etc. – proofs of their simplicity and ignorance, in which his Excellency left Beads and other trifling Trinkets, but took nothing from them'.

Without sufficient time to investigate fully this river of significant size, Phillip elected to return to the ship for the evening and have the exploration continue the following day. But there was one conclusion emerging from the day's activities, after continuous measurement of water depths in the bay had yielded unimpressive results. As the governor would outline in one of his reports: 'It appeared that, though extensive, [Botany Bay] did not afford a shelter from the easterly winds: and that, in consequence of its shallowness, ships even of a moderate draught, would always be obliged to anchor with the entrance of the bay open, where they must be exposed to a heavy sea, that rolls in whenever it blows hard from the eastward ...'

On the 5-mile row back to the anchorage, amid the fading light of that midsummer evening, the rhythmic thump of oars in their slots on the gunwale, the splash of blades dipping into the water, and the wave curling away softly from the bow were the most prominent sounds. The officers were chatting idly until someone peered towards their destination and announced 'the agreeable sight' of three other ships at anchor. *Scarborough*, *Friendship* and *Alexander* had arrived – and within just twenty-four hours of *Supply*. Phillip's ship had obviously not outsailed the others by anywhere near as much as he had hoped. Even more surprisingly, the following day, 20 January, the remainder of the convoy hove into view and entered the bay.

Watkin Tench, the marine officer, and a skilled writer, offered his impressions of the final stages of the passage for the seven rearguard vessels.

> [We] did not regain it [sighting land] until the 19th, at only the distance of 17 leagues from our desired port. The wind was now fair, the sky serene, though a little hazy, and the temperature of the air delightfully pleasant: joy sparkled in every countenance, and congratulations issued from every mouth. Ithaca itself was scarcely more longed for by Ulysses, than Botany Bay by the adventurers who had traversed so many thousand miles to take possession of it ...

He then wrote:

> On the morning of the 20th, by ten o'clock, the whole of the fleet had cast anchor in Botany Bay, where, to

our mutual satisfaction, we found the Governor, and
the first division of transports ...

Thus, after a passage of exactly thirty-six weeks
from Portsmouth, we happily effected our arduous
undertaking, with such a train of unexampled blessings
as hardly ever attended a fleet in a like predicament ...
To what cause are we to attribute this unhoped for
success? I wish I could answer to the liberal manner in
which Government supplied the expedition. But when
the reader is told, that some of the necessary articles
allowed to ships on a common passage ... were
withheld from us ... his surprise will redouble at the
result of the voyage. For it must be remembered, that
the people thus sent out were not a ship's company
starting with every advantage of health and good
living, which a state of freedom produces; but the
major part a miserable set of convicts, emaciated from
confinement, and in want of clothes, and almost every
convenience to render so long a passage tolerable ...

With the entire squadron having arrived safely, this endeavour
could, without question, go down in maritime history as one of
the great voyages of all time. Eleven vessels carrying some 1400
people had crossed more than 17,000 nautical miles of ocean,
much of that distance through hostile and little-known waters.
The duration of the passage was 252 days, and while there had
been loss of life, the death toll (which was never recorded with
great accuracy) could be considered extraordinarily low for the
era – around 3 per cent of the total number. Possibly the most
accurate figure comes from the fleet's chief surgeon, John
White, who recorded forty-eight deaths during the voyage,
along with a birth tally of twenty-eight. The deaths included
thirty-six male convicts, four female convicts, five children of
convicts, one marine, one wife of a marine and one marine's
child. In short, Arthur Phillip had every reason to feel
supremely proud of what had been achieved.

On realising how few deaths there had been in comparison to voyages involving the transportation of convicts to America and the West Indies, King attributed this success to:

> ... the activity & vigilance of the Officers of Marines on
> board the different Transports in compelling [the
> convicts] to be kept constantly clean & wholesome ...
> The abilities of the Surgeon & his assistants were also
> a great means of keeping the Fleet healthy & what
> contributed as much as the above reasons, was
> the goodness of the provisions, which were all
> wholesome & good ...

With all ships in the bay much earlier than expected, pressure increased on the governor to find a site for the settlement. For health reasons if nothing else, it was crucial he got the people, including the convicts, on land as soon as possible. He quickly expanded the exploration of the bay, but the more he looked, the less confident he became in regard to the area's suitability as a colonial outpost. It seemed that no matter where he explored, he found extensive swamps, poor-quality sandy soil or a lack of water. He concluded in his diary: 'no place was found in the whole circuit of Botany Bay which seemed at all calculated for the reception of so large a settlement'.

If one location had any potential, it was Sutherland Point, on the south-eastern shore, where a reasonable run of water had been found. This was enough to tempt Phillip to head there once more, to consider the site in greater detail.

Natives were standing near the tree-line at the point when the bow of Phillip's launch nudged onto its sandy beach, but there was no indication that any challenge might come from them. Comfortable with this impression, Phillip had his men begin evaluating the extent of the water supply. Nagle, who was checking the depth of the stream, explained what followed.

> The Natives Came down to us & Appeared as though
> they did not Approve of Our Visit ... The governor
> Attempted to be Very friendly with them but they
> Came with Spears & a bark Shield ... When we were
> all in the boats [to return to the ships] Excepting
> Captain Ball they begin to be Mischievous ... he took
> one of their Shields & Sit it up against an Old Stump
> of a tree & fired One of his pistols at it which
> frightened them when they heard the report but Much
> More when they saw the ball went through the Shield
> which Cooled them ...

The boats were then rowed 2 miles to the north, back to the anchorage, and by now Phillip was convinced that Sutherland Point was far from ideal. Apart from the freshwater supply being limited, the water around the point was very shallow, which meant that ships would have to anchor a long way off.

Still the survey of the bay continued. King was the officer in charge of another probe that day, which went to the south-west corner of Botany Bay. He found nothing of any note, but he did report on some interesting experiences with the local inhabitants. In the first episode, there was a display of aggression that demanded a response from the Englishmen.

> ... in a very vociferous tone [the people] made signs for
> us to go away & one of them threw a lance [spear] wide
> of us, in order to show the force & power of their arms,
> the distance it was thrown was as near forty Yards, &
> when it was taken out of the Ground it required an
> Exertion to pull it out. As this might be deemed a
> threat ... & seeing that no advantage could be gained by
> a longer stay I joined the party & we went down the
> hill to go to the Boat, we had scarcely got to the foot of
> the hill when a lance was thrown amongst us, but
> without striking any person. As they appeared on the
> top of the Hill & seemed disposed to throw more lances

> I ordered one of the Marines to fire his musket with
> powder only, on which they flew with great haste ...

His second encounter was quite different – it was born of innocent curiosity and humour.

> At the head of the Inlet we met another party of the
> Natives ... & a number came round the boat ... what
> attracted their notice most was our Clothing
> particularly the Great Coats & hats, which they were
> very desirous of obtaining. The natives wanted much
> to know of what sex we were, they certainly took us
> for women as we had not our beards grown. They
> expressed a great desire to have their Curiosity satisfied
> on which I ordered one of the boats Crew to satisfy
> them in this respect. On which they set up a shout, &
> pointed to the Shore where a number of Women &
> Children were sitting all in puris naturalibus ... [I]
> showed a handkerchief which I offered to one of the
> Women [who] came alongside of the Boat, when I
> applied the handkerchief where decency seemed to
> demand it, the natives on the shore & round the boat
> set up another very great shout [of laughter] & my
> female visitor retired ...

When the lieutenant returned to *Supply* at eleven o'clock that evening, 20 January, he met with Phillip, who outlined his concerns about the unsuitability of Botany Bay. The governor went on to say that he intended to take three longboats and row 25 nautical miles north along the coast to Broken Bay, and explore there. On the way, it was also his intention to enter Port Jackson – which Cook had suggested had the appearance of a boat harbour – to see if that waterway might offer a suitable site instead.

In hindsight, it was not difficult for Phillip to understand why Banks and Matra had recommended Botany Bay so highly.

Back in April 1770 while aboard *Endeavour*, they had looked at the bay during autumn and had liked what they saw, but pressure of time hadn't allowed for any extensive exploration there. For Captain Cook, it offered the two things he needed at the time: shelter, and water for his ship. For Phillip, though, his challenge had just become more difficult. He'd arrived in high summer. He had no idea where the settlement would be established, but he did know that if it was at Point Sutherland, his situation would be far from ideal – little fresh water, soil that couldn't support crops, and a bay that would make a far from perfect port. The sooner he looked elsewhere for a solution, the better.

The governor, his chosen officers and the three boat crews were on deck and ready to depart at six o'clock the following morning. Before casting off, he directed King to continue exploring the bay, accepting that there was no certainty a more suitable port would be found. For the same reason, he told his lieutenant governor, Major Robert Ross, that, as it was imperative for the convicts to be off the transports as soon as possible, men were to go ashore and start clearing the land at Point Sutherland.

Phillip needn't have worried, as was obvious in the official report that the British Government would release regarding his arrival in Port Jackson:

> Here all regret arising from the former disappointments
> was at once obliterated; and Governor Phillip had the
> satisfaction to find one of the finest harbours in the
> world, in which a thousand sail of the line might ride
> in perfect security. The different coves of this harbour
> were examined with all possible expedition, and the
> preference was given to one which had the finest spring
> of water, and in which ships can anchor so close to the
> shore, that at a very small expense quays may be
> constructed at which the largest vessels may unload.
> This cove is about half a mile in length, and a quarter
> of a mile across at the entrance ...

Nagle provided a detailed account of the successful find. In his journal, he explains that, during the afternoon of 21 January, the longboats sailed between the two lofty sandstone cliff faces that dominate the entrance to the great harbour, and straight away, everyone was in awe of what confronted them. They were the first Europeans to enter what would soon be recognised as one of the most beautiful and well-protected deep-water harbours in the world – more than 21 square miles of main waterway, comprising sheltered coves, sandy beaches, bays, inlets and a lengthy tributary.

From the outset, there were three options to investigate: a broad waterway directly ahead, to the west; a large bay to the north; and what appeared to be the major part of the harbour, towards the south. On considering the time of day, Phillip chose the waterway ahead as his first point of interest, before turning his mind to deciding where they should go ashore and camp for the night.

The three boats were rowed into what is now known as Middle Harbour. There, the men observed high and heavily timbered hills that ran down to the water's edge for almost the entire area that they explored. They then returned to the harbour entrance where, with little daylight remaining, Phillip had the boats take up a looping course into the bay to the north, to see what could be found there. This bay was about to receive a name that is synonymous with Sydney Harbour. The compiler of Phillip's dispatches provided the detail:

> In passing near a point of land in this harbour, the boats were perceived by a number of the natives, twenty of whom waded into the water unarmed, received what was offered them, and examined the boat with a curiosity which impressed a higher idea of them than any former accounts of their manners had suggested. This confidence, and manly behaviour, induced Governor Phillip, who was highly pleased with it, to give the place the name of Manly Cove ...

Nagle continues the story:

> It then Coming on dark we landed on a Beach on the
> South Side [of the southern headland at the harbour
> entrance] & there pitched Our tents for the Night this
> place was Called Camp Cove – the Marines were put
> on their posts & the Sailors were Employed Variously
> Some getting Out the Cooking utensils Some making
> fires & then shooting the Seine For fish. By the time
> we got Our Suppers it was late in the Night …

While camped on this beach, and with dinner being prepared, another interlude with the indigenous people further convinced Phillip that the locals knew little of what most of the known world took for granted. They lived in caves or the crudest of bark shelters; their food was what they could gather from the land and sea; there had been no evidence of the cultivation of crops; their canoes were little more than long and wide pieces of bark that had been stripped from a tree and lashed at either end; they held no knowledge of sail or the wheel; and their preparation of food was basic, to say the least.

It was on this latter point that the governor was able to interest the locals in a European custom. Details of this cultural exchange were revealed in *The Voyage of Governor Phillip to Botany Bay: With an Account of the Establishment of the Colonies of Port Jackson and Norfolk Island.*

> One man … who appeared to be the chief of this tribe,
> showed very singular marks of confidence in his new
> friends … Under the guidance of Governor Phillip, to
> whom he voluntarily entrusted himself, he went to a
> part of the beach where the men belonging to the boats
> were then boiling their meat when he approached the
> marines, who were drawn up near that place, and saw
> that by proceeding he should be separated from his
> companions, who remained with several of the officers

at some distance, he stopped, and with great firmness, seemed by words and gestures to threaten revenge if any advantage should be taken of his situation. He then went on with perfect calmness to examine what was boiling in the pot, and by the manner in which he expressed his admiration, made it evident that he intended to profit by what he saw. Governor Phillip contrived to make him understand that large shells might conveniently be used for the same purpose, and it is probable that by these hints, added to his own observation, he will be enabled to introduce the art of boiling among his countrymen ...

Phillip himself would note that the Aborigines only broiled their food, from what he could surmise, adding: 'their methods of kindling fire are probably very imperfect and laborious, for it is observed that they usually keep it burning, and are very rarely seen without either a fire actually made, or a piece of lighted wood, which they carry with them from place to place, and even in their canoes ...'.

By four o'clock the following morning, when first light was barely emerging on the eastern horizon, the three longboats had been loaded and every man was ready to continue with the exploration. Once back on the water, the boats spread out across the harbour so that depths could be measured simultaneously in different areas. According to Nagle's recollection, the oarsmen snacked on their breakfast (a few dry ship's biscuits) each time a boat stopped to take a new reading.

Phillip was keen to get to the head of the harbour that day, but because the waterway was 'so large and extensive', his party was only able to reach a cove 4 nautical miles upstream. There – much to everyone's utter delight – they discovered 'a Run of fresh Water Running down into the Centre of the Cove'.

The boats were manoeuvred close to the shoreline so that Phillip, his officers and some of the seamen could step ashore and see what else this cove might have to offer. At the same time, Nagle unwittingly wrote himself into Australian history.

> I being boat keeper had to remain with the boat. I
> hove my [fishing] line over, being 4 or 5 fathom water
> alongside the rocks. I hauled up a large black bream and
> hove it into the stern sheets of the boat. The Governor
> coming down, very much pleased with this cove and
> the situation for a town, he was determined to settle in
> this cove. Coming into the barge, he observed the fish
> I had catched and asked who had caught that fish. I
> informed him that I had. He said, '… you are the first
> white man that ever caught a fish in Sydney Cove
> where this town is to be built' …

Apart from selecting this inlet as the location for the settlement, Phillip decided to name it in honour of his Home Office superior Thomas Townshend – Lord Sydney. Eighteen years earlier, Cook had named Port Jackson after his friend and patron Second Secretary of the Admiralty Sir George Jackson.

After three days of exploration, and with provisions running low, the three boats returned to Botany Bay on 23 January. Besides, there was no time to waste. Immediately on arriving at the anchorage, Phillip advised that a new site had been found and directed that the fleet be ready to sail to Port Jackson the following morning. However, when dawn broke, it was immediately apparent that the decision was not his alone to make.

A 'violent' wind from the east was howling directly into the bay from offshore. Such a headwind would make it near impossible for the ships to sail safely through the entrance – the width of which was no more than half a nautical mile – and establish the desired sea-room. Worse still, the huge seas made the coast a merciless lee shore, so there was no margin for error. As it was, massive, white-capped walls of water were rolling into the bay. Consequently, Phillip had to postpone the departure.

The adverse weather continued into the next day, 25 January, but even so, Phillip decided the fleet would go to sea. While the ships were being prepared, a sight offshore caused immediate concern. In the light of early morning, 'two Strange Ships were seen standing in for the Bay,' King recorded in his journal.

While acknowledging his own incredulity, Tench wrote of the speculation encouraged by the mysterious newcomers.

> I rose at the first dawn of the morning. But judge of my surprise on hearing from a sergeant, who ran down almost breathless to the cabin where I was dressing, that a ship was seen off the harbour's mouth. At first I only laughed, but knowing the man who spoke to me to be of great veracity, and hearing him repeat his information, I flew upon deck, on which I had barely set my foot, when the cry of 'another sail' struck on my astonished ear …

> By this time the alarm had become general, and every one appeared lost in conjecture. Now they were Dutchmen sent to dispossess us, and the moment after storeships from England, with supplies for the settlement. The improbabilities which attended both these conclusions were sunk in the agitation of the moment. It was by Governor Phillip, that this mystery was at length unravelled, and the cause of the alarm pronounced to be two French ships, which, it was now recollected, were on a voyage of discovery in the southern hemisphere. Thus were our doubts cleared up, and our apprehensions banished; it was, however, judged expedient to postpone our removal to Port Jackson, until a complete confirmation of our conjectures could be procured …

King noted that one of the ships was carrying 'a White broad pendant at her main top mast-head & the other a Common White pendant' – signs that led Phillip to 'judge them to be the two Ships under the orders of Monsieur de la perouse'.

His assumption was correct; the French had arrived, just as the British suspected they would! The vessels were Lapérouse's *Boussole* and *Astrolabe*, and their obvious intention was to enter the bay. They too were thwarted by the weather, as, in King's words, 'The Wind coming to blow fresh ... prevented their getting in ...' They then disappeared from view.

Phillip's mind no doubt harked back to a period less than three years before, when he was gathering intelligence in France for the British Government and the Royal Navy. It is likely he knew that as well as being required to report on any settlements the British had established in the South Pacific, one of the secret reasons for Lapérouse's voyage was to visit New Zealand, investigate the quality of the timber there, and consider the possibility of establishing a settlement. Might Lapérouse now also be considering the coast of New South Wales for the same reason, Phillip probably asked himself. If that was the case, it could be said that the arrival of the First Fleet on 20 January 1788 prevented this from happening by just five days.

Maybe it was the presence of the French vessels that had Phillip insist that, regardless of the weather, the fleet be readied to sail. His instinct could well have been that, with the wind having apparently forced the French to abandon their efforts to sail into Botany Bay, they might go north instead to Port Jackson – the last thing the governor wanted. Such a view is reinforced by the fact that, on just about any other day, the prevailing weather would have caused the fleet to remain at anchor and wait for more suitable conditions.

Interestingly, when the French were first sighted, *Supply* was in the process of receiving on board a company of marines and forty convicts. Phillip was determined to sail her to Port Jackson regardless of the stormy weather raging outside the bay.

Obviously, the possibility that the French might beat him into Port Jackson caused the governor to now want as many men as possible aboard his lead ship, so that they could begin clearing the land and have the British colours flying there before day's end.

At the same time, even if the French ships didn't find their way to Port Jackson, they would still be lurking somewhere off the coast. Phillip decided therefore that the British Jack should be flown in all its glory from a prominent position at Point Sutherland – a bold signal of claim to the region. Having accepted that, because of the weather, the rest of the fleet might be forced to remain there for another night, he delivered a strong directive to Ross relating to the possibility that the French might still enter Botany Bay that day. Apart from ordering him to go to Point Sutherland and raise the colours, there was an additional command which was recorded by *Lady Penrhyn*'s master, William Sever, in the following terms: 'he issued orders for no person whatever to be suffered to go on board either of the Ships if they came in, as he did not wish to let them know particulars, especially that we were upon the eve of leaving this place & going to Port Jackson ...'.

As history reveals, this same desire to withhold the merits of this jewel of a harbour from the French would guide Phillip's actions over the ensuing six weeks, during which *Boussole* and *Astrolabe* entered Botany Bay and remained at anchor there. At no time over that period did the British governor extend an invitation to Lapérouse to visit him at Sydney Cove.

Tench would later write of the French sailors, like their English counterparts, enjoying remarkable hauls of fish at Botany Bay.

> The French once caught near two thousand fish in one day, of a species of grouper, to which, from the form of a bone in the head resembling a helmet, we have given the name of light horseman [today, snapper]. Sharks of an enormous size are found here. One of these was caught by the people on board the *Sirius*, which

measured at the shoulders six feet and a half in
circumference. His liver yielded twenty-four gallons of
oil; and in his stomach was found the head of a shark,
which had been thrown overboard from the same ship.
The [natives], probably from having felt the effects of
their voracious fury, testify the utmost horror on seeing
these terrible fish ...

It was early on 25 January, a week after *Supply* had arrived at
Botany Bay, that her anchor was hauled up to the cathead. She
then proceeded towards the entrance under greatly reduced sail
with the twin aims of exiting the bay and showing her fellow
ships how to negotiate the entrance safely. However, as she
approached the exit point, Phillip took stock of the sea
conditions that lay ahead and immediately ordered a change of
plan: common sense and prudent seamanship would prevail.
With wind, wave and tide against him, Phillip had to accept that
it was too dangerous to try to put to sea. *Supply* was then turned
onto a port tack and sailed a short distance to the south, where
she took up temporary anchorage in the lee of Point Sutherland.

Captain Sever, who sailed *Lady Penrhyn* away from the
Yarra Bay anchorage at five o'clock that morning, provided an
overview of this attempt and what subsequently transpired.

... most of the other Ships & we were endeavouring to
work out of the Bay, but were obliged to drop Anchor
again as did also the *Supply* – but about 12 at noon she
[*Supply*] again loosened her Topsails & with the greatest
difficulty got out of the mouth of the Bay. We
endeavoured in vain to follow her, the wind being
directly against us, blowing very strong & rather
increasing. At 2 o'Clock p.m. it blew almost a hurricane,
Thundered, Lightened & rained very much ...

With the tide having just turned, so that by midday it was
ebbing from the bay, Phillip had decided to make a break for

it – even though he knew that wind and wave against tide often made for even more treacherous sailing conditions. Such a bold yet dangerous act might also indicate a precautionary desire to beat the French to Port Jackson, or at least catch them if they were already there.

Rain was pelting down and the wind still howling when Phillip had *Supply* trimmed and positioned for the attempt to sail through the entrance and out to the open ocean. In no time, the robust little ship was pounding her way through the big head seas, and each time she lifted over a large swell and crashed into the trough that followed, spray was hurled high in the air and swept across the deck. As she struggled eastwards under the dreary lead-coloured sky, crewmen standing along the windward rail anxiously scanned the horizon, looking for any sign of Lapérouse's vessels. 'They were out of sight,' wrote King. Had they been seen, Phillip was ready to hoist the British colours high in the rig so that the French would know who they were dealing with.

Through some outstanding sailing and seamanship, *Supply* smashed and bashed her way offshore until finally she held enough sea-room to be safe from the dangers of the lee shore. At that point, she was eased away, with her sails re-trimmed, for a fast, surging run north.

In less than an hour, the southern entrance to Port Jackson was abeam, and before long the call came to wear ship (or gybe), so that she could reach across the wind and into the placid waters beyond. As *Supply* ran down the face of the easterly swells and entered the port, it would later be noted, there was 'no danger entering the harbour but [for] what is visible'. King was similarly impressed, writing: 'The safety & extent of this Harbour, makes it the first port in the World.' And much to everyone's relief, there was no sign of the French.

At seven o'clock, with the sky having cleared and the sun on the verge of disappearing beyond the land lying to the west, *Supply* drifted ever so slowly into picturesque Sydney Cove and her anchor was set. It had taken around two hours to cover the distance from the heads to this cove, during which time the crew had been able to enjoy the magnificent scenery surrounding the waterway. They were equally taken by the high-pitched, incessant drone coming from the millions of cicadas resident in the eucalyptus trees along the shoreline – a summertime signature of the port.

With darkness closing in, everyone would have to wait until sunrise before they could totally appreciate their new environs. Even so, King had already decided on its suitability for the planned settlement, since 'Sydney Cove will admit of the largest Ships lying alongside the Shore'.

Nature's palette of pastel shades coloured the early morning sky at around four o'clock before the sun made its fiery appearance. Almost every man was on deck, preparing enthusiastically for the day ahead. At this hour, the greatest impact on these newcomers continued to be audible rather than visual. They marvelled at the incredible cacophony of sounds coming from the birdlife resident in the cove: screeching lorikeets, cawing crows, plus the cries from other amazing varieties whose names would soon become part of the country's ornithological studies – including magpies, butcher-birds, currawongs and corellas. Still, there was nothing more amazing than the call of the kookaburra – 'the laughing jackass'. They had never heard anything like it!

The convicts and marines were sent ashore as soon as there was sufficient light, the task of the trusted felons being to clear trees where the first part of the camp would be set up. It is possible that this was actually on the western shore and not near the stream at the head of the bay, which is the belief held by many historians.

The judge advocate, David Collins, provided an insightful impression of the labours on that historic first day, 26 January.

... in the course of the day sufficient ground was
cleared for encamping the officer's guard and the

convicts who had been landed in the morning. The spot chosen for this purpose was at the head of the cove, near the run of fresh water, which stole silently along through a very thick wood, the stillness of which had then, for the first time since the creation, been interrupted by the rude sound of the labourer's axe, and the downfall of its ancient inhabitants; a stillness and tranquillity which from that day were to give place to the voice of labour, the confusion of camps and towns, and 'the busy hum of its new possessors' ...

By midday, the felling of trees and the clearing of undergrowth were sufficiently advanced for Arthur Phillip to undertake his first formal event as governor on this foreign shore. The Union Jack had been flying since early morning, probably from the branch of a tree; now, for what would have to pass as the inauguration of New South Wales as an occupied territory of Great Britain, the marines assembled around the flag, while the governor and his officers stood to one side of it and the convicts on the other. King wrote of an event that was conducted with all possible pomp and ceremony: 'His Majesty whose health, with the Queens, Prince of Wales & Success to the Colony was drank, a feu de joie [rifle salute] was fired by the party of Marines & ye whole gave 3 Cheers which was returned by the *Supply* ...'

The true historical significance of this ceremony could never have been appreciated by those present. It was the founding moment for Australia. No nation before then or since has been so informally born from a settlement that had been established to hold convicts in exile.

Back at Botany Bay that same morning, the ten remaining ships in the fleet were being prepared to put to sea and head north to Port Jackson. And then the French reappeared. The masters of the two vessels were obviously still intent on entering the bay, just as Ross wanted his ships out of the waterway as soon as was practicable. Nevertheless, the lieutenant governor chose to delay the departure, in the interests of displaying goodwill towards the visitors. He sent a longboat out from *Sirius* under the captaincy of a lieutenant, whose task it was to head seaward and offer the French any assistance they might require, including guidance to the anchorage.

By the time this diplomatic mission was completed, at ten o'clock, Ross was very anxious to depart, and as a result he decided there was not time for him to go aboard Lapérouse's ship. At least his lieutenant, having spoken with the French nobleman personally, was able to provide Ross with details of their progress since leaving Brest in August 1785.

He said that Lapérouse had informed him that nothing of any great importance had been discovered on the voyage. After rounding Cape Horn and entering the Pacific, *Boussole* and *Astrolabe* cruised north along the coasts of South and North America, visiting the Sandwich Islands on the way, then across to East Asia, and up to Kamchatka Peninsula in the Russian far east – which is where they learned that the British were in the process of sending a fleet to Botany Bay. The two ships then sailed south to the Friendly Islands (Tonga), Îles des Navigateurs (Samoa), the Philippines, Norfolk Island and finally Botany Bay.

During that time, however, a pair of terrible tragedies had befallen the expedition. The first occurred in July 1786, when two longboat crews perished while trying to negotiate rough surf on the north-west coast of North America. Then, in December 1787, *Astrolabe*'s captain, Paul Antoine Fleuriot de Langle, and twelve of his men had been horrifically stoned to death by islanders while on a beach at the Îles des Navigateurs.

With the British ships getting under sail, Tench noted that 'nothing more than salutations could pass between us' as they sailed past the French brigs, which by then were at anchor. With the wind continuing to blow from the east that morning, but somewhat lighter than the previous day, it had been relatively easy for the French to enter the bay. For Ross's fleet, however, the task remained difficult. Despite the wind being softer, the ships would still be confronted by a headwind and head seas as they endeavoured to exit the bay.

This time, Ross and all the ships' masters were determined to follow in *Supply*'s wake. Yet, as Sever would detail, it was another dangerous endeavour that was not without incident.

> We were obliged to work out of the Bay with ye utmost difficulty & danger with many hairbreadth escapes. Got out of the Harbour's mouth abt.
> 3 o'Clock p.m. The *Charlotte* was once in the most imminent danger of being on the Rocks. The *Friendship* & *Prince of Wales* ... came foul of each other ... the *Friendship* carried away her Jib Boom [and] The *Prince of Wales* had her New Mainsail & Main topmast staysail rent in pieces by the *Friendship*'s yard. The *Charlotte* also afterwards ran foul of the *Friendship* & carried away a great deal of the Carved work for her [*Charlotte*'s] Stern, & it was with the greatest difficulty our Ship avoided the same fate, however at last the whole fleet got clear of the Harbour's mouth without any further damage being sustained ...

Sever had no hesitation in ascribing blame for the near carnage. In his journal, he criticised 'the Rashness of the Governor in insisting upon the fleet working out in such weather' and added: 'all agreed it was next to a Miracle that some of the Ships were not lost, the danger was so very great'. There was great relief aboard every vessel therefore as they were finally able to turn to larboard and commence the passage to Port Jackson.

By mid-afternoon, the fleet had safely sailed through the heads and was making its way up-harbour in a favourable breeze. *Sirius*, which was showing the way, then cruised around the eastern entrance to the cove while her square sails were being hauled up and others lowered, before dropping anchor – much to the delight of the men onshore who were clearing the land.

By sunset on 26 January 1788, another historic moment had arrived. The entire First Fleet was now safely within the sanctuary of Sydney Cove.

Ross met with the governor soon after arriving, at which point he relayed the news of the French having entered Botany Bay and details of their voyage to date. He also passed on a request from Lapérouse, about whether one of the British ships due to soon return to England might carry some important dispatches and charts back to the French Ambassador in London. Phillip agreed to the request. Six days later, he had some of his men deliver that message overland to the French expedition leader at Botany Bay, assuring him that the documents would be 'punctually transmitted' to the ambassador. Today, Frenchmans Road in the Sydney suburb of Randwick is the last remaining vestige of the track the men took to Botany Bay.

Yet Governor Phillip still refrained from meeting with Lapérouse during the six weeks that the French were in the bay. This occurred despite officers and men from the British ships travelling cross-country to visit the French at their anchorage, just as some of the Frenchmen trekked to Port Jackson and enjoyed English hospitality there.

The delivery of Lapérouse's papers to London would be recognised as greatly significant in French maritime history, but for the worst possible reason. The men of the First Fleet would be the last to see the French commander and his ships, while the documents that were delivered to the ambassador would be the last ever received from the great explorer relating to his long voyage. Lapérouse, his ships and his men literally vanished after departing from Botany Bay on 10 March 1788. It would not be until 1964 that the fate of *Boussole* and *Astrolabe* was finally confirmed. They had been wrecked in the Solomon Islands, more than 1500 nautical miles to the north-east of the New South Wales coast.

Lieutenant William Bradley's watercolour shows the development of the harbour foreshore: Sydney Cove, Port Jackson. SLNSW a3461012.

Founding of the settlement of Port-Jackson [i.e. Port Jackson] at Botany Bay in New South Wales, designed and engraved by Thomas Gosse (1765–1844), an artist who based his works on descriptions by others who went to New South Wales. National Library of Australia nla.pic-an6016205.

CHAPTER 10

The Colours Are Raised

It was late afternoon on a beautifully warm, clear day when the ten ships reached Sydney Cove and anchored in relatively close proximity to *Supply*. Aside from the excitement filling the air, a very agreeable and symbolic image greeted all those on deck: at the head of the bay, near the tree-line, a Union Jack was flying lazily in the gentle breeze. This was a proud and historic moment. It represented the completion of the initial stage of the plan to create a penal settlement in this part of the world, as well as the first step to gaining a foothold in the region for the Mother Country.

To the same degree, it would prove to be a momentous day in the lives of the indigenous population, members of which now looked on in bewilderment from around the shores of the cove and from the opposite side of the harbour. One can only wonder what was going through their minds as they first watched this armada of alien vessels arrive, and then saw the white-faced people clad in coloured outer skins emerge and head towards shore, carried by huge canoes with sticks poking out the sides … What were these strangers doing? How long would they be here for?

The first Australians arrived in the Sydney region thousands of years ago. But from this particular day, 26 January 1788, the native population's very basic, nomadic and self-sustaining lifestyle would change forever, and the force driving that change was an attitude they could not comprehend. Unbeknown to the natives, these aliens were part of an era in world history when divide and conquer was a fact of life – whereby, with sufficient manpower and firepower, you had every right to lay claim to whatever tract of land you deemed necessary for your national security or advantageous to your people. This was a time when compassionate acts generally ran an acceptable second to victory and, quite often, the annihilation of your enemy. It was under such circumstances that Governor Arthur Phillip came to be in Port Jackson: he was on a mission enshrined by decree from the King of England. Fortunately for the local inhabitants, there was an element of consideration written into this decree, and the leader of the aliens they were watching was well aware of it. Phillip no doubt reminded himself that, on coming into contact with the natives, he was to 'conciliate their affections, enjoining all Our Subjects to live in amity and kindness with them'. Yet the same royal edict stated: 'And if any of Our Subjects shall wantonly destroy them, or give them any unnecessary Interruption in the exercise of their several occupations, it is our Will and Pleasure that you do cause such offenders to be brought to punishment according to the degree of the Offence.'

The plan for the establishment of the first stage of the settlement continued soon after sunrise the following morning, when some minimum-risk convicts were taken to the edge of the bay so that they could get on with the task of tree-felling and clearing the shoreline. This was the first time since leaving England nine months earlier that they had set foot on dry land.

While these felons were considered the most trustworthy, Phillip knew he could not afford to relax security. The same thought caused him to walk around the initial perimeter of the camp and, using a stick, etch a deep line in the dark soil. The provost-marshal – the senior marine officer in charge of security – and the marine guards were then told that this was the boundary, and no convict was allowed to step outside it. Should any do so, they were to be immediately returned to custody aboard their ship.

Collins provided this overview of activities on 27 January:

> The confusion that ensued will not be wondered at, when it is considered that every man stepped from the boat literally into a wood. Parties of people were everywhere heard and seen variously employed; some in clearing ground for the different encampments; others in pitching tents, or bringing up such stores as were more immediately wanted; and the spot which had so lately been the abode of silence and tranquillity was now changed to that of noise, clamour, and confusion: but after a time order gradually prevailed everywhere. As the woods were opened and the ground cleared, the various encampments were extended, and all wore the appearance of regularity ...

There was also an activity away from the camp that, as White reported, delivered an encouraging result.

> The boats sent this day to fish were successful. Some of the natives came into the little bay or cove where the seine was hauled, and behaved very friendly. Indeed they carried their civility so far, although a people that appeared to be averse to work, as to assist in dragging it ashore. For this kind office they were liberally rewarded with fish, which seemed to please them and give general satisfaction ...

In his report, however, Lieutenant Bradley qualified this success with a warning: 'We found Fish plenty altho' the Harbour is full of sharks.'

Within forty-eight hours, Phillip had decided that the time had come to get a better appreciation of Port Jackson and its surrounds, and what benefits they might provide the settlement. He, Captain Hunter and Bradley therefore boarded the launch and set off upstream, intending to see as much as they could in a day. It was a valuable exercise; most importantly, it was apparent that sources of timber, which the settlement would soon be requiring, were readily available. He then commissioned carpenters to build the colony's first vessel, a lighter that could carry logs, shells (for the making of lime) and sand – all essential items for the construction of residences and stores. Another small vessel, designed along the lines of a longboat and rigged with both oars and 'shoulder of mutton' sails, was to be built by the shipwrights and used for survey work on the harbour.

On 29 January, some of the few animals that had survived the voyage from Cape Town – one bull, four cows, a bull calf, one stallion, three mares and three colts – were landed on the eastern headland of the cove, a location that would become known for a brief period as Cattle Point. (Later renamed Bennelong Point, it is now the site of the magnificent Sydney Opera House.) The actual point was then a tidal island, a fact that made containing the livestock considerably easier.

Once the preliminary plan for the settlement was finalised, the next move was to have the governor's portable canvas house and its timber frame sent ashore. The chosen site for the tent was to the east of the freshwater stream, where a small number of convicts would also be accommodated in tents. The marines were allocated a camp site to the south, at the head of the cove and close to the stream, with the main body of convicts quartered in tents on the western shore. Another priority was to disembark the wives and children of the marines, and this occurred as soon as sufficient land had been cleared and accommodation readied.

The building of the first significant structure for the settlement began on 5 February. It was a storehouse to hold the provisions brought ashore from the transports. Unfortunately, there was an unwanted addition among these stores: black rats, which had travelled aboard the ships from England and eaten or spoiled a considerable amount of stores en route. The rodents subsequently took up permanent residency in the country.

At the muster of convicts that same morning, it became apparent that Phillip's 'line in the sand' was ineffectual. Nine of the transportees were missing, including at least one woman. It turned out that they had decamped across land to Botany Bay, hoping to be taken aboard one of the French ships and secreted away from the colony. Lapérouse would have no part of it, however. White explained the consequences for the escapees.

> This refusal obliged them to return; and when they
> came back they were real objects of pity. Conscious of
> the punishment that awaited so imprudent and
> improper an experiment, they had stayed out as long as
> the cravings of nature would permit, and were nearly
> half starved …
>
> A woman, named Ann Smith, and a man have
> never since been heard of. They are supposed to have
> missed their way as they returned, and to have perished
> for want. As the French commodore had given his
> honour that he would not admit any of them on board,
> it cannot be thought he would take them. The convict,
> it is true, was a Frenchman, named Peter Paris, and it is
> possible, on that account, he might have been
> concealed, through pity, by his countrymen, and
> carried off without the knowledge of the commanding
> officer …

Meanwhile, relations with the natives were still at arm's length, but their trust in the visitors was growing, thanks in part to Phillip's attitude towards them. This was helped considerably by the English sharing part of their catch each time they were netting fish. Even so, as Nagle explained, the Indigenous people struggled to comprehend any part of the activities and objects they were observing, particularly the construction of the ships.

> ... the natives would come alongside in their bark
> canoes with amazement, and putting their hands on the
> ship's side with wondering surprise to think what it
> could be made of[.]
>
> Whatever excursions we went on with the
> Governor, he endeavoured to naturalise them, and give
> them clothing and trinkets, and would not permit them
> to be molested by any means, though he run many risks
> of his life by them[.]

The first cause for alarm in the settlement came within two weeks of the fleet's arrival. Surprisingly, while the vast majority of the 1300-plus military personnel, sailors, passengers and convicts had remained remarkably healthy during the voyage out from England, sickness suddenly began sweeping through the fledgling colony. Because of this, there was an urgent need to establish a tent hospital to accommodate the sick. It was erected on the western shore – an area that soon became known as The Rocks because of the predominance of sandstone, which before long was being used for the construction of homes and storehouses.

White, as the principal surgeon, wrote that he was sorry to see that these tents 'were soon filled with patients afflicted with the true camp dysentery and the scurvy. More pitiable objects were perhaps never seen. Not a comfort or convenience could be got for them, besides the very few we had with us ...' He added:

> His Excellency, seeing the state these poor objects
> were in, ordered a piece of ground to be enclosed, for
> the purpose of raising vegetables for them. The seeds
> that were sown upon this occasion, on first appearing
> above ground, looked promising and well, but soon

after withered away, which was not indeed
extraordinary, as they were not sown at a proper
season of the year.

The sick have increased since our landing to such a
degree, that a spot for a general hospital has been
marked out and artificers already employed on it. A
proper spot, contiguous to the hospital, has been
chosen, to raise such vegetables as can be produced at
this season of the year ...

Eleven days after the arrival of the fleet – Wednesday,
6 February – preparations were sufficiently advanced for the
female convicts to be sent ashore. Another surgeon, Arthur
Bowes Smyth, recalled the story that day.

At five o'clock this morning, all things were got in
order for landing the whole of the women, and three of
the ships longboats came alongside us to receive them;
previous to their quitting the ship, a strict search was
made to try if any of the many things which they had
stolen on board could be found, but their artifice
eluded the most strict search, and at six o'clock p.m. we
had the long wished for pleasure of seeing the last of
them leave the ship. They were dressed in general very
clean, and some few amongst them might be said to be
well dressed. The men convicts got to them very soon
after they landed, and it is beyond my abilities to give a
just description of the scene of debauchery and riot that
ensued during the night ...

In no time, Phillip's desire for the continued segregation of the
sexes had become a wasted wish. The premeditated lust that
had, no doubt, been simmering for so long was so
overpowering that not even what White described as 'the most
tremendous thunder and lightning, with heavy rain, I ever
remember to have seen' could curb the revelry. In fact, when

the tempest subsided late that night, many of the participants looked as though they'd been through a mud bath.

Those of a religious persuasion could easily have been convinced that the violence of the thunderstorm represented divine disapproval of such rampant Bacchanalia: six hours in which the wrath of God rained down on the scene with fire and brimstone. Its arrival was signalled late in the afternoon when the sky darkened, the wind went wild and torrential rain began flooding the ground. Soon, savage bolts of lightning were hurtling towards the settlement from the ugly black clouds charging across the sky.

One mighty thunderclap delivered a bolt that went close to achieving a direct hit on the encampment, striking a large eucalyptus tree just a few metres from where the majority of those onshore, including the convicts, were located. It split the tree in two and killed five sheep sheltering in a little shed that had been built for them. The animals were owned by Major Ross and the settlement's quartermaster. For the increasingly unpopular Ross, this unwelcome natural occurrence no doubt added to his deeply unfavourable opinion of Sydney Cove and a country that he would dismiss as the 'outcast of God's works'.

No doubt, the unlawful conjugals were the source of vexation for the colony's chaplain, Reverend Richard Johnson. His duty was to guide the social deviants onto a righteous path, which, as Tench recorded, included furnishing them 'with books, at once tending to promote instruction and piety'. Tench remarked of the challenges that attended the reverend's efforts:

> While they were on board ship, the two sexes had been kept most rigorously apart; but, when landed, their separation became impracticable, and would have been, perhaps, wrong. Licentiousness was the unavoidable consequence, and their old habits of depravity were beginning to recur. What was to be attempted? To prevent their intercourse was impossible; and to palliate

its evils only remained. Marriage was recommended,
and such advantages held out to those who aimed at
reformation …

That same wild and stormy night, there was more partying out on the waters of the cove. In this instance, it was the crewmen aboard the transports, who were celebrating being rid of their human cargo. The task of delivering the wrong-doers to the colony now complete, the tars could look forward to sailing home. Smyth wrote of the celebrations aboard *Lady Penrhyn*:

> The sailors in our ship requested to have some grog to
> make merry with upon the women quitting the ship,
> indeed the Captain himself had no small reason to
> rejoice upon their being all safely landed and given into
> the care of the Governor, as he was under the penalty of
> £40 for every convict that was missing. For which
> reason he complied with the sailor's request, and about
> the time they began to be elevated the tempest came on.
> The scene which presented itself at this time and during
> the greater part of the night beggars every description.
> Some swearing, others quarrelling, others singing – not
> in the least regarding the tempest, though so violent that
> the thunder [that] shook the ship exceeded anything
> I ever before had a conception of. I never before
> experienced so uncomfortable a night, expecting every
> moment the ship would be struck with the lightening.
> The sailors almost all drunk, and incapable of rendering
> much assistance had an accident happened …

Although the storm dissipated around midnight, it remained a thoroughly miserable night for everyone stationed ashore. Tents had been flooded and bedding soaked, but it was something that had to be accepted at this early stage of their pioneering endeavour.

The following day, 7 February, Phillip conducted the colony's first truly formal ceremony. As Collins wrote, this consisted of a public reading of the governor's commission from King George III, which appointed Phillip 'his captain-general and governor in chief in and over the territory of New South Wales and its dependencies'. The proclamation also declared the boundaries of New South Wales, which extended from Cape York (the northernmost point of the coast) to South Cape (the southern extremity of Van Diemen's Land) and inland to a north–south longitude that was almost halfway across the continent. No one yet knew what existed between the east coast of New South Wales and that western boundary – was it one significant landmass, or an archipelago of large islands? The question remained unanswered until 1803, when the intrepid maritime explorer Matthew Flinders completed a circumnavigation, proving that New Holland was the world's largest island, or smallest continent. It was also Flinders who proposed that it be named Australia.

Smyth chronicled much of Phillip's ceremony, which took place on a fine and pleasantly warm summer day.

This morning at 11 o'clock all who could leave the ships were summoned on shore, to hear the Governor's Commission read and also the Commission constituting the Court of Judicature. The marines were all under arms, and received the Governor with flying colours and a band of music. He was accompanied by the judge Advocate, Lieutenant Governor, Clergyman, Surveyor General, Surgeon General etc. After taking off his hat and complimenting the marine officers, who had lowered their colours and paid that respect to him as Governor which he was entitled to, the soldiers marched with music playing, drums and fifes, and formed a circle round the whole of the convicts, men and women who were collected together. The convicts were all ordered to sit down on the ground [and] all

gentlemen present were desired to come into the
centre ... A camp table was fixed before them, and 2
red leather cases laid thereon, containing the
Commissions etc. which were opened and unsealed in
the sight of all present, and read by the judge Advocate
(Captain Collins) ...

With the official part of the ceremony complete, the newly
proclaimed governor then stood in front of the 'First Settlers'
and delivered a powerful directive to the convicts sitting before
him.

The Governor harangued the convicts, telling them
that he had tried them hitherto to see how they were
disposed. That he was now thoroughly convinced there
were many amongst them incorrigible, and that he was
persuaded nothing but severity would have any effect
upon them, to induce them to behave properly in
future. He also assured them that if they attempted to
get into the women's tents of a night there were
positive orders for firing upon them. That they were
very idle – not more than 200 out of 600 were at
work – [and] that the industrious should not labour for
the idle. If they did not work, they should not eat. In
England, thieving poultry was not punished with
death; but here where a loss of that kind could not be
supplied, it was of the utmost consequence to the
settlement, as well as every other species of stock, as
they were preserved for breeding. Therefore stealing
the most trifling article of stock or provisions should be
punished with Death, [and while] such severity might
militate against his humanity and feelings towards his
fellow creatures, yet that Justice demanded such rigid
execution of the Laws and they might implicitly rely
upon justice taking place. Their labour would not be
equal to that of a husbandman in England, who has a

wife and family to provide for. They would never be
worked beyond their abilities, but every individual
should contribute his share to render himself and
Community at large happy and comfortable as soon as
the nature of the settlement will admit of That – they
should be employed erecting houses for the different
officers, next for the marines, and lastly for themselves.

If there was any level of encouragement for the convicts, it
came when the governor declared that through commitment,
good behaviour and strong endeavours, they might soon
'regain the advantages which they had forfeited'. He also
encouraged any who were in a position to marry to do so, and
vowed to promote the well-being of every man, woman and
child placed under his control.

It was a powerful address from the governor to his subjects,
who were then returned to their camps. Smyth's account
continues:

> ... the Governor retired to a cold collation under a large
> tent erected for that purpose to which the general
> officers only were invited and not the least attention
> whatever was paid to any other person who came out
> from England. The Masters of the different ships paid
> him the compliment of attending on shore during the
> reading of the Commission, which they were not under
> any obligation to do, notwithstanding which there was
> no more notice taken of them or even to provide the
> slightest accommodation for them than the convicts
> themselves.

Lieutenant Ralph Clark was more descriptive about the repast,
writing: 'All the officers dined with him on a cold collation;
but the mutton which had been killed yesterday morning was
full of maggots. Nothing will keep 24 hours in this country, I
find ...'

The flag flying at this ceremony was the Union Jack, although a variation from the Union Jack we recognise today. It was officially known as the Jack of Queen Anne – an ensign combining the blue-on-white saltire of St Andrew, and the red-on-white cross of St George. The modern-day version of the Union Jack was introduced on 1 January 1801, when Ireland became part of the union and, accordingly, a saltire representative of St Patrick was added to the Jack of Queen Anne.

Just as there's still considerable debate regarding where Arthur Phillip first landed in Botany Bay, a difference of opinion exists among academics and Australian history buffs relating to where abouts in Sydney Cove he set foot ashore on 26 January 1788, and the site of the ceremonies on that day and 7 February. The idea that the landing and the initial flag-raising ceremony were at one and the same location is given weight by Collins' statement: 'In the evening of this day the whole of the party that came round in the *Supply* were assembled at the point where they had first landed in the morning, and on which a flag-staff had been purposely erected and an union jack displayed ...'

As far as the precise location of this site goes, determining the accuracy of one theory over another is made harder by the fact that the cove's shoreline has changed dramatically since 1788, mainly through the creation of docks and other waterfront facilities. Even so, in 1963, the Sydney City Council deemed that there was sufficient evidence that the site where the flag flew and Phillip delivered his speech was in the vicinity of Loftus Street, about 200 metres south of the current shoreline, and near where the freshwater stream existed. A flagpole was erected there that year to recognise its significance in Australian history. However, in more recent times, further analysis of historical documents has led to a growing belief that the landing and the ceremony took place on the cove's western shore, at The Rocks, about 500 metres north-west of the Loftus Street site, and adjacent to where the international cruise ship terminal is located today.

Given that the western shore was rocky and the southern shore sandy and flat, this more recent theory would appear to be supported by a description in Nagle's journal: 'Eight of us that belonged to the Governors barge pitched our tent by the waterside on a rock near the landing place and the boat in view ...' With the harbour being tidal, it would have been inefficient to land at the head of the cove near the stream, as the longboats would constantly need to be moved away from shore as the tide ebbed. In comparison, the water was deep along the western side, and the boats could come and go at any stage of the tide.

Aside from the logic inherent in such a move, another snippet of information from Nagle's log points to Phillip having landed at The Rocks. Nagle recalled fishing from the governor's boat while waiting at the place where Phillip had recently alighted, noting: 'I hove my line over, being 4 or 5 fathom water alongside the rocks ...' This can only mean that the boats were alongside the shore in deep water, which was only found along the rocky western shore. Those supporting the 'head of the bay' theory have contended that the site was near the freshwater stream, the geography of which featured a gently sloping sandy beach and shallow water.

Sadly though, if the western shore is the correct location, then the manner of its commemoration is a blight on Australian society today. Standing very boldly on this site, which is at the foot of Bethel Steps, is a public toilet block!

February would prove to be a month of milestones – some good, others not so good – as the settlement began to establish a solid foothold around the cove, and with that, forge its own identity. Friday, 8 February – the day after Phillip's proclamation as governor – provided another significant event, when a small open cutter sailed into Port Jackson and cruised up-harbour into Sydney Cove. This moment could be recognised as the first time that the colony received a 'foreign visitor'.

Aboard the cutter was Captain Clonnard, a senior officer whom Lapérouse had sent from Botany Bay to meet with Phillip. The Frenchman was delivering the dispatches that were to be forwarded to his ambassador in London. The governor hosted Clonnard overnight before farewelling him the following morning. A month later, on 10 March, the French ships would sail from Botany Bay, never to be seen again.

On 9 February, the first kangaroo was shot and brought into the camp area, much to the intrigue of the majority of residents. Nagle would later describe kangaroos as the most remarkable of all the local fauna he had seen. 'They leap on the hind legs which is very long and supported by a strong tail,' he wrote. 'Their fore feet is quite short. The she have a false belly, which the young go into when in danger. They leap 20 or 30 feet at a leap. Some [weigh] two hundredweight [100 kg] ...'

Also around this time, it appears that the debauchery that occurred when the women convicts were first brought ashore had swiftly led to wedding bells. In line with the urgings of Reverend Johnson and Phillip, fourteen convict marriages were solemnised during the first week of February. The pairing of William Bryant, a Cornish fisherman, and Mary Braund (as the Exeter Assizes had recorded her surname) was a union that the governor would come to look on with some disfavour in the years ahead, however. Both bride and groom had earlier served time on the prison hulk *Dunkirk*, in Plymouth, before enduring the seven-month voyage to Botany Bay. Mary gave birth to a daughter during the passage from Rio to Cape Town, and named her Charlotte after the ship they had travelled on. Bryant's crime, as recorded in his committal at Bodmin in Cornwall, was 'personating and assuming the names of ... two of his Majesty's Seamen and in their Names feloniously receiving part of their ... wages'. On 22 December 1783, the 26-year-old was sentenced to seven years' transportation.

One union that resulted from the wild and stormy night of 6 February was that of the ironically named Anthony Rope and Elizabeth Pulley, although they would not marry until 19 May. By then, Elizabeth was two months pregnant, and strangely enough, while Rope might have hoped to make an honest woman of her, it was because of their wedding that he almost had an appointment with the hangman's noose. Within days of their celebration, the groom was charged with killing a goat owned by a Lieutenant Johnson, valued at 6 shillings, the meat from which had furnished a pie for the wedding breakfast. Rope claimed that he had merely found the goat lying dead on a track near the settlement, after it had been mauled by a 'wild animal'. The charge did not stand and he was acquitted. Rope and Pulley would eventually be granted freedom and given a parcel of land in the outer west. Today, Ropes Creek, near St Marys, serves as a nominal tribute to their success as farmers in the region.

In a major advancement, the law of the land went into action on 11 February. Under the auspices of Judge Advocate Collins, the colony's criminal court, comprising six officers drawn from the navy and the marines, sat for the first time.

Three convicts were tried on that opening day. The first case was a charge of assault; on being found guilty, the perpetrator was sentenced to receive 150 lashes. In the next one, the accused was sentenced to fifty lashes for stealing a plank, although he was subsequently pardoned by the governor. Finally, there was Thomas Hill, whom the court found guilty of stealing some biscuit from a fellow convict. He was banished to solitary confinement on a 'barren rock' – a rugged, almost treeless, 25-metre-high island midstream in the harbour. Hill would serve a week there, without shelter, in irons, and on rations of bread and water.

Captain Hunter gave this island the appropriate name of Pinchgut, a word that can mean hungry or, in a nautical context, the point where a stream or channel narrows. By the mid-nineteenth century, the island's rocky peak had been levelled and, to counter the threat of a possible Russian attack during the Crimean War, a fort was erected there. Some 8000 tons of sandstone were brought over by boat from the northern side of the harbour to create a Martello tower – the last of its type to be built in the world – and ramparts were also added to this fortification. In 1857, the island was renamed Fort Denison, after the governor at that time.

Collins was evidently disappointed with the leniency of the three sentences. 'The mildness of these punishments seemed rather to have encouraged than deterred others from the commission of greater offences,' he would later write, 'for before the month was ended the criminal court was again assembled for the trial of four offenders, who had conceived and executed a plan for robbing the public store during the time of issuing the provisions ...'

This robbery saw the perpetrators claiming for themselves the same amount of rations as allowed for soldiers and officers. According to Collins, the weekly food allocation for male convicts was '7 pounds of biscuit; 1 pound of flour; 7 pounds of beef or 4 pounds of pork; 3 pints of peas; and 6 ounces of butter', while female convicts received two-thirds of that allowance. With regard to the harsh sentence subsequently passed on the thieves, Collins reasoned: 'we saw with concern, that there were among us some minds so habitually vicious that no consideration was of any weight with them, nor could they be induced to do right by any prospect of future benefit, or fear of certain and immediate punishment ...'.

John White's journal provides further detail on the outcome of this case.

27th February. Thomas Barrett, Henry Lovell, and
Joseph Hall ... were convicted on the clearest evidence,
and, sentence of death being passed on them, they
were, about six o'clock the same evening, taken to the
fatal tree, where Barrett was launched into eternity,

after having confessed to the Rev. Mr. Johnson, who
attended him, that he was guilty of the crime, and had
long merited the ignominious death which he was
about to suffer, and to which he said he had been
brought by bad company and evil example. Lovell and
Hall were respited until six o'clock the next evening.
When that awful hour arrived, they were led to the
place of execution, and, just as they were on the point
of ascending the ladder, the judge advocate arrived
with the governor's pardon, on condition of their being
banished to some uninhabited place ...

Despite the gravity of Phillip's threat regarding the
consequences of lawlessness, the recently appointed judiciary
was kept busy. The hangman at Thomas Barrett's execution, in
fact, was recruited via another case that came before the
criminal court that month, as recorded by White.

27th February. James Freeman was tried for stealing
from another convict seven pounds of flour. He was
convicted and sentenced to be hanged; but while
under the ladder, with the rope about his neck, he
was offered his free pardon on condition of
performing the duty of the common executioner as
long as he remained in this country; which, after
some little pause, he reluctantly accepted. William
Shearman, his accomplice, was sentenced to receive
on his bare back, with a cat-o'-nine-tails, three
hundred lashes, which were inflicted.

Freeman refused to take up his new role there and then,
however, that attitude changed when the provost-marshall and
Major Ross threatened to have him shot by the marines if he
did not proceed with the execution, that of Barrett. Not
surprisingly, having just escaped the noose, Freeman decided
that it was in his best interests to avoid being shot. He therefore

moved Barrett to the gallows and soon afterwards 'turned him off'. According to White's journal, the hangman's services were almost called on again two days later.

> 29th February. Daniel Gordon and John Williams were tried and convicted of stealing wine, the property of Mr. Zachariah Clarke. Williams being an ignorant black youth, the court recommended him to the governor as a proper object of mercy, and he was accordingly pardoned. Gordon, who was another black, had his sentence of death, while at the gallows, changed to banishment with Lovell and Hall …

Confident that Collins was handling legal matters as desired, Phillip pressed on with other important tasks. Less than three weeks after the fleet's arrival in Sydney Cove, he had enacted another requirement of King George III's decree. On 14 February, *Supply*, with Lieutenant King as commander and Henry Ball as captain, sailed out of the harbour and headed to Norfolk Island – a tiny, 13-square-mile dot in the ocean, 900 nautical miles to the east-north-east of Port Jackson. Once there, King's first task was to claim the island in His Majesty's name, before establishing a settlement there.

In addition to her usual number of officers and crew, *Supply* was carrying twelve male and female convicts, the plan being for them to become the initial workforce and backbone of the community. While *Supply* was to return to Sydney Cove, Governor Phillip had provided the mission with supplies to last six months, plus the necessary tools to prepare timber for residences and to cultivate the land.

In early March, Phillip decided to investigate what was to the north, particularly at Broken Bay, so he took the recently built longboat from *Sirius* along with two cutters, and set off on a journey that would end up covering 100 nautical miles. It appears to have been a substantial undertaking, given that the entrance to the bay was only 17 nautical miles away along the coast. There were sixteen oarsmen involved, plus Phillip and five soldiers and officers ('sitters' as the hard-rowing Nagle referred to them), together with supplies to last them one week. But a problem arose even before they had left the harbour. The new longboat proved to be so ungainly and heavy that it couldn't keep pace with the others, so Phillip, not wanting to waste precious time during the expedition, ordered that crew to turn back.

As it was, continual heavy rain marred much of their exploration time, and it also forced the governor to abandon his plan to walk back along the coast to Sydney Cove. Nonetheless, he would record a favourable impression of Broken Bay and particularly of an estuary within it that he named after Britain's prime minister.

> Here the land is much higher than at Port Jackson, more Rocky, and equally covered with Timber, large Trees growing on the summits of Mountains, that appear to be accessible to Birds only ... Immediately round the head land that forms the Southern entrance into the Bay, there is a third Branch, which I think the finest piece of Water I ever saw, and which I honoured with the name of Pitt Water, it is as well as the Southwest branch, of sufficient extent to contain all the Navy of Great Britain ...

There was no doubting that Pitt Water was scenically superb, but it had a significant shortcoming in comparison to Port Jackson: a sandbar near its entrance made the waterway too shallow for large vessels to enter. Also, while Phillip was impressed by what he saw, his hopes of finding some flat land that would be more suitable for farming than that found in Port Jackson were not realised. Had he had the time and inclination to explore the waters further to the west of Broken Bay, the governor would have discovered the Hawkesbury River – a system that arcs 75 miles inland to the west of Port

Jackson and through some of the best farming land imaginable. The existence of this river became known the following year, when it was named the Hawkesbury by Phillip in honour of Charles Jenkinson, the Baron Hawkesbury and first Earl of Liverpool.

The March 1788 exploration was marked by mainly friendly and enlightening contact with the local Aborigines, who had no qualms about revealing part of their lifestyle and cultural attitudes to the visitors. Lieutenant Bradley was particularly impressed, writing: 'One of the Women made a fishing hook while we were by her, from the inside of what is commonly called the pearl oyster shell, by rubbing it down on the rocks until thin enough & then cut it circular with another, shape the hook with a sharp point rather bent in & not bearded or barbed ...'

Phillip's party returned to Sydney Cove on 9 March, the day before the French set sail. Numerous men from the settlement, military and otherwise, had made the 7-mile trek across the relatively flat but bushy land to visit *Boussole* and *Astrolabe*, where they enjoyed 'a very friendly and pleasant intercourse with their officers'. These visits led to information filtering back to the governor that brought a degree of comfort regarding the security of the colony and the coast: the Frenchmen were far from impressed with what they had seen of Botany Bay and its surrounds, such that they intended to present a far from positive report on the region to their government in Paris. This was evident in a journal entry by David Collins, who wrote of Lapérouse's departure: 'the French ships sailed from Botany Bay, bound, as they said, to the northward, and carrying with them the most unfavourable ideas of this country and its native inhabitants; the officers having been heard to declare, that in their whole voyage they nowhere found so poor a country, nor such wretched miserable people ...'.

*

Illness continued to plague the colony and it spared no one. Lieutenant David Collins, like many others, surrendered to dysentery that was so severe, he was not expected to live. The same applied to Reverend Johnson, but like Collins, the chaplain somehow survived this often fatal condition.

Meanwhile, the settlement was alive with industrious activity. During the first weeks of March, a wharf was being built, eight cannons had been landed so that a defence battery could be established on the edge of the harbour, and brick-making was underway at a site about a mile from the settlement. The very first residences had been constructed using cabbage-tree plastered over with clay and a thatched roof. Collins noted that the materials 'formed a very good hovel'.

The first real indication that the settlement would soon be heading towards achieving town status came when the site for the governor's brick residence was selected – atop a rise at the southern end of the cove, where there were pleasant views over the harbour – and the lines of the first roadways were marked out. There were trivialities that had to be dealt with also, such as when hogs began running loose among the tents and huts, causing damage and eating anything they could find. This unexpected nuisance prompted the issuing of an order stating that any such animal found within the camp could be killed by the owner of the damaged property without fear of consequence.

Phillip and his officers were happy to see *Supply* sail back into the harbour on 19 March, the brig having completed her mission to Norfolk Island. The captain, Lieutenant Henry Ball was pleased to advise that, after sighting a spectacular yet small island during the outward voyage from Port Jackson, they had stopped there on the return passage to claim it under British colours. He reported that the island was uninhabited and very scenic; wildfowl were in abundance, as were turtles, in the large lagoon. Ball named it Lord Howe Island in tribute to the then First Lord of the Admiralty.

Supply returned to port at about the same time that three of the transports – *Scarborough*, *Charlotte* and *Lady Penrhyn* – were released from government service, Phillip advising the captains that they were now free to undertake their return voyages when desired. While some saw this as an indication of the isolation the colony would soon encounter, Phillip viewed it as another mark of positive progress. However, things weren't going according to plan in other areas, especially with regard to fostering good relations with the indigenous people.

Collins described one unfortunate incident: 'several convicts came in from the woods; one in particular dangerously wounded with a spear, the others very much beaten and bruised by the natives. The wounded man had been employed cutting rushes for thatching, and one of the others was a convalescent from the hospital, who went out to collect a few vegetables ...' These workers reported that another man had been carried away by the natives after being wounded in the head. Later, a party searching a native hut discovered a shirt and hat, both of which had been pierced by spears. The missing man was never found.

Another concern related to the continued availability of fresh water for the colony. 'The run of water that supplied the settlement was observed to be only a drain from a swamp at the head of it,' the judge advocate wrote. '[To] protect it, therefore, as much as possible from the sun, an order was given out, forbidding the cutting down of any trees within fifty feet of the run ... [as] there had not yet been a finer found in any one of the coves of the harbour ...'

In those autumn months, Collins also recorded the second execution to occur in the colony. Such a judicial act confirmed that youth would not be a mitigating factor when it came to capital punishment.

> The month of May opened with the trial, conviction, and execution of John Bennett, a youth of seventeen years of age, for breaking open a tent belonging to the

Charlotte transport, and stealing thereout property
above the value of five shillings. He confessed that he
had often merited death before he committed the crime
for which he was then about to suffer, and that a love of
idleness and bad connections had been his ruin. He was
executed immediately on receiving his sentence, in the
hope of making a greater impression on the convicts
than if it had been delayed for a day or two ...

While facing these and other challenges, Governor Phillip was
as eager to discover what lay inland, beyond the head of the
harbour, as he was to explore the waterways. His explorations
saw him go as far as he could to the west along the major
tributary entering the harbour, which led to the discovery of
widespread arable land near the headwaters – perfect for crops
that would support the colony. So, within months of the First
Fleet arriving, a satellite settlement was established. In 1791,
Phillip would name it Parramatta – a derivative of the name
the Aborigines had for the region, Burramatta, meaning 'The
place where the eels lie down'. Subsequently, the river leading
to it upstream from Sydney Cove took the same name.

On another excursion, Phillip was able to appreciate the
extent of a large range of mountains in the distance to the
west. They stretched from north to south as far as the eye
could see, and he first named them Carmarthen Hills and
Lansdowne Hills. Known today as the Blue Mountains, they
earned their name via a distinctive haze that almost always
enshrouded them. The blue colour results from the effect that
sunlight has on the mist-like droplets of oil drawn into the
atmosphere from dense forests of eucalyptus trees, and mixing
with dust particles in the air.

Unfortunately for this expedition, a lack of supplies and
the fact that Phillip was suffering severe pain from sleeping on
wet ground forced his party to return to Sydney Cove. As
stated in his report on the excursion, he held 'the general
opinion that the appearance of the country promised the

discovery of a large river in that district'. What he might not have contemplated, though, was the degree to which the mountain range would present a formidable barrier to endeavours aimed at exploring the regions beyond. It would not be until 1813 that Gregory Blaxland, William Lawson and William Charles Wentworth would find a way across the rugged terrain and discover a vast, relatively flat interior. This would lead to the establishment of the colony's first inland settlement, Bathurst, in 1815.

There was bad news awaiting Phillip when he arrived back in the cove. As chronicled by a diarist in England: 'Governor Phillip, on his return from this excursion, had the mortification to find that five ewes and a lamb had been killed very near the camp, and in the middle of the day. How this had happened was not known, but it was conjectured that they must have been killed by dogs [dingoes] belonging to the natives ...'

And there was worse in store.

> No very good fortune had hitherto attended the
> livestock belonging to the settlement, but the heaviest
> blow was yet to come. About this time the two bulls
> and four cows, belonging to Government, and to the
> Governor, having been left for a time by the man who
> was appointed to attend them, strayed into the woods,
> and though they were traced to some distance, never
> could be recovered. This was a loss which must be for
> some time irreparable ...

As much as all these misfortunes posed a serious threat to the future of the settlement, a moment of diversion was not unwelcome. Wednesday, 4 June, presented the fledgling colony with its first chance to stage a royal celebration, that of the birthday of King George III. The activities, which spanned much of the day, involved no small amount of cannon-fire – something that could only have brought considerable fright to the local indigenous people, as the booming sound of each blast echoed around the harbour and across the hills. It was the articulate Collins who again provided details of the event.

> His Majesty's birthday was kept with every attention that it was possible to distinguish it by in this country. The morning was ushered in by the discharge of twenty-one guns from the *Sirius* and *Supply*; on shore the colours were hoisted at the flag-staff, and at noon the detachment of marines fired three volleys; after which the officers of the civil and military establishment waited upon the governor, and paid their respects to his excellency in honour of the day. At one o'clock the ships of war again fired twenty-one guns each; and the transports in the cove made up the same number between them, according to their irregular method on those occasions. The officers of the navy and settlement were entertained by the governor at dinner [lunch], and, among other toasts, named and fixed the boundaries of the first county in his Majesty's territory of New South Wales. This was called Cumberland County, in honour of his Majesty's second brother ... At sunset the ships of war paid their last compliment to his Majesty by a third time firing twenty-one guns each ...

That night, as the silver-white sliver of a new moon descended towards the western horizon, several bonfires were lit as a finale to the celebration. Simultaneously, every member of the colony was permitted to drink to His Majesty's health.

During the festivities, Phillip had planned to lay a foundation stone recognising the creation of what is now known as Sydney, although he intended to name the settlement Albion. The ceremony did not proceed, however, and when it did, some time later, he had changed his mind: it would be

Sydney. The County of Cumberland, which he had already defined, became the largest county in the world. Its area covered the known territory around the settlement – from Broken Bay to the southern part of Botany Bay, and out west to the foothills of the mountains.

Still the task of ensuring the colony's survival went on for the governor. By now, he was coming to realise that a theory he had initially held regarding the local climate was a premature one. He had suggested that the weather pattern could be considered the equal of the finest in Europe. 'The rains are not ever of long duration,' he wrote, 'and there are seldom any fogs: the soil though in general light and rather sandy in this part, is full as good as usually is found so near the sea-coast. All the plants and fruit trees brought from Brazil and the Cape … thrive exceedingly; and vegetables have now become plentiful.' Yet he did display some remarkable foresight in his comment: 'The wines of New South Wales may perhaps, hereafter be sought with avidity, and become an indispensable part of the luxury of European tables.' Three months after expressing these thoughts, the climate was certainly contradicting his expectations. In early August, Sydney Cove was overwhelmed by days of torrential rain that caused havoc and destruction. In Collins' description:

> All public labour was suspended for many days …
> by heavy rain; and the work of much time was also
> rendered fruitless by its effects; the brick-kiln fell in
> more than once, and bricks to a large amount were
> destroyed; the roads about the settlement were rendered
> impassable; and some of the huts were so far injured, as
> to require nearly as much labour to repair them as to
> build them anew. It was not until the 14th of the
> month, when the weather cleared up, that the people
> were again able to work.

While the abundant rain accelerated the growth of new grass for the few irreplaceable animals that remained, it also accounted for the demise of the governor's flock of sheep, when they died suddenly after grazing on grass that was 'rank'. This calamity compounded the loss of six head of cattle some weeks earlier, which in turn spelled the end for the one surviving cow, as Collins explained:

> We had now given up all hope of recovering the cattle
> which were so unfortunately lost in May last; and the
> only cow that remained not being at that time with
> calf, and having since become wild and dangerous, the
> lieutenant-governor, whose property she was, directed
> her to be killed; she was accordingly shot at his farm, it
> being found impracticable to secure and slaughter her
> in the common way.

The rapid depletion of the livestock numbers, the indication that much-needed crops were likely to fail due to poor soil quality and lack of consistent rainfall, and the fact that supplies they had brought from England would not last forever left Phillip only too aware that his colony was in a parlous predicament. Swift action was the best answer, so he ordered that *Sirius* be prepared for a voyage to Cape Town, where a wide range of supplies could be secured for the settlement. It was a gamble, but it was his only option, given that the time of arrival of a second fleet from England was unknown. (No firm plans had been formulated when the First Fleet left England. Phillip could only speculate that this would be more than twelve months after his own arrival in Port Jackson.) Tench touched on the latter issue, lamenting: 'The dread of want in a country destitute of natural resource is ever peculiarly terrible. We had long turned our eyes with impatience towards the sea, cheered by the hope of seeing supplies from England approach ...'

Phillip's original thought was that some of the islands to the north of New Holland might be able to satisfy the colony's needs. This would have made the exercise a relatively brief one, yet there was no certainty of what might be readily available there. Cape Town, although a significantly longer passage, had the advantage of being a known and proven quantity.

There were some perplexing odds for the governor to ponder. The voyage could take *Sirius* up to six months to complete, and while the ship was more than capable of achieving her goal, she would have to survive a circumnavigation of some 12,000 nautical miles on the Great Circle route around the bottom of the globe, while crossing some of the most intimidating stretches of water known to seafarers. Should she founder, there was every chance that the colony would do likewise.

To enable as much cargo as possible to be carried on the return voyage to Sydney, Phillip ordered that *Sirius* sail virtually unarmed and almost stripped bare. Her captain, John Hunter, detailed what was put ashore:

> … eight guns, with their carriages, and 24 rounds of shot for each gun, 20 half barrels of powder, a spare anchor, and various other articles. He [Governor Phillip] also directed that I should leave the ship's long-boat behind for the use of the settlement: this order I confess I with reluctance obeyed, as the want of such a boat has often been very severely felt; at the same time I was desired to endeavour, on my arrival at the Cape, to purchase such a boat for the settlement …

An added complication facing this expedition was that the ship had been in a state of disrepair for some months while the carpenters, in particular, were well occupied with work onshore. Forced to rearrange his priorities, Phillip then directed Hunter to employ 'an old man, the carpenter's yeoman, and a convict caulker' and make good the vessel's shortcomings as quickly as possible.

By 1 October, *Sirius* was considered seaworthy and ready to sail. At the top of the tide that day, Hunter wasted no time in calling for the anchor to be weighed. Soon afterwards, the flagship that had suddenly become the colony's lifeline was riding the ebb tide towards the harbour entrance, carrying nothing more than the heavy cargo of hope of those lining the shore of Sydney Cove, watching her departure.

One of the most reproduced images of the early colony, *The Founding of Australia. By Capt. Arthur Phillip R.N. Sydney Cove, Jan 26th 1788*, was painted by Algernon Talmage (1879-1939) in 1937. According to its identification label, it depicts '1st Lieut. Newton Powell [Fowell']; 'Lieut. P.G. King R.N. H.M.S. *Sirius*'; 'Lieut. George Johnston A.D.C.'; 'Capt. Arthur Phillip R.N.'; 'Capt. David Collins Judge Advocate'; 'Commdr. H.L. Ball R.N. H.M.S. *Supply*'. Mitchell Library, State Library of New South Wales ML 1222 / a128112

CHAPTER 11

The Mercy Mission

Phillip had left the decision about which course the ship should take – east-about or west-about – for Captain Hunter to make once *Sirius* was well clear of the coast and heading towards the Southern Ocean. Hunter found his attention drawn to a more pressing matter first, however. Within forty-eight hours of departure, the weather had turned 'dirty', causing him 'a good deal of concern' – and his journal revealed the basis of his dilemma:

> ... the carpenter reported that the ship, which had hitherto been very tight, now made water. This piece of information, with such a voyage as the *Sirius* was now entered upon, was no doubt very unwelcome; and more particularly so, when it was considered, that the ship's company, from having been long upon salt diet, without the advantage of any sort of vegetables, were not so healthy and strong as a leaky ship might require ...

The issue of whether to continue or retreat quickly fell in favour of sailing on, simply because of the urgency surrounding this mercy mission. And so onto the next question.

Governor Phillip had indicated that he thought a shorter, west-about passage to Cape Town through the Southern Ocean might be more logical, but on considering that such a voyage had never previously been undertaken, Hunter opted to sail the proven track to the east, where strong and favourable westerly winds generally prevailed. The captain's decision was also influenced by the fact that the pounding associated with sailing upwind, which would form a considerable part of the east–west course, would almost certainly worsen the leak, and possibly compromise the ship.

The southern tip of New Zealand was the first objective, from which they would sail well south and towards Cape Horn. From there, it was another 3700 nautical miles across the South Atlantic to Cape Town.

Hunter's concern for the safety of his ship continued to mount as men were soon required to man the pumps every two hours. In that time, more than a foot of water flooded into the hull and was sloshing around from stem to stern. Meanwhile, having crawled through the flooded bilge and into the dark and cramped forward sections, the ship's carpenter discovered that the source of the leak was somewhere in the area of the starboard bow. On closer inspection, as reported to the captain, he suspected that the iron bolts securing the hull planking were most likely incompatible with the copper sheathing covering the underwater sections of the ship: the bolts must have become thinner and weaker due to corrosion, thus allowing water into the hull. (Today, this problem is known as electrolysis.)

It was disturbing news for Hunter, as the entire hull of the ship was fastened using iron bolts. He knew it was possible that *Sirius* could eventually become a sieve, but again, given the importance of this voyage, he could only press on and hope the problem didn't worsen.

Once around the southern tip of New Zealand, the captain adopted the role of explorer. He chose to sail a course that divided the two tracks to the east taken by Cook's ships,

Resolution and *Adventure*, in 1773–74, so that 'if any island lay between the parallels in which the ship sailed, we might have a chance of falling in with them'.

Between 7 and 17 November, with *Sirius* now at 57 degrees south, life became miserable for all on board. The temperature was barely above freezing – indeed, the cask holding fresh water for those on deck, the scuttlebutt, actually froze – and the persistent strong gales were frequently accompanied by showers of snow and hail. A week later, there was another danger: icebergs, the largest of which was estimated to be 3 miles long and 350 feet high. Not surprisingly, Hunter and his men were pleased to be sailing in late spring, because the increased number of daylight hours over those of mid-winter allowed them more time to see the icebergs and take the appropriate avoiding action.

As they approached Cape Horn, there was a surreal experience when the prevailing westerly wind, which would normally drive them east at a considerable rate of knots, disappeared and was replaced by headwinds from the north-east. This made for slow progress towards their goal.

Hunter's major worry now was the declining health of his crew, due to their poor diet while in Port Jackson and in the two months since departure.

> The ship's company began to show much disposition to the scurvy, and what made it more distressing, we had nothing in the ship with which we could hope to check the progress of that destructive disease, except a little essence of malt, that we continued to serve. We had only to hope for a speedy passage to the Cape of Good Hope, where we should, without a doubt, with the good things which were to be had there, be able to re-instate their health perfectly: I was so far from being surprised at this appearance of the scurvy amongst the company of the *Sirius*, so soon after leaving her port, that it was with me rather a matter of wonder that it

had not shown itself sooner; and so it must be with
every person who considers how they had lived since
we left the Cape outward bound [for Botany Bay];
during that time (about 13 or 14 months) they had not
tasted a bit of fresh provisions of any kind, nor had they
touched a single blade of vegetables ...

At last, the much-needed westerlies returned, but the weather remained bitterly cold, which only worsened the condition of many of those who were ailing. Hunter recorded that they had sailed through ice for more than twenty-one days and, in that time, covered a distance of around 2000 nautical miles. *Sirius*'s best average over twenty-four hours had been just 7½ knots. '[The] strong westerly winds with us,' he wrote, 'amply compensated for the northerly and easterly gales which detained us so long between Cape Horn and South Georgia; and it was exceedingly fortunate for us that we were so favoured by the winds, for the ship's company were falling down very fast with the scurvy ...'

The seriousness of this problem was illustrated by the fact that only twelve of the usual twenty men were available to stand each watch, and half of them were not capable of climbing aloft to handle the sails. The first death came on 30 December, with Hunter noting, 'John Shine, a seaman, died of the scurvy.' The same note was written for Joseph Caldwell the following day, so it came as a great relief when land – the hills behind Cape Town – was sighted.

On anchoring in Table Bay after three months at sea, Hunter sent his first lieutenant ashore to meet with the Dutch governor and explain the reason for their presence. The captain was subsequently pleased to learn that Cornelis Jacob van de Graaff, who had been of considerable assistance to the First Fleet more than a year earlier, continued to serve as the Dutch East India Company's senior representative at the Cape. Hunter recorded in his journal that the governor 'very politely informed the officer, that there was great abundance of everything to be had, and that I had nothing to do but to signify in writing the quantity of each article wanted, and directions would be immediately given respecting it'. Of equal satisfaction, van de Graaff granted permission for the forty 'invalids' aboard *Sirius* to be landed ashore, where their recovery would be hastened by a diet comprising a considerable amount of fresh fruit and vegetables.

The achievement of Hunter and his crew quickly became a talking point across the waterfront in Cape Town. The Scottish-born captain wrote with some pride: 'Every person here, with whom any of the officers fell in company, spoke of our voyage from the east coast of New Holland, by Cape Horn, to the Cape of Good Hope, with great surprise, not having touched at any port in our way, and having sailed that distance in ninety-one days …'

*

On 5 January 1789, while *Sirius* was being loaded with stores, a Dutch East India ship sailed into Cape Town from Rio de Janeiro, bringing news that caused Hunter and all his men great sadness. Two of the First Fleet vessels – *Prince of Wales* and the storeship *Borrowdale* – had arrived in Rio via Cape Horn after a nightmare voyage from Port Jackson, during which there had been considerable loss of life. The remaining crewmen were so weak, they'd been unable to sail the vessels into port without assistance from local seafarers. Hunter had no doubt that the reason for this tragedy lay in the decision by the captains, John Mason and Houston Reed, to sail direct to Rio from Cape Horn, rather than via the southern tip of Africa. Had they tracked first to Cape Town, it would have made for a considerably faster passage, and everyone would have enjoyed fresh food and good health much sooner.

Two weeks later, there was more distressing news. When a small Dutch frigate reached Cape Town from Batavia, Hunter learned of a calamity involving another of the First Fleet transports, *Alexander*, under the command of John Shortland. She had been sailing through the tropics in company with *Friendship* when dysentery and scurvy began to rage rampant through both vessels; so brutal was the death toll that, before long, Shortland had seen more than half of the crews of both ships buried at sea. As a result, the only option was to scuttle *Friendship* and transfer her remaining crew to *Alexander*, simply to ensure that one ship might have the necessary manpower to sail the remaining distance to Batavia. But not even that desperate strategy was enough. With the fortunate arrival of the Dutch frigate, the latter's captain had to send officers and men aboard *Alexander* when she was off Batavia, so that the sails could be furled and the ship secured. Hunter's journal reveals the grave situation facing Lieutenant Shortland by that point: 'when he arrived [in Batavia], he had only four men out of the two crews who were capable of standing on the deck ...'.

From the captain down, everyone aboard *Sirius* was elated therefore by the sight that greeted them on 18 February, by which point final preparations were underway for their return voyage. It was *Alexander*, sailing into Table Bay. 'I was going off from the shore, when I discovered the ship coming round Green Point,' Hunter recorded. 'I rowed directly on board, and his people were so happy to see their old friends in Table Bay, that they cheered us as we came alongside ...'

Shortland confirmed the Dutch officer's account of the disastrous voyage to Batavia. These discussions left Hunter in no doubt that his decision to sail east-about to Cape Town had been the right one, as *Alexander*, after heading north from Port Jackson, had taken 137 days just to reach Batavia, a distance of 4000 nautical miles. *Sirius* had covered more than twice that distance in ninety-one days. History would reveal a greater legacy in John Shortland's eventual arrival at the Dutch East Indies capital and his subsequent safe passage home to England. Before leaving Sydney Cove in July 1788, he had been entrusted with the delivery of important government dispatches from Phillip and the manuscript for Watkin Tench's

Narrative of the Expedition to Botany Bay, the latter destined for immediate publication by Debrett's of London.

While in Cape Town, *Sirius* had been heeled over so that the carpenter and other men could attempt to remedy the leak. As expected, the cause was found to be an iron bolt having corroded as a result of contact with the hull's copper sheathing. A wooden plug was hammered into the entry point, although Hunter noted with some consternation that many other bolts were showing early signs of corrosion.

On 20 February, with the captain no doubt dwelling on this and other concerns relating to the long voyage ahead, *Sirius* sailed out of Table Bay with six months' supply of flour and many other items for the colony, along with sufficient provisions for the estimated twelve-week sea passage and for some time after that when the crew would be living aboard in Sydney Cove. As Hunter recorded: 'the ship's hold, between decks, every officer's apartment, and all the store-rooms were completely filled …'.

Sirius was barely around the Cape of Good Hope and heading east when the Southern Ocean hurled its first powerful storm her way. It was blowing so hard, with the seas correspondingly large, that at times all sails normally carried above the main courses were hauled up to the yards and furled. Despite this precaution, damage to the rig was as inevitable as it was unwelcome: the mainmast soon became overloaded and bent alarmingly, causing the trestletrees to splinter.

It was fortunate that this problem was spotted by a tar on his way aloft, so that repairs could be carried out straightaway, because, forty-eight hours later, an even worse storm charged in from the north-east. The new front put the heavily laden, 110-foot brig – which was by then leaking as profusely as she had on the outward voyage – under even greater duress. Hunter did his best to follow the safest possible course in the prevailing conditions, nursing his charge across the huge cresting seas in a south-easterly direction. 'It continued to blow very hard all night, and we shipped much water,' he later reported, 'but the ship having a flush deck, no weight could lay on it, the only danger was that of filling the boats [lashed on deck]; to prevent which, I, after this gale, had them turned bottom up …'.

Sirius was in the middle of a maritime wilderness. With there being no known safe haven in the form of land for at least 2000 nautical miles in any direction, it was a case of pressing on as safely yet expeditiously as possible towards the southern tip of Van Diemen's Land. But as she headed in that direction, yet another challenge emerged. In Hunter's description, a 'most violent gale of wind with thick hazy weather' was now testing the men and the ship.

Of considerable concern also was that, for the past five days, the navigator had been unable to obtain a lunar observation by which to plot *Sirius*'s true position: they were sailing blind, and closing on Van Diemen's Land. Dead reckoning suggested that the ship was safely positioned about 30 nautical miles southward of South Cape, but even so, the lookout and every man on deck strained their eyes northwards into the early morning murk, in the hope of spotting land. Such a sighting would allow the navigator to far more accurately plot their location on the chart.

Eventually, they reached a point where Hunter believed it was safe to change course towards the north-east and subsequently clear Tasman Peninsula, 60 nautical miles away. From there, it was a mere 600 nautical miles to Port Jackson.

But the ship's estimated position was wrong. This fact, allied with a wind blowing with 'great violence' from the south-east, immense breaking seas and poor visibility, created a circumstance from which *Sirius* would be lucky to escape. It was virtually a weather bomb. Instead of being on track to clear the promontory, Hunter's ship was set on a course leading straight to the towering cliffs to the west of it. Suddenly the ship and the colony were on the brink of disaster.

The dreaded threat of a gale-lashed lee shore became a reality by mid-afternoon. Instead of abating, the storm was intensifying, but with it came a blessing of sorts as the thick grey atmosphere of sea mist began to clear. Soon afterwards, the only safety net the ship had – the peering eyes of all on deck – was finally able to register her precarious situation. Hunter's journal entry reflects the urgency that accompanied this: 'it cleared a little in the horizon, and we saw the land bearing east; the haze was such that we could not well guess the distance, but it was very near; on this we wore the ship immediately, and stood to the westward …'.

Hunter was trying to have *Sirius* retrace her track, but the power of the bold, breaking and roaring seas, and the force of the wind in the sails, caused a disturbing amount of leeway, and there was nothing that could be done to prevent it. This new course was towards the south-west, a direction that the captain hoped would provide an offing. *Sirius* was under the minimum amount of sail, enough to propel her forward while minimising leeway – but it was to no avail.

In the late afternoon, land was again sighted, 'close under our lee bow'. There was now no doubt that the ship's predicament was a potentially fatal one: she was trapped by the force of wind and the sea state, and heading for a lee shore. From this moment, every man knew that there was only the finest line between survival and surrender. They could see the massive waves pounding onto the base of the rocky cliffs 'with prodigious force', sending sheets of spray high into the air. Should those rocks be *Sirius*'s destiny, she would be smashed to splinters …

Over the howling wind, orders were shouted again from the quarterdeck for the crew to wear ship and head in the opposite direction. As soon as this was done, the worst possible realisation confronted the captain.

I now found that we were embayed, and the gale not in
the least likely to abate, and the sea running mountain

high, with very thick weather, a long dark night just coming on, and an unknown coast I may call it, close under our lee; nothing was now left to be done but to carry every yard of canvass the ship was capable of bearing, and for every person on board to constantly keep the deck, and attentively to look out under the lee for the land, and as often as it might be discovered, to wear, and lay the ship's head the other way: but as we knew not what bay, or part of the coast we were upon, nor what dangerous ledges of rocks might be detached some distance from the shore; and in our way, we had every moment reason to fear that the next [ledge of rocks] might, by the ship striking, launch the whole of us into eternity.

Our situation was such that not a man could have escaped to have told where the rest suffered: however, whatever might have been the private feelings of each individual, I never saw orders executed with more alacrity in any situation …

In short, *Sirius* was trapped in the confines of the bay and hopelessly incapable of clawing her way to windward to escape.

But suddenly, the unpredictable forces of nature presented an opportunity for deliverance. The wind shifted in their favour by about 45 degrees, enough to allow a change of course which could possibly see *Sirius* clear the promontory that was ahead, and sail into the open sea. In Hunter's words: 'We stood on to the eastward, and the ship, to my astonishment, as well as to that of every person on board, bore such a press of sail wonderfully. We had, about midnight … perceived, through the haze, the looming of that land under our lee, nearly on the beam …'

This was the situation he had hoped for – and the first sign that they might just escape tragedy after all.

The ship continued to be pressed as hard as possible on her course, with captain and crew ever hopeful that the wind would hold its favourable direction. When daylight came, they still hadn't cleared the cliffs, but there was a growing belief that they would. 'I observed the looming of a high and very steep point of rocky land,' Hunter continued, 'and the sea foaming with frightful violence against it. I made no mention of it … as it was now on our beam … there could be no danger from it, we should soon pass it …'

The captain's journal confirms that his pursuit of safety was determined and relentless. He was pushing his ship to her limit: 'The ship was at this time half buried in the sea by the press of sail, since she was going through it (for she could not be said to be going over it) at the rate of four knots …' The fortuitous change in the direction of the wind and the remarkable efforts by every member of the crew were duly rewarded. *Sirius* 'soon shot past this head', Hunter reported, adding:

I do not recollect to have heard of a more wonderful escape. Everything which depended upon us I believe, was done; but it would be the highest presumption and ingratitude to Divine Providence, were we to attribute our preservation wholly to our best endeavours: His interference in our favour was so very conspicuously manifested in various instances, in the course of that night, as I believe not to leave a shadow of doubt, even in the minds of the most profligate on board of his immediate assistance!

But *Sirius* had not escaped unscathed. The force of wind and sea had caused the ship to be 'exceedingly disabled'. Her wooden figurehead, under the bowsprit – a carved effigy of the Duke of Berwick – had been ripped from the hull by the waves, while on deck the sheer power of the broken seas charging across the ship had torn many of the thick timber handrails from their mountings. The damage to the bowsprit was such that the jib boom, spritsail yard and fore topgallant mast had to be lowered to the deck to ease the stress and thus preserve the rig. Of equal concern was the integrity of the ship: after the pounding she had taken in the storm, she was leaking worse than ever. The only godsend was that the pumps, mounted on deck, were still able to cope.

Battered and weather-beaten, *Sirius* was sailed cautiously over the remaining 550 nautical miles to Port Jackson, reaching there on the afternoon of 9 May. After 219 days away, 168 of which were at sea, she limped into Sydney Cove just before dark, to the exuberant joy of every man, woman and child in the settlement.

Watkin Tench documented the historic moment: 'At sunset … the arrival of the "*Sirius*", Captain Hunter, from the Cape of Good Hope, was proclaimed, and diffused universal joy and congratulation. The day of famine was at least procrastinated by the supply of flour and salt provisions she brought us …'

CHAPTER 12

Trials and Tribulations

In the seven months that *Sirius* was absent, a number of milestones had been achieved at Sydney Cove. Less gloriously, though, confrontations continued to occur with the Aborigines, and there had been numerous breaches of the law by both marines and convicts.

Within days of John Hunter's departure for Cape Town on 1 October 1788, the settlement's first bridge had been assembled, with a gang of convicts providing labour. Understandably, it was an extremely basic structure: a number of large logs rolled together to span the stream running into the cove. As a result, it was now easier, and a shorter distance, for settlers to cross to the other side.

Not long after the bridge was completed, convicts were employed about a quarter-mile upstream from the waterfront, excavating three large holes in the sandstone alongside the stream in the form of tanks. The plan was to channel water into these tanks – the largest of which was 16 feet deep and held more than 5000 gallons – so that they remained full, thus guaranteeing the colony a constant supply. Also, to ensure the water remained as fresh as possible, a wooden fence was erected around the ditches to prevent access by livestock and wild animals. This undertaking led to the little waterway becoming known as the Tank Stream. Its headwaters originated in a swamp half a mile to the south, where the northern section of Hyde Park, in the heart of Sydney, is located today.

But in 1788 those tanks were not even being considered. At that time, Arthur Phillip was possibly thinking that only a crystal ball could provide the answers relating to the future of his distressingly remote and famine-ravaged community. His hopes were in the hands of the Almighty; it was as if the governor was walking blind into whatever lay ahead. The ocean that swept the coast of New South Wales and beyond held the answers to every one of his questions: Where was *Sirius*? Had she made it to Cape Town intact? When might the first support ship arrive from England?

As Phillip well knew, it was imperative that he develop a survival strategy independent of whatever a sail on the horizon might promise. The colony had to become self-sufficient through the effective cultivation of crops. He had already decided to establish a farming area 11 miles upstream from Sydney Cove, at a site he would name Rose Hill (later renamed Parramatta) in honour of George Rose, the Secretary of the Treasury under William Pitt. This area was chosen because the soil there was of a high quality and free from rocks and stones – two factors that had thus far bedevilled farming efforts around the settlement. Even so, all attempts at farming were incredibly laborious, no matter the location. For some unknown reason, no beasts of burden – workhorses or bullocks – were included as part of Phillip's fleet, so the only way to work the land was by hand, with hoes and other tools. It would be no different more than a year later, when James Ruse, a Cornish farmer turned thief, was permitted an allotment. Ruse later became the first emancipated convict to receive a land grant for farming in New South Wales. After enduring the back-breaking effort inherent in preparing land using such basic implements, he was rewarded by producing some of the colony's first successful crops, small though they were.

Another new development during the final months of 1788 was the introduction of clothing that would become synonymous with convict life. Fittingly, it was David Collins, the settlement's chief law enforcer, who explained how this outfit came into existence.

> In order to prevent, if possible, the practice of thieving, which at times was very frequent, an order was given, directing that no convict, who should in future be found guilty of theft, should be supplied with any other clothing than a canvas frock and trousers. It was at the same time ordered, that such convicts as should in future fail to perform a day's labour, should receive only two thirds of the ration that was issued to those who could and did work ...

Collins added that while the distribution of such a uniform might have appeared trivial, it served 'to show the nature of the people by whom this colony (whatever may be its fate) was first founded'. This could be considered a step towards 'establishing good order and propriety among them, and for eradicating villainy and idleness'.

That December, Phillip took a small group of men on a five-day excursion by boat to Botany Bay, in order to convince himself, once and for all, that the waterway was unsuitable for the establishment of a major settlement. Collins confirmed this intention and noted that the governor 'returned well satisfied that no part of the extensive bay was adapted to the purpose'.

Meanwhile, the judge advocate continued to find himself occupied with his duties on the criminal court, and inevitably with cases involving repeat offenders. Some four months beforehand, the community had been abuzz with the news that a prisoner, James Daley, had discovered gold on the harbour foreshore – only for the truth to emerge that it was nothing but a ruse, part of a plan to escape. On confessing to this 'falsehood', Daley was sentenced to receive 100 lashes, and from then on to wear a canvas frock with the letter R sewn onto it, so that he could be distinguished from the other convicts as a rogue. By the end of the year, however, Daley's luck had run out, after he was convicted of committing numerous thefts across the settlement. When admitting to his crimes, he identified two women as having been the recipients of some of the stolen goods, both of whom were subsequently arrested. Only one of the women was punished in the form of public humiliation. She was sentenced to wear a canvas frock with 'R.S.G.' (receiver of stolen goods) across it. Daley's punishment was terminal: he was hanged.

Late in December, Phillip resolved to address the vexed relations with the local indigenous people, who, according to Collins, were 'becoming every day more troublesome and hostile'. Having exhausted every avenue of peaceful co-existence, Phillip decided that the only option was to capture two of their number and hold them in the settlement, in the hope that he might come to understand their language and attitudes, while simultaneously convincing them of the colony's peaceful intentions. Two officers were commissioned for the task, but they were only able to capture one young man, the second having escaped by jumping into the harbour. Details were provided by Tench.

> The governor sent two boats, under the command of Lieutenant Ball of the 'Supply', and Lieutenant George Johnston of the marines, down the harbour, with directions to those officers to seize and carry off some of the natives. The boats proceeded to Manly Cove, where several Indians were seen standing on the beach, who were enticed by courteous behaviour and a few presents to enter into conversation. A proper opportunity being presented, our people rushed in among them, and seized two men: the rest fled; but the cries of the captives soon brought them back, with many others, to their rescue: and so desperate were their struggles, that, in spite of every effort Pursuant on our side, only one of them was secured; the other

> effected his escape. The boats put off without delay;
> and an attack from the shore instantly commenced:
> they threw spears, stones, firebrands, and whatever
> else presented itself at the boats ...

Tench added that the 'prisoner', who had been tied to a thwart, let out 'the most piercing and lamentable cries of distress' on realising that escape was impossible. 'His grief soon diminished,' Tench continued, 'he accepted and ate of some broiled fish which was given to him, and sullenly submitted to his destiny ...'

Once at Sydney Cove, the naked Aborigine, who was believed to be about thirty years old, was presented to Phillip, before being dressed in clothes – an experience that was obviously quite alien to him. Still, he remained relatively calm. Since all attempts to learn his name had proved unsuccessful, the governor decided that it should be 'Manly', in recognition of the manly behaviour of his fellow tribesmen in the cove where he was captured. Within six weeks, it would become apparent that his Aboriginal name was Arabanoo.

Collins explained what happened immediately after the man's arrival: 'A slight iron or manacle put upon his wrist, and a trusty convict appointed to take care of him. A small hut had been previously built for his reception close to the guardhouse, wherein he and his keeper were locked up at night; and the following morning the convict reported, that he slept very well during the night, not offering to make any attempt to get away ...'

Arabanoo very quickly adapted to his new life in the settlement, so much so that before long he was dining at the governor's abode, enjoying fish, duck, pork and many other unfamiliar foods. 'Bread he began to relish,' wrote Tench, 'and tea he drank with avidity: strong liquors he would never taste, turning from them with disgust and abhorrence. Our dogs and cats had ceased to be objects of fear, and were to become his greatest pets, and constant companions at the table.'

The first New Year's Day to be celebrated in New South Wales was marked by a holiday for everyone, the suspension of all labours and the hoisting of the colours at the small waterfront fort which, by then, had been completed. It was now high summer and the temperatures were taking a toll. On 8 January, the mercury rose to an almost inconceivable 105 degrees Fahrenheit (40.5 degrees Celsius) in the shade.

The desperate circumstances the colony faced through rapidly depleting food supplies and poor crops were compounded in March 1789 by a plague of rats, after the hundreds that had survived the voyage from England rapidly multiplied onshore. They invaded warehouses, residences and gardens, and there was no way of stopping them. Still, it was the human pilfering that same month that truly shocked the colony.

It was discovered that someone had entered the allegedly secure storehouse and stolen a considerable amount of highly prized provisions. On investigation, the authorities learned that the thief had used replicas of three keys to gain access to the store. Much to everyone's disappointment, the culprit was soon found to be a former soldier – one Private Joseph Hunt. This man already had a blemished record within the colony. A few weeks earlier, he had been the recipient of 700 lashes (two sessions of 350, dealt three weeks apart) after a court martial declared him guilty of abandoning his post while on guard duty. This time though, Hunt didn't go to trial; he 'rolled over' and provided evidence for the Crown. As revealed by Collins:

> ... he accused six other soldiers of having been
> concerned with him in the diabolical practice of
> robbing the store for a considerable time past of liquor
> and provisions in large quantities. This crime, great
> enough of itself, was still aggravated by the manner in
> which it was committed. Having formed their party,
> seven in number, and sworn each other to secrecy and
> fidelity, they procured and altered keys [and] ...

whenever any one of the seven should be posted there
as sentinel during the night, two or more of the gang,
as they found it convenient, were to come during the
hours in which they knew their associate would have
the store under his charge ... until they had procured as
much liquor or provisions as they could take off ...

The six were declared guilty in a unanimous vote and
'sentenced to suffer that death which they owned they justly
merited'. The judge advocate's view was: 'A crime of such
magnitude called for a severe example ...'

On 27 March, the half-dozen offenders were hanged in full
public view from a specially prepared scaffold erected on the
western side of the cove. Tench's words reflect the shock of the
moment: 'An awful and terrible example of justice took
place ... which I record with regret, but which it would be
disingenuous to suppress. Six marines, the flower of our
battalion, were hanged by the public executioner, on the
sentence of a criminal court, composed entirely of their own
officers ...'

Four of the hanged marines had already visited court,
during the colony's first murder trial. On 17 November the
previous year, they were charged with being involved in a
brawl that caused the death of another soldier, Thomas
Bulmore. The fight related to a convict woman, and the men
were believed to be drunk at the time. The charges were
downgraded to manslaughter, and all were declared guilty.
Each received 200 lashes as punishment.

In the first week of April, by which point *Sirius* was still a full
month away from reaching Port Jackson, the eyes of every
settler in the cove were increasingly trained down-harbour
with expectation. When the square sails of a vessel finally did
arrive on the waterway, not only did they belong to the wrong
ship, *Supply*, but they brought with them alarming news from
Norfolk Island.

It was, in Collins' description, a 'chimerical scheme' hatched by the convicts against Philip Gidley King – a ploy that, had it not been foiled at the last minute, would have seen the lieutenant governor 'secluded from society, and confined to a small speck in the vast ocean, with but a handful of people'. The intention of the renegades was not to harm anyone on the island, but simply to escape to Otaheite, where they hoped to establish their own settlement. While cleverly thought out, the plot unravelled once details were revealed to King's gardener by the convict woman who was 'cohabitating' with him.

According to Collins, the plan was 'intended to be effected on the first Saturday after the arrival of any ship in the bay, except the *Sirius* (because of her size and number of crew)'. His report continued:

> The capture of the island, and the subsequent escape of the captors, was to commence [on that day] as it had been for some time Mr. King's custom on Saturdays to go to a farm which he had established at some little distance from the settlement, and the military generally chose that day to bring in the cabbage palm from the woods. Mr. King was to be secured on his way to his farm. A message, in the commandant's name, was then to be sent to Mr. Jamison, the surgeon, who was to be seized as soon as he got into the woods; and the sergeant and the party were to be treated in the same manner. These being all properly taken care of, a signal was to be made to the ship in the bay to send her boat on shore, the crew of which were to be made prisoners on their landing; and two or three of the insurgents were to go off in a boat belonging to the island, and inform the commanding officer that the ship's boat had been stove on the beach, and that the commandant requested another might be sent ashore; this also was to be captured: and then, as the last act of this absurd

scheme, the ship was to be taken, with which they
were to proceed to Otaheite ... They charitably
intended to leave some provisions for the commandant
and his officers, and for such of the people as did not
accompany them in their escape ...

Having received the tip-off from his gardener, King had taken
all the necessary steps to put down the rebellion and ensure
that it could never happen again. Collins remarked that the
plot's uncovering was a 'truly providential circumstance', and
as a consequence, 'many of the colonists afterwards were
indebted for their lives'.

Meanwhile, Phillip continued to have his own pressing
problems to confront. With it not being known when, or even
if, *Sirius* would return with the urgently needed supplies, every
possible effort had to be made to cultivate crops. The farm at
Rose Hill was still some time away from becoming sufficiently
productive, but more frustrating was that the one established
in the desirously named Farm Cove, immediately to the east
of Sydney Cove, had proved to be an utter failure. Captain
Hunter would later write of the disappointing results:

There have been several attempts made by the gentlemen
here, who had little farms in the neighbourhood of
Sydney Cove, to raise grain of different kinds, for the
purpose of feeding a few pigs, goats, or poultry; but
although their endeavours seemed for a time to promise
an ample reward, for the corn shot up very quickly, yet it
no sooner formed into ear, than the rats (with which, as
well as other vermin, this country is over-run) destroyed
the whole of their prospect: the Indian corn, which was
remarkably promising, was destroyed in a night; but I am
sorry to say, that such of the corn as had escaped the
vermin, notwithstanding its very promising appearance
in the beginning, turned out the most miserable empty
straws I ever beheld ...

And the month of April brought yet more disaster to the beleaguered colony, as an infectious disease ravaged the local Aboriginal population between Broken Bay, Botany Bay and inland (and later, well beyond), killing thousands. According to some medical experts, the epidemic had the signature of smallpox, leading to widespread suggestions that the virus was introduced by the white settlers. Others have speculated that it was chickenpox or something similar. Due to an absence of any clearly defined medical evidence, the cause of this epidemic will probably remain unknown forever.

Writing in the 1980s, author P.H. Curson observed that it was common during this era for medical practitioners to misdiagnose an ailment as smallpox – a point that would appear to be relevant when reading accounts of the 1789 epidemic. While this particular tribulation did not affect the European visitors directly, for some, it was no less distressing to have to witness. Tench provided this viewpoint:

> An extraordinary calamity was now observed among the natives. Repeated accounts brought by our boats of finding bodies of the Indians in all the coves and inlets of the harbour, caused the gentlemen of our hospital to procure some of them for the purposes of examination and anatomy. On inspection, it appeared that all the parties had died a natural death: pustules, similar to those occasioned by the small pox, were thickly spread on the bodies; but how a disease, to which our former observations had led us to suppose them strangers, could at once have introduced itself, and have spread so widely, seemed inexplicable …

Collins expounded a theory that such a disease was no stranger to the Aboriginal population.

> The cause of this mortality remained unknown until a family was brought up, and the disorder pronounced

to have been the smallpox. It was not a desirable
circumstance to introduce a disorder into the colony
which was raging with such fatal violence among the
natives of the country; but saving the lives of any of
these people was an object of no small importance, as
the knowledge of our humanity, and the benefits
which we might render them, would, it was hoped,
do away [with] the evil impressions they had received
of us. From the native who resided with us we
understood that many families had been swept off by
this scourge, and that others, to avoid it, had fled into
the interior parts of the country. Whether it had ever
appeared among them before could not be discovered,
either from him or from the children; but it was
certain that they gave it a name (gal-gal-la); a
circumstance which seemed to indicate a pre-
acquaintance with it ...

Such a theory could be interpreted as supporting another
belief – that the epidemic originated in the most northern or
north-western parts of the country, where the local population
had come into contact with visitors from Asia.

As the epidemic spread, the colony soon had its own
reason to grieve. Arabanoo, who had successfully been
assimilated into the community, contracted the mysterious
disease and died within six days. His presence had delivered
many of the benefits that Governor Phillip had hoped for; in
fact, apart from providing insight into the ways of the
indigenous people, 'Manly' had become the nexus between
two vastly different cultures. Tench elaborated:

To convince his countrymen that he had received no
injury from us, the governor took him in a boat down
the harbour, that they might see and converse with him:
when the boat arrived, and lay at a little distance from
the beach, several Indians who had retired at her

approach, on seeing Manly, returned: he was greatly
affected, and shed tears. At length they began to
converse. Our ignorance of the language prevented us
from knowing much of what passed; it was, however,
easily understood that his friends asked him why he did
not jump overboard, and rejoin them. He only sighed,
and pointed to the fetter on his leg, by which he was
bound ...

A Royal Marine since his teens, thirty-year-old Tench had
already spent a considerable amount of time studying the
Aboriginal population while in Sydney, and the epidemic that
killed Arabanoo and so many others caused him great distress.
After he returned to England in December 1791, Tench would
continue to present his thoughts and theories on the possible
cause. In his second book, *A Complete Account of the Settlement
at Port Jackson*, he asks a series of questions that still defy
definitive answers:

> ... is it a disease indigenous to the country? Did the
> French ships under Monsieur de Lapérouse introduce it?
> Let it be remembered that they had now been departed
> more than a year; and we had never heard of its
> existence on board of them. Had it travelled across the
> continent from its western shore, where Dampier and
> other European voyagers had formerly landed? Was it
> introduced by Mr. Cook? Did we give it birth here? No
> person among us had been afflicted with the disorder
> since we had quitted the Cape of Good Hope,
> seventeen months before. It is true, that our surgeons
> had brought out various matter in bottles; but to infer
> that it was produced from this cause were a supposition
> so wild as to be unworthy of consideration ...

Saturday, 10 May 1789. As the new day welcomed the sun on
the morning after *Sirius* had come to anchor in Sydney Cove,

small boats shuttled back and forth between ship and shore, transferring the precious cargo to makeshift warehouses, the little vessels like ants taking pieces of a prized kill back to their nest. There was close to 60 tons of wheat, flour and barley aboard the ship – enough merely to ease the settlement's famine woes, not to solve them. Regardless, the entire community appreciated how fortunate they were to receive this bounty, particularly on hearing Hunter's report that, just days earlier, *Sirius* had been 'in the utmost peril of being wrecked' on the coast of Van Diemen's Land.

Soon enough, John Hunter would recognise the true extent of this good fortune. After carrying out a close inspection of *Sirius*, shipwrights confirmed that the pounding she took in the storm while trying to round Tasman Peninsula had made her structurally deficient: she was incapable of undertaking another ocean voyage. Her hull had been weakened so much that, had she been punished by another malevolent and unforgiving storm while on approach to Port Jackson, she could well have been lost without trace.

While Hunter and his crew counted their blessings, the fact that their ship could no longer put to sea was a serious blow to the struggling colony. *Sirius* was a vital lifeline, and it was crucial that she be strengthened and made ocean-ready immediately. A survey of 'a convenient retired cove on the north shore' of the harbour, less than 2 miles from the settlement, proved it to be a suitable site for her careening and repairs. As Collins explained, it was the urgency surrounding her repair that saw this bay chosen over Sydney Cove: 'She could have been refitted with much ease at Sydney; but there was no doubt that the work necessary to be done to her would meet with fewer interruptions, if the people who were engaged in it were removed from the connections which seamen generally form where there are women of a certain character and description ...'

With this work being carried out in July, Captain Hunter was able to join the governor for two expeditions to Broken Bay, the aims of which were to survey the waterway before exploring the river known to run to the west. The plan saw boats sailing north to the bay while the governor's party travelled overland, along the coast via long, sandy beaches and over headlands. The river was negotiated on the second visit, which was when Phillip named it the Hawkesbury. He and his party ventured more than 70 nautical miles upstream to a place he named Richmond Hill. Shallowing water was just one reason for the decision to return home. The other factor concerned the height of floodwaters in this part of the river: as Hunter observed, logs and other debris that could only have come from the peak of a flood were seen lodged 'in the cliffs ... from thirty to forty feet above the common level of the river'. It was almost beyond comprehension, and certainly something they did not wish to confront.

Phillip decided that he and some of the party, including Hunter, would return to Sydney Cove overland from Pitt Water, via an inland route. But on reaching the north-west arm of Port Jackson (Middle Harbour), their progress was blocked by the waterway, and there seemed no easy way around it. While they could have tried to find its headwaters and cross there, with supplies running low, they were under pressure to take the shortest route. Hunter explained what followed, including how the colony's first catamaran came into existence.

> We found this morning a canoe upon the beach, with which we had no doubt of getting two men across the water, who could in a short time walk over to the cove where the *Sirius* lay [opposite Sydney Cove in Port Jackson]; but this prospect was disappointed by the first man who entered the canoe having overset her, and she immediately sunk, and he was obliged to swim ashore: after this we went to work and made a catamaran, of the lightest wood we could find, but when finished and launched, it would not, although pretty large, bear the weight of one man ...

Two brave tars then offered to swim the 400 yards across the waterway, but before doing so, they had a solid swig of rum – Dutch courage to help them on their way. Had the intrepid pair known that these waters were shark-infested, they might just have kept drinking. Both men made it to the other bank before crossing the hills to the bay where *Sirius* was docked. Acting on Hunter's orders, they then arranged for a boat to row around to where the party was waiting, and ferry everyone back to Sydney Cove.

Ensconced in his official residence, up on the hill to the south of the cove, Governor Phillip had many matters to deal with during the spring of 1789. One priority was to capture two more Aborigines so that he could continue with his efforts to bridge the cultural divide and establish a peaceful environment. As before, the indigenous people of Manly were chosen as the most suitable, and on 25 November, two men were captured there and taken back to the settlement. The first was named Bennelong, the other Colbee. Although the latter escaped within a matter of days, Bennelong stayed and adapted to British colonial culture remarkably well. He learned to speak English and also took a liking to English fare and alcohol. Initially he resided with Phillip, but before long he had adapted to his new lifestyle so well that he was accommodated in a small hut built especially for him at what is now named Bennelong Point.

But while Phillip's intercultural initiative showed foresight on his part, it was a relative sideshow to the crises that were engulfing the colony. By late October 1789, over a year after *Sirius* had departed on her mercy mission, an even worse famine was confronting the settlers. The local farms had still not produced suitable crops, and the two years of provisions put aboard the ships prior to leaving England were all but gone. This meant that even with the stores that *Sirius* had delivered from Cape Town, there was less than five months of provisions left. And there remained the uncertainty of when the first ship carrying relief supplies would arrive from England. The worst possible scenario, assuming that the ship did not founder on its voyage, was fifteen months away – a thought that no one wanted to entertain. Not even hauls of fish from the harbour and the (relatively unsuccessful) shooting of kangaroos could ease the predicament.

Tench's words in early 1790 painted an utterly disconsolate picture of life in the settlement:

> Our impatience of news from Europe strongly marked
> the commencement of the year. We had now been two
> years in the country, and thirty-two months from
> England, in which long period no supplies, except what
> had been procured at the Cape of Good Hope by the
> 'Sirius', had reached us. Famine besides was
> approaching with gigantic strides, and gloom and
> dejection overspread every countenance. Still we were
> on the tiptoe of expectation ...

Phillip had to accept that he was the captain of a sinking ship, one that appeared to have no lifeboats. Desperate measures were demanded of him, and options ebbed and flowed in his mind like waves washing onto a beach. Then, thanks to the application of every piece of tenacity, logic and determination he possessed – the very traits that had contributed to his being selected as Governor of New South Wales – he devised a plan that just might keep the colony afloat until the first rescue ship arrived.

Put simply, *Sirius* would sail for China in March and acquire a cargo of essential supplies, but of equal importance, en route she would deliver convicts, marines, animals and more to Norfolk Island, where they would take up residence. In addition, *Supply* was to accompany *Sirius* to the island with passengers and equipment, after which she would return to Port Jackson. As Collins explained, with the colony's supplies ever dwindling, the need for fewer mouths to feed at Sydney Cove was the biggest influence on the governor's decision.

> Lieutenant King having constantly written in high
> terms of the richness of the soil of Norfolk Island, the
> governor, on comparing the situation of the convicts
> there and in this settlement, where their gardens had
> not that fertility to boast of, and where the ration from
> the store was, with too many, hastily devoured ...
> determined to detach a large body of convicts [200 in
> all], male and female, together with two companies of
> the marines. Some immediate advantages were
> expected to be derived from this measure; the garden
> ground that would be left by those who embarked
> would be possessed by those who remained, while the
> former would instantly on their arrival at Norfolk
> Island participate in the produce of luxuriant gardens,
> [and] in a more constant supply of fish ...

This resolution to commit to Norfolk Island was a bold one. As expected, Phillip commissioned Hunter to oversee the maritime element of the mission.

Bringing the governor a tinge of personal satisfaction perhaps, it presented Phillip with the chance to relieve himself of the bane of his life – the much-disliked Lieutenant Governor Robert Ross. Aside from his objections regarding the suitability of Sydney Cove, Ross had long tended to disagree with most of what Phillip chose to do or say. And there was no hiding the marine commander's contempt for New South Wales, about which he wrote: 'I do not scruple to pronounce that in the whole world there is not a worse country than what we have yet seen of this. All that is contiguous to us is so very barren and forbidding that it may with truth be said, here Nature is reversed ...'

The island's current lieutenant governor, Philip Gidley King, would obviously be unaware of the new venture until the ships arrived. The fact that Ross was there to replace him need not have worried the 31-year-old Cornishman. Far from his removal being a demotion, King would learn on arrival in Sydney that, as Governor Phillip's trusted and capable deputy, he was to sail to England on the first available ship and report direct to the British Government on the development of the colony. Phillip hoped that by having a man on the ground with the ability to answer all questions, he would then be able to count on continuing support from within the hallowed chambers of Whitehall and Westminster. The colony had been weighed down in its infancy by many unexpected problems – the result of a lack of knowledge about the destination on the part of the government.

All their chosen representative in New South Wales had to do now was ensure that it lasted long enough to receive the benefits of that support.

The fauna and flora of the new colony were painted and sketched by numerous artists. Kangaroo by Peter Mazell (dates unknown). National Library of Australia nla.pic-an7890412.

Echidna by Aylmer Bourke Lambert (1761–1842). Mitchell Library, State Library of New South Wales PXD 1098/vol. 1 / a5203027.

CHAPTER 13

Life and Death

On 6 March 1790, the two vessels, both riding low in the water due to the burden of their cargo, sailed from Sydney Cove and out towards the heads. *Sirius* was not expected to return before mid-year while *Supply*, soon to be the colony's only support ship, was due back in Port Jackson during the first part of April.

The two brigs took with them close to a large percentage of the population of the settlement. Although the number varies considerably across numerous historical documents, John Hunter wrote of receiving the following official order from Phillip:

> ... to embark the lieutenant-governor, with one company of marines, and the officers, baggage, and also 186 convicts; in all, 221 persons; with such a proportion of the remaining provisions and other stores, as the settlement at that time could furnish; and I was directed to land them upon Norfolk Island: Lieutenant Ball, commander of his Majesty's armed tender, *Supply*, was ordered under my command, and he also embarked a company of marines, and twenty convicts.

Twenty-seven children of convicts were included in the total also, and among the non-human cargo was a meagre collection of livestock and poultry.

As much as all hearts were set on little else but survival, there was an important historical fact associated with this mission. Among their number was the first convict to be emancipated in New South Wales, John Irving, who had been granted his freedom less than a week before departure. He had been sentenced in England to 'seven years beyond the seas' for larceny, after stealing a silver cup from a home in the Lincolnshire town of Grantham. On the voyage to Botany Bay, he had proved himself to be a man of good character when working as a surgeon's assistant. Phillip was so impressed by Irving's ongoing commitment to the colony that he appointed him to the same role at Norfolk Island.

On board *Sirius* as she rounded the tree-covered Bradley's Point (now Bradleys Head) and the settlement gradually disappeared from view, David Collins looked back and lamented: 'the little society that was left in the place was broken up, and every man seemed left to brood in solitary silence on the dreary prospect before them'. Once the ship reached the harbour entrance, however, such a thought was the farthest thing from his mind.

Both vessels were on the edge of coming to grief, even before reaching the open ocean. It happened just as the sails were being trimmed for the new course, towards the eastern horizon, when the wind faded in an instant to the faintest breath; the sails fell limp and began slatting in response to the roll of the ocean swell, and both ships stopped making headway. Soon the force of the waves and the influence of the tide were combining to move the brigs in the wrong direction: they were heading straight for the rocks. Collins told of the unfolding drama: 'everybody on board thought of no other but that we should have been drove onshore. [If we had,] the ship would have been in pieces in a few minutes from the great sea that was breaking on the rocks and most of us onboard would have been lost. [But] … by great good fortune a puff of wind shoved us clear out of the harbour as it did the *Supply* …'

Sirius had come disturbingly close to being washed onto the sheer grey sandstone cliffs of the harbour's northern headland. After the near-miss in Storm Bay, off Tasman Peninsula, salvation had smiled on her once again.

The new breeze – a perfect south-westerly – soon had the pair making good speed on a direct course towards the island, which was some 900 nautical miles away to the east. But the breeze continued to strengthen, and this, coupled with rising seas, then made for an uncomfortable ride for those struggling to gain their sea legs, even though the ships were sailing downwind. While the well-seasoned tars relished the speed, Ralph Clark was one of many who succumbed to seasickness. 'I am a poor soul at sea for I am mostly always seasick,' he wrote, resignedly, 'as was everybody in the ship a few hours after we got out of the harbour.' As usual, things were far grimmer where the convicts were: 'between decks there [is] Such a disagreeable Smell from the women that are Sea Sick that it is enough to Suffocate one – there is [65] convict women on board for Norfolk and there is not one but what is Sea Sick'.

The wind stayed in their favour, as did the current once they were offshore. In the early hours of 13 March, just after four bells had rung to signal two o'clock, there was little surprise when an alert lookout on *Sirius* shouted out that he could distinguish the shadowy outline of the island, off the bow. This sighting caused no alarm, despite the darkness: there was still ample sea-room between the ship's position and the island, a flat-topped pinnacle of a subterranean mountain. Its highest point, Mount Bates, peaks at just 1000 feet above sea level.

Hunter called for the ship to be brought-to and allowed to drift casually until sunrise, at which point, sails were then set and trimmed so that she could proceed safely to the lee of Cascade Bay, on the north-eastern shore, the opposite side to the island's main anchorage. *Sirius* arrived at Cascade Bay at the anchorage during the afternoon, and over the next forty-eight hours, all the marines and convicts were transported ashore by boat. In total, 270 people were landed from the two ships, and subsequently accommodated in small huts on the other side of the island. The plan to offload the stores and the animals had to be swiftly abandoned, however, after a rapid and unfavourable change in the weather appeared out of nowhere. As a result, it became imperative that *Supply* and *Sirius* head back to sea for safety. Hunter explained what followed.

> ... we were now driven out of sight of the island ...
> I was also acquainted with the many difficulties which
> Lieutenant Ball, commander of the *Supply*, had met
> with in the different voyages he had made from Port
> Jackson to this island with provisions; and the length of
> time he had, in some of these voyages, been obliged to
> cruise before he could have any access to the shore; so
> continually does the surf break all round it. These
> considerations gave me much anxiety and uneasiness ...

A welcome change in the weather conditions on 19 March allowed both ships to return to the island, where this time they made for Sydney Bay (now Slaughter Bay), on the south-west side. For Hunter, with *Supply* having gone ahead and anchored in the bay, and a flag flying onshore signalling that it was safe for boats to begin transporting stores, there was no hesitation for him deciding to sail his ship towards the anchorage in the bay.

It was eleven o'clock in the morning, on a sunny and pleasant early autumn day, when the anchor was released from the cathead aboard *Sirius*. As soon as the call came that the bower had taken a bite, an order was hollered for the boats to be hoisted out, loaded and rowed to the nearby sandy beach. With only some of the crew being required for this task, their off-watch shipmates took the opportunity to go fishing. 'All the seamen that could muster hook & line was catching groupers, not thinking of any danger,' Jacob

Nagle recalled of the drama that was soon to unfold. 'Captain Ball of the *Supply* [then] hailed us and informed Captain Hunter that the swell of the surf having hold of us, we were too close [to] a reef of sunken rocks, which lies off the west point of the bay ...'

It took no more than a hasty glance over the bulwark for Hunter to realise the presence of considerable danger: the outline of the reef was obvious and far too close for comfort. In an instant, urgency rushed through the ship. Orders were shouted from the quarterdeck and men scrambled about – some rushing up the ratlines like startled chimps, others to their posts on deck – all doing what they could to prevent *Sirius* from striking the rocks. The threat was worsening by the minute, with the wind having suddenly turned onshore and increasing in strength at a rapid rate of knots – such that *Sirius* was now stretching back on her anchor cable and into shallower water. Each fresh gust of wind, each surge of a new wave, moved the ship precariously closer to doom.

Because *Supply* had the ability to sail upwind, and slightly more sea-room in her favour inside the bay, Ball was able to set sail, beat to windward and move off to safety. But only by the narrowest of margins. *Sirius* was incapable of sailing upwind anywhere near as well, and her captain could only hope for a miracle to save the ship.

In a desperate bid to escape the seemingly ravenous reef, once he had sufficient sail set to attempt to make headway, Hunter shouted for the anchor warp to be hacked through with an axe and let run. The captain was applying every piece of seafaring skill he could muster, but the ungainly ship couldn't achieve what was being asked of her. On this day, Hunter's vast experience was no match for the forces of nature.

> I plainly perceived that we settled so fast to leeward
> that we should not be able to weather it: so, after
> standing as near as was safe, we put the ship in stays
> [attempted to tack]; she came up almost head to wind,

but the wind just at that critical moment baffled her,
and she fell off again: nothing could now be done, but
to wear her round in as little room as possible, which
was done, and the wind hauled upon the other tack,
with every sail set as before; but, still perceiving that
the ship settled into the bay, and that she shoaled the
water [sailed into shallower water], some hands were
placed by one of the bower anchors [in readiness to
release it], in five fathoms water; the helm was again
put down, and she had now some additional after-sail,
which I had no doubt would ensure her coming
about; she came up almost head to wind, and there
hung some time; but by her sails being all aback, had
fresh stern way [was moving backwards]: the anchor
was therefore cut away [released from the cathead],
and all the halyards, sheets, and tacks let go, but before
the cable could be brought to check her, she struck
upon a reef of coral rocks which lies parallel to the
shore, and in a few strokes was bulged ...

Each time all 511 tons of his ship were lifted by the might of a
large wave and then dumped unceremoniously onto the reef
with a sickening thud, hull planks burst open like breached
staves in a busted barrel. Nagle recorded how 'as the rocks cut
her bottom away the ballast fell out ... four foot of water
flowed fast in the hold'. From that moment, *Sirius* had met her
match. Hunter therefore turned his attention to doing
everything possible to save the lives of all on board. Only after
that was achieved did he try to save what he could of the ship's
cargo. His account continues:

When the carpenter reported to me, that the water
flowed fast into the hold, I ordered the masts to be cut
away, which was immediately done. There was some
chance, when the ship was lightened of this weight,
that by the surges of the sea, which were very heavy,

> she might be thrown so far in up the reef, as to afford
> some prospect of saving the lives of those on board, if
> she should prove strong enough to bear the shocks she
> received from every sea. After the masts were gone, all
> hands were employed in getting out of the hold such
> provisions as could be come at, and securing them
> upon the gun-deck, that they might be at hand in case
> any opportunity offered of floating them on shore ...

The people watching from land felt shocked and helpless as the three towering timber masts, along with their yards and sails, and the ribbon-like captain's pennant, were sent crashing over the side in a splintered, tangled mess. It was like witnessing a beautiful swan being shot in flight and plunging to earth in a fatal spiral. As noted by Nagle, the sight proved too much for some: 'the women on shore set up such cries lamenting and hallowing on the beach that the Governor was compelled to send soldiers to drive them off the beach and compel them to remain in their huts ...'

Ralph Clark, who observed the tragedy from the beach, scribbled a flurry of notes that considered the consequences of so valuable a loss.

> Gracious God, what will become of us all? The whole
> of our provisions in the ship now a wreck before us – I
> hope in God that we will be able to save some, if not
> all – but why do I flatter myself with such hopes? There
> is at present no prospect of it – except that of starving.
> What will become of the people that are on board? No
> boat can go alongside for the sea. And here am I, who
> has nothing more than what I stand in and not the
> smallest hope of my getting anything out of the ship –
> everybody expects that she will go to pieces when the
> tide comes in ... I am so low that I cannot hold the
> pencil to write – in short, my pocket book is full and
> will not hold any more ...

By nightfall, when the tide was rising, the height and power of the seas grew even more, hammering the stricken vessel even harder. With it now unsafe for anyone to remain on board, Hunter made the call to abandon ship. Before the crew departed, he issued two orders, the first of which, in Nagle's words, was that the men 'open the aft hatchway and save all the liquor that could be got at to prevent the seamen from [stealing it and] getting drunk'. Then, in line with the captain's second instruction, 'we began to secure our clothing in our chests & lashed them well with cords & hove them overboard thinking the surf would take them on shore'. Misfortune governed this last effort, however, as Nagle revealed: 'But being a strong current setting to the westward they were carried to sea and we lost all but what we had on.'

Hunter and some forty others then made their way through the surf by clinging on to a timber grating that had been attached to a hawser stretched between the ship and a tree on the beach. It was a miracle that no lives had been lost, although Clark recounted a close call that came his way.

> I was very near drowned … when I was going off on
> the raft to assist the people that were coming on shore
> [when] one of the convicts who could not swim, fell off
> the Raft and pushed me along with him, in which case
> we should both have been drowned if I could not have
> swimmed – for I was obliged to swim back to the shore
> with him holding fast to me by the waistband of my
> trousers. When I got on shore he was almost dead but
> he soon recovered … I took a stick out of one of the
> Sergeants hands and gave him a damned thrashing for
> pulling me off the raft with him …

When Hunter finally reached the beach, he looked back at the wreck with dismay and frustration. Yet he could remain comfortable in the knowledge that this tragedy had come about more through misfortune than bad management, at an isolated island where there was no sheltered harbour to accommodate ships. It was all open sea around Norfolk's mostly rocky, 18-mile perimeter.

With the livestock and poultry still aboard *Sirius*, their welfare now became a matter of considerable concern – particularly given that vital provisions for the colony would surely be lost or ruined. As a result, Hunter directed two convicts to swim out to the ship and save whatever animals they could. 'They got on board and throw a great number of hogs, goats and fowls over board,' wrote Clark. Having found some alcohol on the ship, the pair then chose to reward themselves for their efforts by getting horribly drunk. And before long, they'd decided that it would be an equally good idea to set fire to the hulk …

Amid the high emotions onshore, there was panic when the first wisp of smoke was seen. Hunter agreed to allow one brave convict to swim out to the ship. Once there, he extinguished the fire before electing to stay with the drunks until morning, just to ensure their thoughts of arson did not return.

Throughout that night, *Sirius* was pounded by the thundering surf. So it was somewhat surprising when morning's light on 20 March revealed her to still be relatively intact. Nagle would later credit the workmanship that he and others had put into strengthening her hull as having been responsible for saving countless lives. '[Her] upper works was as strong as wood, copper & iron could make a ship,' he wrote with obvious pride. 'We put 28 strong riders into her, copper bolted in Port Jackson of the country oak, which saved us, or otherwise nothing could resist so tremendous a surf as there is on that Island …'

His pride could well have been justified, as the shattered hulk that was once the flagship of the First Fleet, and before that the former HMS *Berwick*, continued to resist the might of the seas. Renamed after a bright southern star, the ship had twice escaped the ocean's gallows in recent times, first in

Storm Bay, then while departing from Port Jackson for this
new island home. But now her day of reckoning had arrived.

At last, after five days of this onslaught, conditions were
sufficiently benign for the younger and more agile sailors to
venture aboard *Sirius* and salvage what they could. A
dangerous and arduous task, for much of the time they were
up to their chests in water, while the remnants of the heavy
timber ship creaked, groaned and moved all around them.
Each day, they managed to bring ashore between twenty and
thirty casks – a moderate success.

While the struggle to recover cargo and livestock
continued, one particular breed of birdlife – a pair of pigeons –
had survived the wreck of *Sirius* and would go on to populate
the island with their offspring. When detailing the story at a
later date, Nagle revealed that these birds had been a welcome
part of much of the First Fleet voyage and the early days of the
settlement.

> … while at Rio de Janeiro, in a strong gale of wind, a
> pigeon was blown off from the shore and lit on board
> of us. We cut his wings and let him run on the quarter
> deck, and when at the Cape of Good Hope, laying in
> Table Bay in a strong SE wind, another pigeon was
> blown off and lit on the cathead and permitted herself
> to be taken. [We] cut her wings and put it with the
> other. They happened to be a pair, he and she. When
> their wings grew, they would take a flight from the
> ship in the wide ocean but would return to the ship
> again, and by those two pigeons all the breed sprung
> from on Norfolk Island, which was numerous when I
> left it. The Lieutenant Governor had pigeon houses
> built for them, but they would visit and go on board
> the wreck of the ship daily looking for food …

Over the days before salvage work could begin, Hunter had
put the time to good use. The crew from *Sirius* had trekked

across the island, back to Cascade Bay, to receive cargo from
Supply, which was anchored offshore. While Hunter's men
were there, it was decided that twenty-two of their lot would
board *Supply* and sail back to Port Jackson when she departed
on 24 March. King also joined the ship. His replacement,
Robert Ross, immediately adopted a heavy-handed, arrogant
approach to governing, which would almost cause the failure
of the island settlement over the years ahead.

Hunter opted to stay on Norfolk Island with his remaining
men. The problem was, with the intention having been that
Sirius would depart for China, their unexpected presence put
extra pressure on food supplies. 'We were now upon this little
island 506 souls, upon half allowance of provisions,' Hunter
acknowledged, 'and that could, with our present numbers, last
but a very short time; as the supply intended for the island was
yet on board the *Sirius*; and consequently its safety very
uncertain ...'

When *Supply* hoisted sail and headed west, Hunter and all
others 'entertained a glimmering of hope that she might, in
the course of five or six weeks, return to us with the very
comfortable news of arrivals from England'. This would prove
to be a forlorn hope. It would be eleven months before a vessel
reached the island with supplies, and to repatriate the
shipwrecked sailors to Sydney Cove.

In the months before Phillip announced his plans for easing the
food crisis in early 1790, he and Captain Hunter had established
a signal station on the southern headland at the entrance to Port
Jackson. Should any ship approach the port, the marines
stationed there were to raise a flag to the top of a high pole,
which was visible from Sydney Cove. This signal was the centre
of attention every day while the remaining members of the
colony eagerly awaited any sign of the support ship from
England.

Such an air of excitement came on 5 April when a sail
appeared on the horizon ... But disappointment soon followed

once it was realised that the new arrival was *Supply* returning to port from Norfolk Island. Nevertheless, Phillip decided to go down-harbour and welcome the ship. Tench, who was invited by the governor to join him, takes up the story.

> Having turned a point about half way down [Bradleys Head], we were surprised to see a boat, which was known to belong to the *Supply*, rowing towards us. On nearer approach, I saw Captain Ball make an extraordinary motion with his hand, which too plainly indicated that something disastrous had happened; and I could not help turning to the governor, near whom I sat, and saying, 'Sir, prepare yourself for bad news.'

With the loss of *Sirius*, the prospect of failure now loomed large for Phillip. Added to the contrary forces of nature, the undermining attitudes of some of his militia and the absence of support from England, it put his dream of establishing a self-sufficient colonial outpost on the verge of ruin. And apart from the alarming food crisis confronting the local settlers, Norfolk Island, which had promised so much as a producer of crops, was also on the brink of failure.

Famine was the enemy, and Phillip treated it that way. He decided to make one last stand to defend his garrison, by calling together a 'council of war'. All civil and military personnel who were thought to be able to contribute something to the cause were summoned to an evening meeting in mid-April, the sole purpose of which was to plan a strategy for survival. It was quickly confirmed at the meeting that at the current rate of rations, there was sufficient food to last about ten weeks. As Tench noted in his journal, those present agreed on some immediate changes.

> Several regulations for the more effectual preservation of gardens, and other private property, were proposed, and adopted and after some interchange of opinion,

the following ration was decreed to commence
immediately, a vigorous exertion to prolong existence,
or the chance of relief, being all now left to us. Two
pounds of pork, two pounds and a half of flour, two
pounds of rice, or a quart of pease, per week, to every
grown person, and to every child of more than
eighteen months old. To every child under eighteen
months old, the same quantity of rice and flour, and
one pound of pork ...

Tench then elaborated on the condition of that food. It was
not good.

When the age of this provision is recollected, its
inadequacy will more strikingly appear. The pork and
rice were brought with us from England. The pork had
been salted between three and four years, and every
grain of rice was a moving body, from the inhabitants
lodged within it. We soon left off boiling the pork, as it
had become so old and dry, that it shrunk one half in
its dimensions when so dressed. Our usual method of
cooking it was to cut off the daily morsel, and toast it
on a fork before the fire, catching the drops which fell
on a slice of bread, or in a saucer of rice. Our flour was
the remnant of what was brought from the Cape, by
the *Sirius* and was good. Instead of baking it, the
soldiers and convicts used to boil it up with greens ...

In a gesture that David Collins would describe as 'a motive
that did him immortal honour', Phillip chose to lead by
example. 'The governor ... in this season of general distress,
gave up three hundred weight of flour which was his [own]
private property,' the judge advocate recalled, 'declaring that
he wished not to see anything more at his table than the ration
which was received in common from the public store, without
any distinction of persons; and to this resolution he rigidly

adhered, wishing that if a convict complained, he might see that want was not unfelt even at Government house.'

The meeting endorsed two other important decisions. A far greater effort would now be made to catch fish in the harbour. For this purpose, every available small boat would be used in the hope that seafood could become a fresh alternative to the salted meat. Tench wrote: 'officers, civil and military, including the clergyman, and the surgeons of the hospital, made the voluntary offer, in addition to their other duties, to go alternately every night in these boats, in order to see that every exertion was made'. Additionally, onshore, the best marksmen among the marines and trusted prisoners would hunt kangaroos in the quest for fresh meat.

While these plans were designed to keep at bay the inevitable, in the absence of relief from England, all attendees at the meeting recognised that there was one remaining opportunity to save the colony. It was another gamble: *Supply* would sail for Batavia, secure supplies there and return to Port Jackson as quickly as the winds would allow.

Phillip and his subordinates knew that, while their hearts were willing them to believe that a supply ship would arrive any day, it hadn't happened, and it might not. Maritime experience suggested that one of three things could have occurred: the ship's departure had been delayed, she had come to grief en route, or the vessel had been forced to return to England. The fact that no ship had arrived in over two years was testament to this belief.

Supply's modest size and displacement meant that she could not carry sufficient quantities of flour, beef, pork, rice and other vital provisions to last the colony for eight months, so the ship's captain, Henry Ball, was directed to charter a suitable vessel in Batavia for the task. With the loss of the fleet's flagship so fresh in everyone's mind, Collins expressed the widely held concern about this new mission, writing: 'it was painful to contemplate our very existence as depending upon her safety; to consider that a rough sea, a hidden rock, or the violence of elemental strife, might in one fatal moment precipitate us, with the little bark that had all our hopes on board, to the lowest abyss of misery ...'.

The tiny *Supply* sailed out of Port Jackson on 17 April 1790 carrying an important passenger – Lieutenant King. The governor had commissioned him to join a Europe-bound vessel in Batavia, so that he could reach London and deliver highly important dispatches to the government.

It seems that everyone who was left in the colony watched *Supply* set sail and head down-harbour. 'We followed her with anxious eyes until she was no longer visible,' Tench confirmed. 'Truly did we say to her "*In te omnis domus inclinata recumbit*" [On thee repose all the hopes of your family]. We were, however, consoled by reflecting that everything which zeal, fortitude, and seamanship could produce was concentrated in her commander ...'

As *Supply*'s topsails disappeared behind the tall eucalypts covering Bradley's Point, those whose hopes she carried returned to what had become an everyday chore – the procurement of food, in the hope of supplementing the paltry rations. Their plight was obvious to the eye: across the community, from convict to marines and their families, they were starting to take on the appearance of filthy and emaciated social derelicts. Clothes were like rags and uniforms tattered. It was not unusual to see a marine wearing what was left of his dirty and dusty uniform, but without shoes, because they were worn out.

With the dawning of each day, all eyes in the settlement turned towards the east, in the desperate hope that a flag might be seen flying high at the harbour lookout station. But on every occasion, the same level of disappointment prevailed.

As the days ticked by through April and May, the ravages of hunger were compounded by despondency. Both marines and prisoners became sapped of energy, so much so that they were unable to complete the tasks assigned to them. Thieving from vegetable gardens was rife, despite Phillip having ordered the highest level of punishment for such a crime. One convict, who had been caught stealing potatoes from the chaplain's garden, was sentenced by the criminal court to the ultimate corporal punishment of 300 lashes. But it didn't end there: as a further deterrent to all in the colony, the man's flour ration was stopped for six months. Desperation meant that not even the governor's garden was safe from thieves – despite it being known that he distributed whatever fresh vegetables he could to the neediest in the community. Temptation could prove too much also when it came to the hauls of fish caught for the benefit of the colony. A convict was dealt 100 lashes after he had secreted in a boat some of the fish he'd caught during a night-time excursion. But while food-related thefts were the most prevalent crimes, robbery of all sorts continued unabated; again, regardless of the brutal punishments being meted out by the court. One convict was hanged after being found guilty of breaking into a house.

The depression that accompanied this daily struggle for survival missed no one in the colony, not even the judge advocate himself. Around this time, Collins wrote in a letter to his father:

> I find that I am spending the Prime of my Life at the
> farthest part of the World, without Credit, without ...
> Profit, secluded from my Family, ... my connexions,
> from the World, under constant Apprehensions of
> being starved ... All these Considerations induce me ...
> to embrace the first Opportunity that offers of escaping
> from a Country that is nothing better than a Place of
> banishment for the Outcasts of Society ...

Perhaps it was the severe rationing that persuaded Bennelong to escape and return to his people. He had been in the colony for nearly six months when, on 3 May, he decided to absent himself with great stealth. The fact that his disappearance went unnoticed for some time allowed him to get well beyond the limits of the search that was subsequently undertaken by some of the marines.

The onset of a cold southern-hemisphere winter exacerbated the misery at Sydney Cove, but still every morning started with the hope that their distant flagpole would signal an end to the suffering. That moment finally came forty-seven days after *Supply*'s departure for Batavia. Tench wrote of the unbridled excitement:

> At length the clouds of misfortune began to separate, and on the evening of the 3rd of June, the joyful cry of 'the flag's up' resounded in every direction.
>
> I was sitting in my hut, musing on our fate, when a confused clamour in the street drew my attention. I opened my door, and saw several women with children in their arms running to and fro with distracted looks, congratulating each other, and kissing their infants with the most passionate and extravagant marks of fondness. I needed no more; but instantly started out, and ran to a hill, where, by the assistance of a pocket glass, my hopes were realized. My next door neighbour, a brother-officer, was with me, but we could not speak. We wrung each other by the hand, with eyes and hearts overflowing ...

Tench then joined Governor Phillip aboard a small boat and sailed down-harbour to welcome the new arrivals. The marine officer continued:

> As we proceeded, the object of our hopes soon appeared: a large ship, with English colours flying, working in, between the heads which form the entrance of the harbour. The tumultuous state of our minds represented her in danger; and we were in agony. The weather was wet and tempestuous but the

body is delicate only when the soul is at ease. We
pushed through wind and rain, the anxiety of our
sensations every moment redoubling. At last we read
the word 'London' on her stern. 'Pull away, my lads!
She is from Old England! A few strokes more, and we
shall be aboard! Hurrah for a bellyfull, and news from
our friends!' Such were our exhortations to the boat's
crew ...

While Phillip elected to return to Sydney Cove in another
boat and welcome the ship there, Tench and others continued
on. Soon they had pulled alongside the vessel, *Lady Juliana*,
and were clambering up her topsides and onto the deck. They
learned that it had been an eleven-month passage and that as
well as bringing some supplies, she had aboard 225 convict
women. But there was another cargo that was of immediate
interest to everyone in Tench's unofficial welcoming party.

'Letters, letters!' was the cry. They were produced, and
torn open in trembling agitation. News burst upon us
like meridian splendour on a blind man. We were
overwhelmed with it: public, private, general, and
particular. Nor was it until some days had elapsed, that
we were able to methodise it, or reduce it into form.
We now heard for the first time of our sovereign's
illness, and his happy restoration to health. The French
revolution of 1789, with all the attendant circumstances
of that wonderful and unexpected event, succeeded to
amaze us ...

Lady Juliana made her way up-harbour at a slow rate of knots,
before turning to port and entering Sydney Cove, where the
best bower was released amid adulation from the sorry-looking
individuals lining the shore. News flowed freely from both
sides; for the settlers, it was heartbreaking to learn that another
ship, *Guardian*, carrying two years' worth of supplies for the

colony, would have arrived in March had she not struck an iceberg in the Southern Ocean and been forced to return to Cape Town (where she eventually sank). This information tormented Phillip immensely. If only *Guardian* had been able to hold her course and reach Sydney on schedule, there would have been no need for the emergency measures that resulted in *Sirius* becoming wrecked on Norfolk Island.

Although some would not categorise *Lady Juliana* as being officially part of the Second Fleet to New South Wales, her involvement in the support of the colony certainly warranted that title. Little more than two weeks after her splendid arrival on 3 June, the flag was flying once more at South Head, bringing further joy in the settlement. The Second Fleet storeship *Justinian* duly entered the harbour, loaded with a large cargo of supplies, and carrying the first detachment of what became known as the New South Wales Corps.

Tench's account reflects the elation initiated by *Justinian*'s arrival, as well as wonderment at her remarkable passage from England, under Captain Benjamin Maitland.

> ... our rapture was doubled on finding that she was
> laden entirely with provisions for our use. Full [food]
> allowance, and general congratulation, immediately
> took place. This ship had left Falmouth on the
> preceding 20th of January, and completed her passage
> exactly in five months. She had stayed at Madeira one
> day, and four at Sao Tiago, from which last place she
> had steered directly for New South Wales, neglecting
> Rio de Janeiro on her right, and the Cape of Good
> Hope on her left; and notwithstanding the immense
> tract of ocean she had passed, brought her crew without
> sickness into harbour. When the novelty and boldness
> of such an attempt shall be recollected, too much
> praise, on the spirit and activity of Mr. Maitland,
> cannot be bestowed ...

Over the following days, Phillip hosted officers and non-commissioned officers from the newly arrived ships and the corps. While doing so, he was pleased to announce that a dispatch he had received from King George III decreed that land grants would be made to members of the militia who elected to stay in the colony beyond the completion of their term.

The three remaining ships in this flotilla – the convict transports *Surprize*, *Neptune* and *Scarborough* – were also at anchor in Sydney Cove within a matter of days. Although they too brought relief to the colony in the form of supplies, their voyages to this far-flung destination told a tale that contrasted sharply with the laudatory reports of Maitland's passage. The loss of life among the convicts was nothing short of abhorrent: more than a quarter of the 1006 prisoners who were embarked in England had died en route. An obvious reason for this death toll was the gross neglect of their well-being by the three ships' captains, whose contracts saw them paid per head on departure, not on the number they delivered alive.

The governor was appalled at this outcome, and, across the community, there was more than general disgust at the transport commanders' lack of human compassion. Phillip was also losing faith in the British Government: he was convinced that the Home Office and parliamentarians were now treating the little colony as nothing more than a dumping ground for prisoners. This in turn fostered a belief in him that, among the decision-makers in London, any initial desire for New South Wales to serve as the foundation for a strong British presence in the region had all but been abandoned. So incensed was Phillip that he had no hesitation in sharing his displeasure with Lord Grenville of the Home Office. In a letter dated 17 July 1790, he wrote:

> The sending out of the disordered and the helpless
> clears the gaols, and may ease the parishes from which
> they are sent; but, sir, it is obvious that this settlement,

instead of being a colony which is to support itself,
will, if the practice is continued, remain for years a
burthen to the mother country. The desire of giving
you full and clear information on this head has made
me enter into this detail. Of the nine hundred and
thirty males sent out by the last ships, two hundred and
sixty one died on board and fifty have died since
landing. The number of sick this day is four hundred
and fifty; and many who are not reckoned as sick have
barely strength to attend to themselves ...

This second consignment of convicts represented only a small
proportion of the total of 63,000 who would be shipped out of
England to New South Wales between 1788 and 1830. By
comparison, only 14,000 free immigrants arrived during that
same period. The first eleven free immigrants arrived from
England in 1793.

There was room for sentimentality, if not compassion,
aboard *Scarborough*, the 430-ton transport that had already
endured an eventful passage with the First Fleet – including
the thwarting of a convict mutiny, and a place among the
vanguard of ships led by Phillip in *Supply*. Before subsequently
departing for China, her captain, John Marshall, had thought
it best to leave behind his faithful dog, Hector. On *Scarborough*'s
return two years later with the Second Fleet, David Collins
wrote of the heart-warming scene that unfolded.

An instance of sagacity in a dog occurred on the arrival
of the *Scarborough*, too remarkable to pass unnoticed.
Mr Marshall, the master of the ship, on quitting Port
Jackson in May 1788, left a Newfoundland dog with
Mr Clark, which he had brought from England.

On the return of his old master, Hector swam off
to the ship, and getting on board, recognised him, and
manifested, in every manner suitable to his nature, his
joy on seeing him; nor could the animal be persuaded

to quit him again, accompanying him always when he
went on shore, and returning with him on board ...

The rehabilitative effect provided by the wide range of
provisions was evident across the community within weeks,
and with it came a lift in the spirits of all – settlers, marines
and convicts alike. Nature similarly returned to a bountiful
mood, delivering the largest catch of fish that had been
achieved since the First Fleet's arrival. In a single day, the small
boats cast their nets just twice for a haul of some 4000 salmon-
like fish, all weighing around 5 pounds.

Another day brought tragedy, however, for the team of a
small boat assigned to trawl for fish in the harbour. Once again
it was Tench who supplied a report of the incident, which
came soon after a whale had surfaced near the boat.

> Sensible of their danger, they used every effort to avoid
> the cause of it, by rowing in a contrary direction from
> that which the fish seemed to take; but the monster
> suddenly arose close to them, and nearly filled the boat
> with water. By exerting themselves, they baled her out
> and again steered from it. For some time it was not
> seen, and they conceived themselves safe, when, rising
> immediately under the boat, it lifted her to the height
> of many yards on its back whence slipping off, she
> dropped as from a precipice and immediately filled and
> sunk. The midshipman and one of the marines were
> sucked into the vortex which the whale had made, and
> disappeared at once. The two other marines swam for
> the nearest shore; but only one reached it, to recount
> the fate of his companions ...

Ironically, this same whale was implicated in an incident in
September when Phillip almost lost his life. The giant
mammal had remained in the harbour since the episode with
the small boat, until it beached itself and died in Collins Flat,

near Manly, at the northern end of the harbour. Having rejoined his people since escaping from Sydney Cove, Bennelong was feasting with them on the carcass of this monster when some fishermen from the settlement entered the bay. Bennelong beckoned the visitors over, before carving off a piece of whale flesh and asking that they take it back to Governor Phillip as a token of his goodwill. Soon afterwards, as fate would have it, the fishing party met with the governor, who was coming down the harbour aboard his launch. They informed Phillip of Bennelong's gift, in addition to relaying the Aborigine's promise that he would return to Sydney Cove if the governor could first meet him at Collins Flat. So Phillip immediately made for that location.

While taking muskets ashore was standard in such situations, Phillip decided to eschew security and avoid causing alarm. Instead, he had the launch remain close to shore, with men ready at the oars in case a rapid retreat was called for. The governor then walked up the beach to beyond the tree-line, where he came upon a large group of Aborigines, including not just Bennelong but Colbee, the earlier escapee from the colony.

Bennelong moved forward to welcome Phillip, carrying what was later described as 'a remarkable good spear', measuring some 12 feet in length. The Englishman was so impressed by this weapon that he asked if he could take it back to Sydney Cove with him as a gift, but Bennelong refused, and simply dropped it in the long grass alongside him. Lieutenant Henry Waterhouse provided a report of what followed.

> During [the] time perfect harmony subsisted. The
> natives now seemed closing around us which the
> Governor took notice of, and said he thought we had
> better retreat as they had formed a crescent with us in
> the centre; there were then 19 armed men near us and
> more in great numbers that we could not see ... Just as
> we were going Bennelong pointed out and named

> several Natives that were near, one in particular to
> whom the Governor presented his hand and advanced
> towards him, at which he seemed frightened and
> seized the spear Bennelong had laid in the grass, fixed
> his throwing stick [to it] & immediately threw it
> with astonishing violence ... The spear entered the
> Governor's right shoulder just above the Collar bone
> and went through about 3 inches just behind the
> shoulder blade close to the backbone. I immediately
> concluded the Governor was killed as it appeared to
> me much lower [in his body] than it really was, and
> supposed there was not a chance for any one of us to
> escape ...

With the point of the spear protruding from his back, Phillip did his best to run to the boat while holding on to the shaft, which was projecting out in front of him. But it was a hopeless exercise, with the end of the shaft continually bouncing along the ground. The agony he was experiencing was far too great for him to keep going. Waterhouse's account continues: 'He then begged me for God's sake to haul the spear out which I immediately stopped to do, and was in the act of doing it when, I recollected I should only haul the barb into his flesh again [if I did so] ...'

Waterhouse elected to break the shaft as close as he could to the barb, but while doing this 'another spear came & just grazed the skin off between the thumb and forefinger of my right hand'. He added: 'Spears were then flying very thick, one which I perceived fell at Capt Collins' feet as he was calling to the boat's crew.'

Once Phillip had been helped into the boat, the oarsmen began rowing their hearts out. Among the rowers was Jacob Nagle, who would write that he and his team 'pulled the boat to Sydney Cove with all our might'.

To the 51-year-old Arthur Phillip and to all those around him, his situation appeared terminal. Waterhouse, who was

Taking of Colbee & Benalon. 25 Novr 1789, by William Bradley. As the
settlement became established Phillip continued to make contact with the
local inhabitants, by force if necessary. Late in 1789, Williams Bradley
was among a group that captured two Aboriginal men, Colbee and
Bennelong, from Manly Cove. Colbee soon escaped but Bennelong
stayed and learned to speak English. Mitchell Library, State Library of New
South Wales Safe 1/14 Opp p.182 / a3461012

In an extraordinary act of confidence, Bennelong (above left) and another
Aboriginal man, Yemmerrawannie, (above right) travelled to England with
Phillip in 1792. It was a death sentence for Yemmerrawannie, who died of
an infection in London. Bennelong eventually made it back home,
returning to the ways of his countrymen, which he declared preferable to
those of Europeans. Dixson Galleries, State Library of New South Wales DGB
10, 13 / a1256013 (Bennelong). DGB 10, 14 / a1256014 (Yemmerrawannie).

physically supporting the governor in the boat, wrote that he was 'perfectly collected but conscious that a few hours must fix the period of his existence'.

In Nagle's recollection, Phillip bore the duration of the passage with great patience, but while doing so, 'he made his will and settled his affairs, not expecting to live'. The former American colonist concluded his account with a note that possibly underplayed the drama of the moment: 'As soon as we arrived, the doctor drew the spear out of his body and stopped the blood. Though it was unexpected, the Governor recovered ...'

CHAPTER 14

Bolters by Land and Sea

The arrival of the Second Fleet in June 1790, along with confirmation that more vessels from England would follow, brought renewed hope for the future at Sydney Cove. Positive attitudes seemingly grew in proportion to the expanding waistlines of men and women who had previously felt forgotten and abandoned by the Mother Country.

One group within the community were still not content with their lot, however, simply because they had a completely different agenda when it came to where they were headed in life. These were the convicts who thought of nothing but escape from New South Wales – the would-be 'bolters'. Regardless of the opportunities that life here might offer in the long term, numerous transportees looked on the grimy English dungeons and prison hulks they had departed as preferable to the hardship they were forced to endure in this godforsaken penal settlement. The punishing climate, the gut-wrenching famine and having family and friends half a world away convinced them that the only thing to do was make a break for it and try to find their way home.

These convicts knew that to escape from the cove would not be difficult. So the question was where to escape to. A colony in such a distant land meant that its isolation made it a giant natural prison: even if a prisoner should bolt for freedom, their chances of survival were next to none. The extent of the landmass to the north, south and west was as unknown as the dangers harboured there, while to the east lay a vast moat in the form of endless ocean.

Although the sea provided the most logical escape route for some, the associated problems were immense. The distance to the nearest civilised port could only be approximated, but it was certainly more than 1500 nautical miles. And, while the length of such a passage was not insurmountable, the fact remained that, apart from *Supply*, the only available craft in the colony were small open boats, which made escape by ocean a highly dangerous prospect. Not surprisingly therefore, the majority of those desperate to decamp elected to do so over land, despite the life-threatening experiences they might confront – be they from the terrain, the weather, the venomous wildlife or hostile Aborigines.

From the early 1790s, there were countless escapes by convicts but few, if any, brought success. Many bolters were known to have suffered gruesome deaths through exhaustion or dehydration, while others surrendered to the environment and staggered back to the settlement, looking, as David Collins is reputed to have said, 'so squalid and lean, the very crows would have declined their carcasses'.

Watkin Tench revealed an episode where prisoners absconded en masse on a 'flight of fantasy' that reflected blind optimism as much as ignorance of the geography of the region.

> A very extraordinary instance of folly stimulated [by] desperation occurred … among the convicts at Rose Hill. Twenty men and a pregnant woman suddenly disappeared with their clothes, working tools, bedding, and their provisions which had been just issued to them. The first intelligence heard of them was from some convict settlers, who said they had seen them pass, and had enquired whither they were bound. To which they had received for answer, 'to China'. The extravagance

and infatuation of such an attempt was explained to
them by the settlers; but neither derision, nor
demonstration could avert them from pursuing their
purpose. It was observed by those who brought in the
account that they had general idea enough of the point
of the compass in which China lies from Port Jackson, to
keep in a northerly direction.

In the course of a week the greatest part of them
were either brought back by different parties who had
fallen in with them, or were driven in by famine.
Upon being questioned about the cause of their
elopement, those whom hunger had forced back, did
not hesitate to confess that they had been so grossly
deceived as to believe that China might easily be
reached, being not more than 100 miles distant, and
separated only by a river. The others, however,
ashamed of the merriment excited at their expense,
said that their reason for running away was on account
of being overworked and harshly treated, and that they
preferred a solitary and precarious existence in the
woods to a return to the misery they were compelled
to undergo. One or two of the party had certainly
perished by the hands of the natives, who had also
wounded several others …

Captain Tench added a footnote that read: 'I trust that no man
would feel more reluctant than myself to cast an illiberal
national reflection … but it is certain that all these people were
Irish.'

The first desertion by sea came in September 1790, after
five convicts employed on the farm at Rose Hill stole a punt to
get them downriver to the harbour. There, under the cover of
darkness, they transferred to a small boat and rowed their way
out of Port Jackson. Their intention was to navigate across the
Pacific Ocean, all the way to Otaheite – which they were
obviously unaware was some 3500 nautical miles away to the

east. The few items they took with them indicated as much: just a week's worth of supplies, three iron pots and a few utensils.

After the five men had disappeared, it was assumed by all that, in Collins' words, 'from the wretched state of the boat wherein they trusted themselves, [it] must have proved their grave'. Such an assumption would prove grossly premature when, five years later, the escapees were found living among a tribe of Aborigines some 90 nautical miles north of Port Jackson. The judge advocate explained that they were discovered only after a British ship had been blown off course on approach to Sydney.

> [HMS] *Providence* met with very bad weather on her passage from the Brazil coast, and was driven past this harbour as far to the northward as Port Stephens, in which she anchored. There, to the great surprise of Captain Broughton, he found and received on board four white people, (if four miserable, naked, dirty, and smoke-dried men could be called white,) runaways from this settlement. By referring to the transactions of the month of September 1790, it will be found that five convicts, John Tarwood, George Lee, George Connoway, John Watson, and Joseph Sutton, escaped from the settlement at Parramatta ... Four of these people (Joseph Sutton having died) were now met with in this harbour by the officers of the *Providence*, and brought back to the colony. They told a melancholy tale of their sufferings in the boat; and for many days after their arrival passed their time in detailing to the crowds both of black and white people which attended them their adventures in Port Stephens, the first harbour they made ... They spoke in high terms of the pacific disposition and gentle manners of the natives ... Each of them had had names given him, and given with several ceremonies. Wives also were allotted them, and one or two had children. They were never

> required to go out on any occasion of hostility, and
> were in general supplied by the natives with fish or
> other food, being considered by them … as unfortunate
> strangers thrown upon their shore … and entitled to
> their protection …

If the breakout by Tarwood and company wasn't inspired by Captain William Bligh's superhuman small-boat journey following the mutiny aboard his vessel, HMS *Bounty*, then the next attempt certainly would be. The recently departed ships of the Second Fleet had brought news of the April 1789 mutiny, and of the 47-day voyage that Bligh and his loyal crewmen subsequently undertook in an open boat measuring no more than 23 feet long. In the face of searing tropical heat and relentless salt spray, the captain had led all seventeen of his charges to safety, covering 3600 nautical miles of storm-tossed ocean – from Tonga to Timor – with virtually no instruments for navigation and only a minuscule amount of food and water.

The 1791 escape from Port Jackson, led by Mary and William Bryant, still enjoys a prominent place in the annals of maritime history. After learning that these bolters undertook the endeavour in a similar boat to that used by the *Bounty* loyalists, Tench would write that due to '[the] escape of Captain Bligh, which was well known to us, no length of passage or hazard of navigation, seemed above accomplishment'. There is then no doubt that the Bryants' exodus was inspired by Bligh's almost inconceivable journey.

Early on at Sydney Cove, William Bryant's fishing abilities had been recognised by Governor Phillip, as a result of which the Cornishman was put in charge of the boats working the harbour. However, he fell from grace when, at the height of the 1789 famine, he was caught concealing fish aboard his boat, his intention being to sell them on the black market. As well as receiving 100 lashes, William was immediately evicted from the relatively comfortable hut he shared with Mary and little Charlotte. Yet he was still retained as a fisherman –

Collins noting that Bryant was 'too useful a person to part with and sent to a brick cart'. When he received his prescribed dose of corporal punishment, the raw pain accompanying each lash from the cat-o'-nine-tails made him ever more determined to abscond. And now, Captain Bligh's trans-ocean achievement had showed him and Mary that such a flight from captivity was more than possible. Not even the presence of a newborn son, Emanuel, could diminish the couple's resolve; the children would be going with them.

Initially, the Bryants trusted only each other, but when *Supply* returned to Sydney Cove in October 1790 with provisions from Batavia, an unexpected opportunity presented itself. In the ship's wake was the Dutch snow, *Waaksamheyd*, which Captain Ball had chartered to bring additional cargo to the settlement. Bryant established a healthy rapport with Deter Smit, *Waaksamheyd*'s captain, and within two weeks of their first meeting, Bryant was confident enough to discuss with the Dutch mariner his plans for escape. Smit's reaction was surprisingly sympathetic, probably because he was unimpressed with the dogged negotiations then underway with Phillip, regarding the possibility of *Waaksamheyd* recovering the *Sirius* crew from Norfolk Island and returning them to England.

Smit provided considerable assistance to the Bryants' plan, initially in the form of advising on and mapping a course to Kupang, the same port in Timor that had been the destination for Bligh's small-boat voyage. Before long, the Dutchman's support had extended to the provision of a chart, a compass, a navigation quadrant, two muskets, ammunition and food – all essential items that the convict then secreted under the floorboards of the hovel in which he and his family were living. Among other necessaries, Bryant also acquired carpenter's tools (so that their chosen boat could be modified as needed or repaired at any time), a fishing net, fishing equipment and additional food supplies.

With almost everything in place, the Bryants then sought seven fellow convicts who might be willing to join them on this daring escapade. William and Mary had thought carefully about who to select, and everyone they approached signed up. On doing so, each man vowed not to divulge details of the proposed voyage to anyone, not even to their wives or partners – and each of the new conspirators kept to this promise.

Surprisingly, it was Bryant himself who almost brought the plan unstuck, when he was, according to Collins, 'overheard consulting in his hut after dark, with five other convicts, on the practicability of carrying off the boat in which he was employed'. Whoever it was that heard this conversation then advised the governor, who immediately 'determined that all his proceedings should be narrowly watched [by the guards], and any scheme of that nature counteracted'.

For the Bryants, their co-conspirators' contract of silence was a satisfying reward – the secret remained safe. It justified the couple's patience and attested to the trustworthiness of the people they had invited to be part of the crew. Their prime criteria were compatibility across the group and that each man be able to contribute something to the voyage, particularly with regard to sailing and rowing the boat. These men also needed to hold no qualms about becoming bolters, and be fully aware of the severe punishment awaiting any fugitive who was captured and returned to the colony.

All of the Bryants' men were concerned that staying in Sydney might well mean starving to death as a consequence of famine. The most important crew-member was probably William Morton, a convict who had five years of his sentence still remaining. Apart from being adept at handling a boat, he held a basic knowledge of navigation, which was every bit as vital to their chances of success as good seamanship.

Among the Bryants' seven recruits, Morton was one of four who had arrived with the Second Fleet, the others being Samuel Broom, William Allen and Nathaniel Lilly. The latter pair obviously felt that they had nothing to lose by being part of this scheme, seeing as they'd been transported for life. From the original consignment of convicts, James Cox was similarly destined to be a permanent resident of the colony, while Samuel Bird and James Martin had two years or less of their sentences left to serve. It is quite possible that few details of their voyage would ever have surfaced had it not been for Martin's so-called *Memorandoms* – recollections that were scrawled onto scraps of paper sometime later by Martin and two of his fellow escapees.

Ironically, according to the judge advocate, William Bryant believed that his own 'term of transportation' had 'recently expired', with seven years having passed since he was sent down at Bodmin in December 1783. For some unknown reason, the former fisherman had not been released for repatriation to England, and there was no indication as to when that might happen. Mary still had two years to serve.

To give themselves the greatest possible chance, the Bryants had set their sights on stealing the best available boat: the governor's 23-foot, six-oared cutter. Having served as a fishing boat during the famine, this craft had recently been overhauled and fitted with new masts, sails and oars. For the would-be bolters, a long and patient wait now ensued until the circumstances were right – specifically, when there was no large vessel in port that had the speed to pursue them.

The moment finally came on the night of 28 March 1791. With *Supply* having sailed for Norfolk Island six days before, *Waaksamheyd* had departed for England that day, taking with her Captain Hunter and many of the survivors of the *Sirius* wreck, who had earlier been brought back to Sydney. Making the 28th even more suitable for the Bryants and their team, there was no moon; they could escape under the heaviest possible cloak of darkness.

In the dead of night, when the only sound came from a soft breeze rustling the leaves of eucalyptus trees, the eight men and Mary – who still had baby Emanuel 'on the breast' – crept and crawled their way to the waterfront where the cutter was secured to shore. Working as silently as possible, the men then loaded the boat with all the equipment, in addition to provisions that included 100-weight of flour and rice, 14 pounds of pork and 8 gallons of water. For Mary, her challenge was to keep the two children warm and quiet, until the time came for the three of them to be helped aboard. After climbing over the gunwale and onto the floor of the boat, she then stepped over the athwartships seats, taking the children aft, where they all sat low in the stern sheets.

Finally, the remaining men clambered into the boat, took to the oars and, with great stealth, began rowing slowly and deliberately out onto the waters of Sydney Cove. With each stroke, they dipped their oars into the ink-black water with the greatest of care, ensuring there was not even the sound of a splash. The tension among the group was such that all were struggling to breathe, but with each cautious haul on the oars, they were now making good their escape. Once clear of the cove, they could relax a little. There were no known challenges to come on the 5 miles they would cover to the harbour entrance, but once there, they had to hope that the blackness of the night would conceal them from the lookouts stationed on South Head. If they were spotted, the convicts had the advantage of a head start over any small boat that might be sent out from the cove to pursue them. Additionally, given this cover of night, even the most eagle-eyed of sentries would be unable to tell whether the fugitives had followed a course to the north, east or south after exiting the heads.

Proof that there had been a breakout from the colony came the next morning, with the discovery of a letter written by James Cox to his partner, Sarah Young, a convict who had arrived with the Second Fleet. In it, he bequeathed to her what little property he had left behind, and confirmed that he was escaping because, faced with a life sentence, there was no chance of him ever being able to return to England. Collins wrote that further evidence of the convicts' departure came when 'in the path [they took to the boat] were found a hand-saw, a scale and four or five pounds of rice, scattered about in different places, which, it was evident, they had dropped in their haste'.

Once clear of the heads, the escapees' course was to the north along the same coast that Captain Cook had sailed more than twenty years earlier, all the way to the tip of Cape York. Fair weather continued, and approximately 60 miles north of Port Jackson, the seas were sufficiently benign for them to guide their boat onto the shore at what James Martin described as 'a little creek (we call it fortunate Creek)'. It is highly probable that this was Glenrock Lagoon, a few miles south of where the city of Newcastle is located today.

The escapees were relieved to come across food in the form of a 'varse Quantity of Cabage tree' and 'a varse Quantity of fish', and have a pleasant encounter with the local Aborigines, who 'went away very much satisfied' after they'd been given some clothing and other items. This stop also resulted in the Bryants and their group becoming arguably the first Europeans to discover coal in New South Wales. Martin noted that they 'found a Quantity of fine Burn Coal', with Bryant adding that it was 'as good as Coals as any in England'.

After forty-eight hours onshore, the fugitives continued north until, two days later, they entered what could only be Port Stephens, as Martin wrote: 'Made a very fine harbour Seeming to Run up the Country for Many miles and Quite Comodious for the Anchorage of Shipping ...' It was a welcome find, because, with the shelter this waterway provided, they were able to carry out repairs on their already leaking boat. Less fortunately, the indigenous people were nowhere near as hospitable as those encountered at Glenrock Lagoon, forcing the visitors on a number of occasions to beat a hasty retreat to their boat and move on.

Soon after they'd continued sailing north from the bay, the intrepid voyagers were made aware of the dangers they would be facing from tempests on the high seas. In no time, a ferocious wind from the south was creating rising seas –

conditions that forced them to take up an offshore course until
they were 'Quite out of sight of Land'. It was impossible for
the men to row in such conditions, so they could only set the
smallest of sails, in order to provide some level of control over
the boat, and run with the weather. When they were finally
able to change course and close on the coast, the size of the
surf breaking onto the beaches made it impossible to reach
shore, where they had dearly hoped to find water and food. As
a result, the little cutter was forced to stay at sea for a period of
'near three weeks', in Martin's estimation, and for most of that
time, the crew struggled to keep the craft 'above Water'.

Not only was the boat now leaking more than ever, but
the seas were continually sweeping over the gunwale and
swamping the bilge. Soon the plight of all aboard was so dire
that the men were bailing around the clock, while a wet and
miserable Mary Bryant sat huddled in the stern, doing her
utmost to shelter Charlotte and Emanuel. Once the vile
weather had abated and they were finally able to reach shore,
the only thing available for caulking the cracks between the
planks was tallow – something that was destined to wash out
in no time when they were back at sea.

While the wind generally remained in their favour from
the southern sector of the compass, it was the annual tropical
wet season, where torrential rain and perilous storms were facts
of life. The foul weather brought with it more large, and
disturbingly powerful, breaking seas, which once more tested
to the limit the crew's seafaring skills and the boat's
seaworthiness. Judging by the sketchy details contained in
Memorandoms, it appears that one such storm charged in from
the south as the fugitives were closing on what is thought to be
Moreton Bay, east of Brisbane. Martin wrote: 'Sea Breaking
over us Quite Rapid ... we were Obliged to throw all our
Clothing overboard ... to lighten our Boat ...' When they
arrived at the entrance to the bay, it was pitch dark and there
was a brutal sea still running. The convicts' salt-lashed eyes
could not locate anywhere to land – all they could see were

breaking waves, every one of which had the potential to claim the small boat and its occupants. So it was decided to cast the anchor, in the hope that they could ride out the storm, at least until daylight. The anchor held, but they were forced to continue bailing into the night – until, at two o'clock in the morning, their worst fear was realised.

Martin scribbled that the anchor warp snapped and 'we were drove in the Middle of the Surf Expecting every Moment that our Boat would be Staved to Pieces & every Soul Perish but as God would have [it] we Got our Boat safe on Shore without any Loss or Damage [except for the loss of an oar]'. Having endured such an ordeal at the hands of the elements, the Bryants and their companions decided to spend some time on land, to recover their strength and search for food and water. Ever present in the back of everyone's mind, though, was the thought that Governor Phillip might have initiated a search for them in a similarly small boat. The moment they felt fit enough, they had no choice but to resume their arduous journey.

It continued to be a trial of seamanship and human mettle. On land, they were regularly confronted by hostile Aborigines who, on many occasions, could only be deterred from making an attack via the discharge of a musket over their heads. At sea, on one night in early May, the terrified crew 'expected … to go to the Bottom', according to Martin, who admitted to 'thinking every Moment to be the Last' with this ocean 'running Mountains high'. At one point during the passage, aided no doubt by William Morton's navigational instincts, it was estimated that they had been blown 90 nautical miles offshore. But most remarkable throughout this entire ordeal was Mary Bryant's relentless determination to protect and care for her babies, even though mother and children were, due to such a poor diet, 'in a bad Condition'.

The lack of fresh water was a constant concern, but it seemed that whenever they were heading for their last drop, they would be blessed by the 'wet season'. The weather would turn in their favour and send rain-laden clouds their way. Every time it looked like raining, the men prepared to spread out the boat's mainsail, in order to catch the life-preserving fluid and direct it into the communal water cask.

The further the escapees from Sydney Cove sailed north, so the threats from the coral-strewn waters of the Great Barrier Reef became more real. Navigating a path through the reefs became a nervous exercise, demanding great caution and concentration, yet this region also presented numerous opportunities to go ashore on some of the small islands, where the men could catch turtles for fresh meat and, hopefully, find fresh water.

After voyaging 1500 nautical miles to the tip of Cape York, the salt-caked, weather-beaten and sunburnt individuals were confronted by a new menace, in the form of extremely hostile islanders aboard outrigger canoes. At one stage, after rounding the cape, the fugitives were greeted by a fusillade of arrows fired from one of these swift-sailing canoes. With return musket-fire proving ineffective as a deterrent, it was only thanks to a favourable breeze, and the grace of God, that the convicts were able to escape without injury.

Once that threat was behind them, they were able to safely sail across the Gulf of Carpentaria in less than five days, before turning north-west to Timor. On 5 June, they eventually found the Dutch settlement in Kupang. This incredible undertaking by the Bryants and their comrades had taken a day under ten weeks to complete, and for five of those ten weeks, their open boat was pelted with heavy rain and challenged by frightening seas. Having reached the port, the nine adult escapees could've been forgiven for believing that they were now safe, but that was not the case.

Back in Port Jackson, a prophetic David Collins had already commented in his diary: 'What story they could invent on their arrival at any port, sufficiently plausible to prevent suspicion of their real characters, it was not easy to imagine …' In fact, the fugitives had concocted such a story during the voyage, and initially, it appeared to work its magic. Martin explained that when they were greeted by the Governor of Kupang, Timotheus Wanjon, Bryant 'represented himself as a Mate of a Whale Fisher that was lost, and all but themselves perished, and had written a very ingenuous account of their misfortunes that gained them protection'. Martin also reported that the entire group was welcomed to Government House, where Wanjon 'behaved extremely well to us, filled our Bellies & Clothed Double with ever that was wore on the Island'.

The ruse lasted about two months, and – according to one of the stories, anyway – it was undone by that old adage, 'Loose lips sink ships'. In this instance, the lips were probably William Bryant's, and alcohol-infused. The tale goes that, following an argument with Mary, Bryant ended up betraying them all by telling the Dutch governor that they were escapees from Sydney Cove, and that the cutter had sailed from there to Kupang.

Another version has it that the captain of a Dutch East Indiaman challenged the validity of their story, at which Mary Bryant and a member of the crew high-tailed it into the nearby woods. They were caught, brought back to the settlement, and on being questioned, the pair confessed to being escaped convicts from New South Wales.

Whatever the cause of their unveiling, Wanjon was far from impressed by the subterfuge. He immediately took the group into custody and confined them to the town's jail, known as 'the Castle', with a view to having them shipped back to England as prisoners as soon as possible. That opportunity came after some genuine survivors of a shipwreck arrived in Kupang by small boat on 15 September. Coincidentally, the demise of their ship had come about as a consequence of the mutiny aboard Bligh's command, HMS *Bounty*. This group was led by the notoriously tough Captain Edward Edwards, a man who had been ordered by the British Government to sail to Otaheite aboard HMS *Pandora* and arrest any of the *Bounty* mutineers who remained on the island. This he did, but on the return voyage, *Pandora* was wrecked on the northern fringe of the Great Barrier Reef, taking with her thirty-one of her 134 crew, and four of the fourteen captured mutineers, all of whom had been locked in a cage-like box on the ship's aft deck. Governor Wanjon gladly gave Edwards charge of the convicts, and on 5 October, they were divided among three vessels sailing to Cape Town via Batavia. Martin wrote that, under Edwards' orders, all of them had 'Both legs [put] in Irons called the bilboes'.

Unfortunately, by the time these ships reached Cape Town, both William Bryant and twenty-month-old Emanuel had died. Samuel Bird, William Morton and James Cox were dead also, the latter having committed suicide by jumping overboard while his ship was sailing through the Sunda Strait.

Once at the Cape, there was a strange coincidence: the first England-bound ship to arrive was HMS *Gorgon*, on her way home after carrying cargo and convicts to Port Jackson as part of the Third Fleet. Among those on board for this return passage was a contingent of First Fleet marines led by Robert Ross, Watkin Tench, William Dawes and Ralph Clark – all of whom were well aware of the amazing escape that the Bryants had orchestrated. While the surviving fugitives, including little Charlotte Bryant, were put aboard *Gorgon* and placed in confinement, the scene became even more surreal with the addition of the *Bounty* mutineers and the survivors from *Pandora*. Tench spent considerable time with the convict escapees, who, in his words, had 'boldly pushed out to sea, determined to brave every danger and combat every hardship, rather than remain longer in a captive state'.

He went further in expressing his obvious admiration for their endeavour:

> I confess that I never looked at these people without
> pity and astonishment. They had miscarried in a heroic
> struggle for liberty after having combated every
> hardship and conquered every difficulty ...

> The woman, and one of the men, had gone out
> to Port Jackson in the ship which had transported
> me thither. They had both of them been always
> distinguished for good behaviour. And I could not but
> reflect with admiration at the strange combination of
> circumstances which had again brought us together,
> to baffle human foresight and confound human
> speculation ...

Tench advised Mary and her fellow absconders – James Martin, Samuel Broom, William Allen and Nathaniel Lilly – that as a consequence of their disappearance, Governor Phillip had ordered that no small boat longer than 14 feet was to be built in the colony. It was considered that boats of this length were too small to make open-ocean passages such as the Bryants had undertaken.

Gorgon arrived in England in early June 1792, and sadly, four-year-old Charlotte was among a number of children who died during the passage. Clark wrote that the children were 'going very fast ... the hot weather is the reason for it'. Charlotte's tiny body was 'committed to the deep' on the same day she died.

All five convicts appeared in court in London within days of their arrival and were subsequently committed to Newgate Prison. They were held there while awaiting a final decision on their future, knowing that escaping from transportation usually brought the death penalty. The magistrate they appeared before, Nicholas Bond, struggled with his task, stating that he had 'never experienced so disagreeable a task as being obliged to commit them to prison, and assured them as far as lay in his power he would assist them'. During their court appearance, the prisoners had all attested to Bond that 'they would sooner suffer death than return to Botany Bay ...'. One week later, the group returned to court to be told that they had escaped death – but they would remain in jail until their pre-existing sentences had expired.

However, a tide of public sentiment in support of these intrepid individuals was growing across England, primarily through the press in London. Mary Bryant was dubbed 'the Girl from Botany Bay', and esteemed lawyer and author James Boswell soon took up her cause and that of her associates, petitioning authorities on their behalf. His efforts were rewarded when Mary was released from prison as a free woman in May 1793. In November that year, a justifiably proud Boswell wrote that 'all four men had been set at liberty and had been at my door'.

Back in Sydney, around the time that the escapees arrived in England and were packed off to Newgate, Arthur Phillip was dealing with an ongoing health issue. The constant pain he had been experiencing in his side, possibly due to poor diet during the famine, was becoming worse, and although it was most definitely not his intention to abandon the colony, he had written to the government in 1790, requesting permission to return home for medical attention. It had taken two years for his request to reach London and for the reply – approving his return – to be delivered to him in Sydney.

The first available ship heading to England was *Atlantic*, a large merchant vessel that had just delivered supplies to the colony from China. So, accompanied by two Aboriginal men, Bennelong and Yemmerrawannie, the governor stepped aboard the ship for his voyage home. It was noted in official records that on the morning of 11 December 1792, *Atlantic* 'weighed anchor and by 8 o'clock was clear of the Heads'.

As *Atlantic*'s turbulent wake burbled away from her full-buttocked stern and meandered across the trailing wave crests, and the towering cliffs at the entrance to Port Jackson dimmed in the distance, the colony's first governor could only look back and wonder what its future might hold. Would it succeed, or would it fail? Only some of his long-held visions for New South Wales had been realised. And he still hoped that, due to his efforts in laying the foundation for this

British outpost, it might one day be recognised as a milestone in world history.

With this in mind, he would have recalled the words he wrote to Lord Sydney in a letter dated July 1788: '... nor do I doubt but that this country will prove the most valuable acquisition Great Britain ever made ...'.

It remained his earnest desire to return, once he had regained his health, and complete his mission, but that was not to be. It was not until 1796 that he was considered well enough to return to duty, and when he did, he was assigned to active service as commander of various Royal Navy ships, including the 98-gun HMS *Blenheim*. Shore postings followed in 1798, and the following year, his outstanding achievements were officially recognised when he was appointed Rear Admiral of the Blue. In 1805 he retired to live in Bath with his second wife, Isabella, whom he had married in 1794.

Arthur Phillip – the founder of a nation – died on 31 August 1814, aged seventy-five. He was buried in the church of St Nicholas, Bathampton. Three months prior to his death, he was promoted to the position of Admiral of the Blue.

With his seafaring ability and fluency in German, French and Portugese, Arthur Phillip made a useful spy for the British government. He was sent to assist the Portugese in their conflict with the Spanish, eventually taking command of a vessel transporting convicts from Rio de Jeneiro to Colonia do Sacramento, gaining experience that would prove useful some years later. Dixson Galleries, State Library of New South Wales DG 233 / a2828001.

Glossary

abaft Towards the stern of a ship; 'abaft the beam' means aft of
abeam

abeam A point 90 degrees out from anywhere along the
centreline of a ship

adjutant A military officer who acts as an administrative
assistant to a senior officer

a-lee To leeward, as in 'the helm is to leeward'

anchor Bower, the biggest anchor; stream, the next largest
anchor; kedge, a smaller anchor for special purposes, usually
stored below decks

anchor stocks The heavy timber crossbar at the top of the
anchor

athwartships Directly across the ship, from side to side

baffling winds An erratic wind that frequently changes
direction

ballast Any heavy material (such as gravel, iron, lead, sand,
stones) placed in the hold of a ship to provide stability

beam ends The sides of a ship; 'on her beam ends' is used to
describe the rolling effect of very rough seas on a ship which
is almost on her side and possibly about to capsize

beat, to Sail upwind

belay, to Secure a rope

belaying pins Wooden pins found around the mast at deck
level, or at the side of a ship, which are used to secure a rope

bend/unbend sails, to Attach or remove sails from their yards

best bower   The starboard of the two anchors carried at the
     bow of the ship; that on the port side was known as the
     smaller bower, even though the two were identical in weight

bilge   The curved part of a ship's hull immediately above the
     keel

bitt   A vertical post set on the deck of a ship, used to secure and
     tie ropes or cables

bitthead   The top of the bitt

block   A single or multiple sheaved pulley

boatswain/bosun   Warrant or non-commissioned officer
     responsible for the maintenance of the ship's rigging, anchors
     and cables

bower   Bow anchor or cable

bowsprit   A pole extending forward from a vessel's bow

brace   A rope or line attached to the end of a yard which is
     either eased or hauled in so that the sail is trimmed to suit
     the wind direction

brig   A two-masted square-rigger

bring   To cause a ship to turn into the wind or come to a stop

bulwarks   The planking along the sides of a ship above the
     upper deck which acts as a railing to prevent crew and
     passengers from going overboard

buntlines   Ropes tied to the foot of a square sail that keep it
     from opening or bellying when it is being hauled up for
     furling to the yard

burthen   Displacement

cable   1. A long, thick, heavy rope attached to the ship's anchor;
     2. A naval unit of distance – ten cables is 1 nautical mile

capstan   A large waist-high vertical winch turned by crew
     manning the capstan bars, which lock into the head of the
     winch; the crew walk in a circle to work the winch; used to
     raise the anchor and other heavy objects

careen   To heel a ship over on one side or the other for cleaning,
     caulking or repairing

carronade   A short-barrelled limited-range gun used for close-
     quarter action; enormously destructive to a ship's timbers

cathead A sturdy timber projection near the bow to hold the anchor

cat-o'-nine-tails A lash used as a form of punishment aboard a naval ship

caulking Material making the ship watertight (such as cotton fibres or oakum) forced between the planks to stop leaks

cay A low bank or reef of coral, rock or sand

chains The area outside the ship where the deadeyes, rigging and other hardware come together to support the mast

clew The bottom corners of the square sail, or the lower aft corner of a triangular sail

clew up To draw up a square sail to the yard by hauling on the clew lines

close-hauled Sailing with the sails trimmed in as close as possible to the centreline; allows the ship to sail as close to the direction of the wind as possible

collier A cargo ship that hauls coal

commander The next rank above lieutenant in the Royal Navy prior to the introduction of the rank of lieutenant-commander in the early twentieth century

coxon/coxswain The helmsman of a ship's boat

cutter A fast sailboat with one mast that carries several headsails

Deadeye A round- or triangular-shaped hardwood disc with a grooved perimeter and one or more holes through it; used to tension or tighten a shroud or stay; the most common type has three holes

dead reckoning The method for estimating a vessel's current position based on its previously determined position then advanced by estimating speed and course over an elapsed time

deck beams Timbers running from side to side of a ship to support the deck

doldrums A region of the ocean near the Equator characterised by calms, faint breezes or squalls

Downs, the An anchorage off the coast of England between Dover and Deal

draught The measurement from the waterline to the deepest point of the vessel in the water

driver boom The yard carrying the driver, a square sail set from the peak of the gaff on the mizzen mast

embayed Trapped within the confines of a bay and unable to sail into safe water

fathom A unit of measurement for depth; 1 fathom is 1.83 metres or 6 feet

fetters A chain or manacle used to restrain a prisoner, usually placed around the ankles

fine off the ... bow Just off the centreline looking forward

fire ship A vessel filled with combustibles and explosives, which, having been set aflame, is released to drift among enemy ships to destroy them

fore castle/foc'sle/fo'c's'le The living quarters in the bow of the ship where crew is accommodated

foremast The first mast, or the mast fore of the mainmast

fothering Sealing a leak by lowering a sail over the side of the ship and positioning it to be sucked into the hole by the rushing sea

freeboard The distance from the water to the ship's gunwale

frigate A three-masted sailing warship with two full decks, and only one gun deck; usually armed with 30–44 guns, located on the gun deck

futtock An iron plate in the ship's topmast for securing the rigging

grapnel A small anchor with four or five 'arms' used for anchoring a small craft and as a grappling hook

great cabin An interior, windowed area of the ship spanning the width of the stern; traditionally, this was the captain's private quarter, subdivided by partitions at his discretion

grog A mixture of rum and water served to a ship's crew

guinea An English gold coin worth £1 and 1 shilling

gunwale/gunnel The top edge of the planking at the sides of the ship, named for the place where a crewman rested his gun to take aim

gybe Changing from one tack to the other away from the wind; turning the ship's stern through the wind; see also 'wear ship'

HMS His/Her Majesty's ship

halyard A rope used for raising or lowering a sail, yard, spar or flag

haul up or haul onto the wind To change a ship's course so that it is sailing closer to the direction from which the wind is blowing; at the same time the ship's sails are trimmed to suit the new course

hawse holes Cylindrical holes in the bow of a vessel for the anchor cable to run through

hawser A cable or rope used for mooring or towing a ship

headed When the wind changes direction so that it is coming from a point closer to the ship's bow, causing the vessel to change course to leeward so that it can continue sailing effectively

heel To tilt to one side

helm The apparatus used to steer the vessel by moving the angle of the rudder

hove Raised or lifted with effort or force, particularly the anchor

hove to Slowing a vessel's forward progress by fixing the helm and foresail so that the vessel does not need to be steered; a procedure usually applied in very rough weather

hull The main body of the ship

hull-down Where the hull of a vessel is not visible because it is below the horizon, but the rig can be seen

jib A triangular headsail set from the foremast which is the foremost sail

jury-rig A temporary rig put up in place of a mast that has broken or been carried away

kedge A small anchor used to keep a ship steady and clear from her bower anchor

knot A unit of speed equal to 1 nautical mile per hour or approximately 1.151 miles (1.852 km) per hour

larboard The old name for port, the left-hand side of the ship; the term 'fine on the larboard bow' refers to an area just off the vessel's centreline, looking forward on the port side

lead-line A sounding line with a lead weight at one end used to record the depth of water under the ship

leadsman The man who, standing in the chains, heaves the lead to take soundings

league A unit of distance used in the eighteenth century equal to 3 nautical miles

lee The sheltered side

leeward The direction away from the wind; opposite of 'windward'

leeway Drifting sideways

lieutenant Lowest rank of commissioned officer in the Royal Navy, prior to the introduction of the rank of sub-lieutenant in the twentieth century

log 1. A device for measuring a ship's speed; 2. A record of a ship's movements and the weather, for navigational purposes, and general and pertinent information regarding incidents, observations and shipboard routine, usually kept by the captain, master and lieutenant

luff The leading edge of a fore-and-aft sail; or to change course into the wind so that the sails flap

lying to/lying a-hull Waiting out a storm by lowering all sails and letting the vessel drift

main course The lowest square sail

mainmast The tallest mast on a vessel

make fast To secure a line

mal de mer Seasickness (Fr.)

marines Seaborne contingent of soldiers

master The most senior non-commissioned officer or warrant officer in the Royal Navy in the eighteenth century, responsible for the navigation of the ship, subject to the command of its officers

masthead The very top part of a mast

mate Assistant warrant officer to a senior warrant officer, hence bosun's mate and master's mate

mizzen The sail set from the aftermost mast

mizzen mast On a ship with three masts, this is the mast nearest the stern

nautical mile A mathematical calculation based on the circumference of the earth at the Equator

oakum Old pieces of rope picked to shreds and tarred for use as caulking; known as rope junk

offing Distance from shore, land or other navigational hazards

one hundredweight 50 kilograms

packet A vessel that transports passengers, mail and goods between two ports at regular intervals

painter A mooring line; usually a light line attached to the bow of a small boat

pawl A hinged or pivoted catch on a ratchet wheel which prevents it from slipping back

pinnace A small vessel with two fore-and-aft rigged masts, which can be rowed or sailed, and usually carries men between ship and shore

poop deck The short deck towards the stern above the quarterdeck of a ship

pooped To have a wave break over the stern of the ship and onto the deck

port The left-hand side of a vessel

post-captain An alternative form of the rank of captain, distinguishing those who were captains by rank from officers in command of a naval vessel who were recognised as captain regardless of rank, and commanders who received the title of captain regardless of whether they were in command or not

pounds, shillings, pence English currency

put the wheel/helm down To turn the steering wheel in a particular direction

quadrant A very simple instrument used to determine the altitude of a heavenly body

quarterdeck The upper exposed deck at the stern of the ship from the mainmast to the back, usually the territory of the ship's officers

quit the chains, to When the crewman heaving the lead to check the water depth leaves his post in the chains and returns to the deck

ratlines Bands of rope lashed across the shrouds like steps that allow crew to easily climb aloft

reciprocal course/track To return along a course from whence one came

reef/reefed To take in or reduce the area of a sail without furling it

refit To repair or restore a vessel

rhumbline The shortest distance in a straight line between two points free of obstruction

rigging All ropes, wires and chains used to support the masts and yards

schooner A fore-and-aft rigged vessel, originally with two masts, but later with three or more; designed for blockade-running and as a fast naval vessel

seine net A fishing net weighted so that it trawls along the seabed

sextant A navigational instrument used to measure the angle of elevation of an object above the horizon

sheave The grooved and revolving wheel fitted within a block over which a rope travels

Sheerness docks An important naval dockyard at Sheerness, on the Isle of Sheppey, in the Thames estuary

sheet A rope attached to either of the lower corners (clews) of a square sail or the aftermost lower corner of a fore-and-aft sail; also the rope used to control the boom of the mainsail or mizzen/spanker

sheet anchor Traditionally the largest of a ship's anchors carried so it can be quickly dropped in the event of an emergency

ship of the line A sailing warship built to fight in the traditional line form of naval battle in the late eighteenth and early nineteenth centuries, whereby ships formed a line so they could fire broadsides at the enemy

shroud The standing rigging on the ship that provides lateral support to the mast

slatted A sail flopping backwards and forwards in near windless conditions

sloop A single-masted sailing ship usually carrying a mainsail and a single jib or headsail

slops Ready-made clothing from the ship's stores sold to seamen

snow The largest of two-masted sailing vessels which primarily acts as a merchant ship

spanker A large fore-and-aft sail set from the mizzen (aft-most) mast using a gaff – a wooden spar which supports the top of the sail

spars A general term relating to all the poles in a vessel's rig, such as masts, yards, booms and gaffs

Spithead A stretch of water at the eastern end of the Solent located between Portsmouth and the Isle of Wight

spritsail A four-sided sail set from a sprit, which usually extends beyond the end of the yards

square-rigger A ship using square sails as its principal form of sail

starboard The right-hand side of a vessel

stay A long large rope which acts as a piece of standing rigging to support the mast either athwartships or fore-and-aft

sternsheets The stern area of an open boat

strake A line of planking on the side of a vessel

strike To remove and lower yards and topmasts to the deck

tack A manoeuvre; and a corner of a sail

taffrail The upper rail of the aft rail at a ship's stern

tar A nickname for a lower-deck sailor derived from the fact that their canvas coats and hats were waterproofed with tar

tender A small vessel that attends a man-of-war, primarily in harbour; usually used to carry munitions, provisions, mail and dispatches to and from the ship

timoneer An alternative term for the helmsman

topgallant In a square-rigged ship, the spars and rigging at the very top of the masts above the topsails

topmast The second section of mast above the deck fixed to the top of the lower mast and which supports the topgallant mast

toss oars To place the oars in their rowlocks and put the blades in the water

trestletrees Framing comprising two short, strong parallel timbers fixed fore-and-aft on the opposite side of the lower masthead to support the topmast, or at the top of the topmast to support the topgallant mast

uncleat To untie from a cleat, a T-shaped, low-profile anchor point for securing lines

waist (of the ship) The middle part of the upper deck of a ship, between the quarterdeck and the forecastle

warp A rope attached to a ship which is used to move it from one place to another by men pulling on it when the ship is in harbour; hence, warping means to move or reposition a ship by hauling on a line or anchor line

wear ship To manoeuvre a square-rigged ship to change course by turning the stern through the wind so that the wind comes onto the opposite side of the ship; today it is referred to as a gybe

weather helm To counter the tendency of a sailing vessel to turn towards the direction of wind by turning the helm

windage The exposed part of a ship's hull and rig of a vessel causing wind resistance

windlass A horizontal and cylindrical barrel used as a lifting device for a rope or anchor cable, turned by rods called handspikes

yard A slender wooden spar slung at its centre on the forward side of a mast on a square-rigged ship

yardarm The outer end of each yard from where, on square-rigged ships, signal flags were flown, or where men sentenced to death following a court martial were hanged

List of Ships
and Known Officers,
Men and Families

- Transports

- Store Ships

- Naval Escorts

TRANSPORTS

Alexander

Ship type: Convict transport – three-masted bark (the largest ship of the fleet)

Dimensions: 452 tons, 114 ft long, 31 ft wide

Owner: William Walton & Co.

Launched: 1783, Hull, England

Master/Captain: Duncan Sinclair

Surgeon: William Balmain

Fate: Little is known after her return to England. No record of her after 1808.

Crew

Allen, Robert – Seaman
Ashley, John – Seaman
Bailey, Alexander – Seaman
Bones, James – 3rd Mate
Burns, Edward – Seaman
Cross, Edward – Carpenter
Dearing, William – Ship's Boy
Dixon, William Archer – Seaman
Donovan, Stephen – 2nd Mate
Dooat, Joseph – Seaman
Ellis, John – Boatswain RN
Floan, Richard – Seaman
Frazer, Thomas – Ship's Boy
Goodall, William – Corporal
Harris, Isaac – Seaman
Harrison, Richard – Seaman
Hawk/Hawks, John – Seaman
Healey, Anthony – Seaman
Kelly, John – Ship's Cook
Lewis, John – Seaman
Long, William Aston – 1st Mate
McGill, John/James – Seaman
Moor, John – Seaman
Morris, William – Seaman
Ranson, Robert – Seaman

Shortland, John Snr – Lieutenant
    Naval Agent
Shortland, Thomas George – 2nd
    Mate
Sinclair, Duncan – Ship's Master
Steward, William – Seaman
Stokell, James – Seaman
Stone, Jacob – Sailmaker
Summers, Thomas – Seaman
Tool, Philip – Seaman
Trimmings, Thomas – Ship's
    Steward
Waugh, William – Carpenter
White, John – Ship's Boy
Winter, John – Seaman

Marines and Family

Archer, Isaac – Private
Asky/Askew, Richard – Private
Baxter, William – Private
Bishop, Elias – Private
Bramage, Thomas – Private
Brannon, John – Private
Brough, Ralph – Private
Dargan, Peter – Private
Dew, William – Private
Dinger, Edward – Private
Dinger, Elizabeth – Marine's Wife
Dowlan, William – Private
Edmonds, William – Private
Fishburn, Andrew – Private
Gilbert, Stephen – Private
Grant, James – Drummer
Hailey, John – Private
Harp, Thomas – Private
Hayes, John – Private
Johnstone, John – 1st Lieutenant
Jones, John – Private
Kennedy, John – Sergeant
    (transferred from *Prince of Wales*
    at Rio)

Kennedy, Mary – Marine's Wife
    (transferred from *Prince of Wales*
    at Rio)
Kirby, James – Private
Knight, Isaac – Sergeant
Lewis, John – Private
Lewis, Joseph – Private
Lynch, Mortimore/Morty –
    Private
Mapp, James – Private
Martin, Thomas – Private
McCalden/McCalder, Joseph –
    Private
Munday, John – Private
Munday, Ann – Marine's Wife
Munday, Edward – Marine's Child
Nation, Gabriel – Private
Nevitt, Thomas – Private
Perry, William – Sergeant
Perry/Scoble, Ann – Marine's Wife
Pugh, John – Private
Roberts, William – Private
Shairp, James Maitland – 1st
    Lieutenant
Simmons, William – Private
Smith, William – Corporal
Strong, William – Private
Swinerton, Thomas – Private
Wherritt, James – Private
Winstead/Wixted/Wixstead, John
    – Corporal

Civilians

Clark, Zachariah – Contractor's
    Agent (transferred from
    Scarborough)

TRANSPORTS

Charlotte

Ship type: Convict transport – three-masted, fully square-rigged ship
Dimensions: 335 tons, 105 ft long, 28 ft wide
Owner: Unknown
Launched: 1784
Master/Captain: Thomas Gilbert
Surgeon: John White (Surgeon-General)
Fate: Sold to a merchant in Quebec in 1818. Lost off the coast of
    Newfoundland that year.

Crew

Caird, David – 1st Mate
Gilbert, Thomas – Ship's Master
Lavender, George – Boatswain RN
Lodwick, Archibald Andrew
    ('William') – Seaman
Moore, William – 2nd Mate
Riddel, John – Seaman
Rimmer, Joseph – Seaman
Smith, Edward – Seaman
Storey, John – Seaman

Marines and Family

Baker, James – Private
Baker, William – Corporal
Brixey/Brexley, Charles –
    Corporal
Brown, Thomas – Private
Chapman, Thomas – Corporal
Chapman, Elizabeth – Marine's
    Child
Chapman, Jane – Marine's Wife
Chapman, Jane – Marine's Child
Cheslett, George – Private
Chew, John – Private
Connell, Patrick – Private

Cook, Benjamin – Drum Major

Cook, Mary – Marine's Wife (died 17 October 1787 at Cape Town)

Creswell, Daniel – Private (died 30 November 1787 at sea)

Creswell, Susanna – Marine's Wife

Dwan, Edward – Sergeant

Dwan, Jane – Marine's Wife

Dwan, Edward – Marine's Child

Edmondstone, William – Private

Goodwin, Phillip – Private

Howell, John – Private

Hunt, Joseph – Private

King, William – Private

Maxwell, James – 1st Lieutenant (transferred from *Prince of Wales* at sea)

McManus, James – Private

Mitchell, William – Private

Odgers, Edward – Private

Overton, Edward – Private

Tench, Watkin – Lieutenant Captain

Timins, Thomas – 1st Lieutenant (transferred from *Prince of Wales* at Cape Town)

Tynan, Thomas – Private

White, James – Private

Civilians

Broughton, William – Servant (to Surgeon-General John White)

TRANSPORTS

Friendship

Ship type: Convict transport – two-masted brig
Dimensions: 278 tons, 75ft long, 23ft wide
Launched: About 1784
Master: Francis Walton
Fate: Scuttled in the Strait of Makassar on 28 October 1788 during her
    return voyage to England as a result of insufficient crew being able to
    sail her due to scurvy.

Crew

Allen, William – Seaman
Arndell, Thomas – Assistant
    Surgeon
Barnes/Barns, Robert – Boatswain
Bruce, William – Cook
Cockran, Robert – Seaman
Craven, James – Seaman
Duhig, Cornelius – Seaman
George, Robert – Seaman
Henderson, George – Seaman
Hern, William – Ship's Steward
Lawrence, Robert – 1st Mate
Lewis, Thomas – Seaman
Mckay, Allen – Seaman

Morris, John – Seaman
Philpot, John – Seaman
'Rodney' – Ship's Boy
Sandell, Richard – Seaman
Smith, Richard – Seaman
Vallance, Patrick – 2nd Mate
    (transferred from HMS *Sirius*
    and died 29 October 1787 at
    Cape Town)
Walton, Francis – Ship's Master

Marines and Family

Bishop, Thomas – Private
Browning, William – Private
Carver, John – Private

Chipp, Thomas – Private
Clark, Ralph – 2nd Lieutenant
Cottrell, Thomas – Private
Cusley, Benjamin – Private
Dempsey, William – Private
Dukes, Richard – Private
Ellis, William – Private
Faddy, William – 2nd Lieutenant
Folly, John – Private
Godfrey, William – Private
Green, Charles – Private
Griffiths, John – Private
Hughes, William – Drummer
Jones, Thomas – Private
McCarthy, John – Private
McDonald, Alexander – Private
Mason, William – Private
Meredith, James – Captain
Norris, William – Private
Plowman, James – Corporal
Plyer, George – Private

Roberts, John – Private
Rowden, Thomas – Private
Russell, John – Private
Russell/Pound, Elizabeth –
    Marine's Wife
Russell, Mary – Marine's Child
Russell, Thomas – Marine's Child
    (born 12 August 1787 at Rio)
Stephens, Robert – Private
Stewart, Peter – Private
Stewart, Margaret – Marine's Wife
Stewart, John – Marine's Child
Stewart, Robert – Marine's Child
Thatcher, John – Private
Watts, John – Private
Williams, Thomas – Private
Young, Thomas – Sergeant
Young, Elizabeth – Marine's Wife
Young, John – Marine's Child
Young, Thomas – Marine's Child

TRANSPORTS

Lady Penrhyn

Ship type: Convict transport – fully-rigged ship
Dimensions: 338 tons, 103 ft long, 27 ft wide
Owner: Curtis & Co., London
Launched: 1786, London (had no time for sea trials prior to departing for Botany Bay)
Master/Captain: William Cropton Sever
Surgeon: John Turnpenny Altree (superseded by Arthur Bowes Smyth at Tenerife)
Fate: Returned to England via China with a load of tea. Later operated on the London-to-Jamaica run after returning to London. Captured in the West Indies in 1811.

Crew

Anderson, William – Seaman
Anstis, Nicholas – 1st Mate
Ball, Thomas – 3rd Mate
Bentley, Joshua – Seaman
Bruce, William – Seaman
Clay, Charles – Seaman
Clement, John – Seaman
Curtis/Crudis, William – Quartermaster
Davis, Thomas – Seaman
Dawson, Richard – Ship's Boy
Dean/Dease, Edward – Seaman
Downey, Joseph – Quartermaster
Duncan, David – Ship's Boy
Fisher, John – Seaman
Gunthorpe, William – Boatswain
Henderson, William – Seaman
Hill, Henry – Seaman (deserted 3 September 1787 at Rio)
Holmes, James – 4th Mate
Marshall, William – Seaman

Measures, Timothy – Seaman
Mooring, William – Seaman
Roach, Charles – Quartermaster
Scriven/Screven/Shewing, Philip
   – Seaman
Sisson, First name unknown –
   Cook
Squires, James – 2nd Mate
Theakston/Fixton, Joseph –
   Seaman
Young, Richard/William – Ship's
   Steward

Marines and Family
Anderson, Alexander – Corporal
Bramwell, Thomas – Private
Campbell, James – Captain
Campbell, James Duncan (child
   relation of Captain James
   Campbell)

Clements, Henry – Private
Colethread, John – Private
Colethread, James – Marine's
   Child
Collins, William – 2nd Lieutenant
Evans, Humphrey – Private
Hallam, William – Private
Haswell, Thomas – Private
Jackson, Thomas – Private
Jackson, Agnes – Marine's Wife
Johnston, George – 1st Lieutenant
McCann, Joseph – Private
Ross, Alexander John – Marine's
   Child
Rosser, Henry – Private
Watts, John – Lieutenant
Wilkins, John – Private

Civilians
Smith, James – Peace Officer

TRANSPORTS

Prince of Wales

Ship type: Convict transport – fully-rigged ship
Dimensions: 350 tons, 103 ft long, 29 ft wide
Owner: James Mather
Launched: 1786, River Thames
Master/Captain: John Mason
Surgeon: Unknown
Fate: After returning to England on what was a troubled voyage, *Prince of Wales* operated around the coast of England until 1797, after which time she was sent to Fort Royal, Martinique. Nothing else is known of her.

Crew

Butler, Daniel – Seaman
Hosburn, Robert – Seaman
Mason, John – Ship's Master
Moore, Samuel – Seaman
Nelson, George – Cook
Porter, James – Ship's Boy
Richardson, Joseph – Seaman
Rogers, William – Seaman
Wilkinson, Joseph – Carpenter
Younginson, Yorgan – Seaman
(drowned at sea 23 November 1787)

Marines and Family

Barrisford, John – Private
Barrisford, Hannah – Marine's Wife
Clayfield, William – Sergeant (transferred from *Alexander* at Rio)
Clayfield, Rachel – Marine's Wife (transferred from *Alexander* at Rio)
Creswell, John – 1st Lieutenant (transferred from *Charlotte* at Cape Town)

Davey, Thomas – 1st Lieutenant

Davis, John – Private

Davis, Martha – Marine's Wife

Davis, Jane – Marine's Child (born 9 May 1787 at sea – died 13 July 1787 at sea)

Dougherty, Arthur – Private

Dougherty, Judah/Judith – Marine's Wife

Dougherty, Daniel – Marine's Child (born 10 July 1787 at sea)

Gough, Thomas – Corporal

Gough, Johanna – Marine's Wife

Gough Joseph – Marine's Child

Harmsworth, Thomas – Private

Harmsworth, Alice – Marine's Wife

Harmsworth, Ann – Marine's Child

Harmsworth, John – Marine's Child

Harmsworth, Thomas Jnr – Marine's Child (born 1 December 1787 at sea)

Hume, John – Sergeant

Hume, Sarah – Marine's Wife

Manning, James – Private

Nash, William – Private

Nash/Haynes, Maria – Marine's Wife

Parfett, John – Drummer

Parfett, Sarah – Marine's Wife

Parfett, James – Marine's Child

(born 1 June 1787 at sea)

Poulden, John – 1st Lieutenant (transferred from *Charlotte* at Cape Town)

Richards, Laurence – Private

Richards, Mary – Marine's Wife

Richards, Samuel – Marine's Child (born 9 October 1787 at sea)

Ryan, Robert – Private

Scott, James – Sergeant

Scott, Jane – Marine's Wife

Scott, Elizabeth – Marine's Child (born 29 August 1787 at Rio)

Tolan, Michael – Private

Turner, John – Private (transferred from *Sirius* at Cape Town)

Turner, Susannah – Marine's Wife (transferred from *Sirius* at Cape Town)

Wright, Henry – Private

Wright, Ann – Marine's Wife

Wright, Mary Ann – Marine's Child

Wright, Matthew – Private

Wright, Elizabeth – Marine's Child (born 17 October 1787 at Cape Town)

Wright, Mary – Marine's Wife

Civilians

Alt, Augustus Theodore Henry – Surveyor

TRANSPORTS

Scarborough

Ship type: Convict transport – fully-rigged ship
Dimensions: 430 tons, 111 ft long, 30 ft wide
Owner: Thomas George and John Hopper
Launched: 1782, Scarborough, England
Master/Captain: John Marshall
Surgeon: Dennis Considen
Fate: Took part in the Second Fleet then operated on the London-to-St Petersburg route before carrying cargo from London to the West Indies. Last records were with the Lloyds' register in London in 1805. Her fate after that is unknown.

Crew

Butler, Michael – Seaman
Caffery, George – 2nd Mate RN
Dawson, Given name unknown – 1st Mate
Fawley, John – Seaman
Marsh, George – Seaman
Marshall, Given name unknown – Seaman (brother of Ship's Master)
Marshall, John – Ship's Master
Mason, Thomas – Seaman

McCarty, Charles – Boatswain
Mead, William – Seaman (died 21 May 1787 at sea)
Meredith, Frederick – Steward
Plaisted, William – Seaman (died 22 May 1787 at sea)
Walton, James – Apprentice
Wilson, Thomas – 2nd Mate

Marines and Family

Abbott, Joseph – Drummer
Brown, John – Private

Brown, John – Private
Bullmore, Thomas – Private
Cable, William – Private
Campion, Edward – Sergeant
Chadwick, William – Private
Clayton, John – Private
Clinch, Richard – Sergeant
Connor, Martin – Corporal
Coward, Joshua – Private
Douglas, William – Private
Easty, John – Private
Escott, John – Private
Freeborne, Alexander – Drummer
Gannon, John – Private
Hand, Abraham – Private
Harper, Joseph – Private
Haynes, Luke – Private
Hurst, Mark – Private
Jones, John – Private
Jones, William Sega – Private
Kellow, Robert – 1st Lieutenant
Knight, Richard – Private
Knight, Thomas – Private
Lee, James – Private
Long, John – 2nd Lieutenant
    (transferred from *Sirius* at sea)

Lucas, Thomas – Private
McAvenaugh, Barney – Private
Mee, Francis – Private
Mountstephens, Robert –
    Drummer (transferred from
    Sirius at sea)
Nicholas, Richard – Corporal
O'Brien, Thomas – Private
Phillips, Thomas – Private
Redman, John – Private
Redman, Michael – Private
Redman, Elizabeth – Marine's
    Wife
Redman, James – Marine's Child
Reed, Anthony – Private
Ross, Robert – Major and
    Lieutenant Governor
    (transferred from *Sirius* at sea)
Shea, John – Captain
Smyth, Thomas – Corporal
Spencer, Thomas – Private
Thompson, Robert – Private
Wall, William – Private
Woodhouse, Thomas – Private
Woods, John – Private

STORE SHIPS

Borrowdale

Ship type: Three-masted, square-rigged man-of-war transport
Dimensions: 272 tons, 75 ft long, 22 ft wide
Owner: Unknown
Launched: 1785, Sunderland, England
Master/Captain: Hobson Reed
Surgeon: Unknown

Crew included:
  Brown, James – 1st Mate
  Campbell, Donald – Seaman
  Malton, John – Seaman
  Martin, Charles – Seaman
  Powel, Thomas – Seaman
  Reed, Joseph – Seaman
  Taylor, Robert – Seaman
  Williams, Richard – 2nd Mate

Marines:
  Brown, James – Private
  Brown, Elizabeth – Marine's
    Wife

Fate:
  Disappeared from records after
    her return to England.

STORE SHIPS

Fishburn

Ship type: Three-masted, square-rigged man-of-war transport
Dimensions: 378 tons, 103 ft long, 29 ft wide
Owner: Leighton Co.
Launched: 1780, Whitby, England
Master/Captain: Robert Brown
Surgeon: Unknown

Crew included:
  Armstrong, Archibald – 2nd Mate
  Cockett, William – Seaman
  Dane/Dean, George – Seaman
  Hisclope, George – Seaman
  Hoggot, Thomas – Boatswain (died 8 January 1788)
  Robinson, Andrew – Cook
  Ryan, Thomas – Seaman

Fate: Disappeared from records after returning to England.

STORE SHIPS

Golden Grove

Ship type: Three-masted, square-rigged man-of-war transport
Dimensions: 331 tons, 103 ft long, 29 ft wide
Owner: Leighton Co.
Launched: 1780, Whitby, England
Master/Captain: William Sharpe
Surgeon: Unknown

Crew included:
  Hart, John – 1st Mate
  Hay, George – Able Seaman
  More, Stephen – Steward
  Simms, William – Seaman
Civilians included:
  Barnes, Samuel – Servant to Reverend Johnson
  Barnes, Mary – Servant's Wife
  Johnson, Reverend Richard – Chaplain
  Johnson, Mary – Chaplain's Wife

Fate:
  Worked the London-to-Jamaica run after returning to England.
    Disappeared from records after 1804.

NAVAL ESCORTS

HMS *Sirius*

Ship type: Flagship – naval warship – 20 guns
Dimensions: 540 tons, 110 ft long, 32 ft wide
Launched: As HMS *Berwick*
Master/Captain: 2nd Captain John Hunter RN
Surgeon: George Bouchier Worgan
Fate: Returned to Cape Town for supplies. Later sailed to Norfolk Island
and sank on 14 April 1790.

Naval Officers

Alt, Matthew Bowles –
Midshipman RN
Bradley, William – 1st Lieutenant
RN
Brewer, Henry – Midshipman RN
Ferguson, John – Midshipman RN
Fowell, Newton Digby –
Midshipman RN
Harris, John – Midshipman RN
King, Philip Gidley – 2nd
Lieutenant RN
Maxwell, George William – 3rd
Lieutenant RN
Nairn, James – Corporal RN
Ormsby, Charles Cutts –
Midshipman RN
Raper, George – Midshipman RN
Southwell, Daniel – Midshipman
RN
Waterhouse, Henry – Midshipman
RN

Crew

Anderson, John – Able Seaman
Bayne, David – Able Seaman
Beard, William – Able Seaman
Bell, Jonathon – Able Seaman
Berriman, John – Purser's Steward
Boyce, Benjamin – Able Seaman
Brody, Walter – Armourer

Brooks, Deborah – Boatswain's
Wife
Brooks, Thomas – Boatswain
Bryant, John – Able Seaman
Bryant, William – Master's Mate
Buckley, Stephen – Boatswain's
Mate
Buddle, Daniel – Able Seaman
Burne, Terrance – Able Seaman
Caldwell, Joseph – Gunner
Cavenaugh, Owen – Able Seaman
Cleverly, Joseph – Able Seaman
Conway, John – Able Seaman
Coventry, James – Quartermaster
Cunningham, James – Master's
Mate
Daveny, Thomas – Able Seaman
Davies, David – Able Seaman
Davis, John – Gunner's Mate
Desmond, Thomas – Able Seaman
Deverlier, John – Able Seaman
Dodd, Henry/Edward – Able
Seaman
Doyle, Luke – Able Seaman
Drummond, John – Quartermaster
Eldridge, George – Able Seaman
Ellis, Walter – Able Seaman
Fellows, Joseph – Quartermaster
Fitzgerald, Henry – Able Seaman
Fombell, Furzey – Able Seaman
Freeman, Thomas – Clerk (to
Captain Hunter)
Gordon, James – Able Seaman
Greaves, George – Boatswain's
Mate
Hacking, Henry – Quartermaster
Hambly, William – Carpenter's
Mate
Harragan, Cornelius – Able
Seaman
Heatherly, James – Carpenter

Henderson, Robert – Able Seaman
Hibbs, Peter – Able Seaman
Hill, Francis – Master's Mate
Hopkins, Morris – Able Seaman
Howlett, John – Able Seaman
Hunter, William – Able Seaman
Jamison, Thomas – Surgeon's 1st
Mate
Johnson, James – Able Seaman
Jones, John Benjamin – Able
Seaman
Joseph, Paul – Able Seaman
(deserted 14 September 1787 at
Rio)
Keltie, James – Master (from
August 1787), (transferred from
Fishburn at Rio)
Kerr, Hugh – Coxswain
Kerr, John William – Able Seaman
Knight, William – Carpenter
Lewis, James – Able Seaman
Livingstone, John – Carpenter's
Mate
Lowes, John – Surgeon's 2nd Mate
Lyons, Michael – Able Seaman
Mara, John – Gunner's Mate
March, William – Carpenter
McDonald, John – Able Seaman
McNeal, John – Able Seaman
Middleton, John – Able Seaman
Miles, John – Able Seaman
Mitchell, William – Boatswain's
Mate
Monk, George – Sailmaker's Mate
Moore, Henry – Able Seaman
Morley, James – Able Seaman
Morton, Micah – Master
(discharged ill 2 September
1787 at Rio)
Murley/Morley, Roger –
Sailmaker's Mate

Nagle, Jacob – Able Seaman
Neldor, Philip – Able Seaman
Palmer, John – Purser
Parker, Charles – Carpenter
Parker, John – Master at Arms
Parker, Robert – Armourer
Paul, James Douglas – Cook
Paynter, James – Carpenter
Phillips, David – Carpenter
Phillips, Thomas – Quartermaster
Poate, James – Carpenter's Mate
Pritchard, William – Able Seaman
Proctor, James – Gunner
Punton, John – Able Seaman
Reed, David – Able Seaman
Reid, William – Able Seaman
Rider, George – Able Seaman
Roberts, Peter – Able Seaman
Robertson, John – Able Seaman
Ross, Alexander – Quartermaster
Ross, Peter – Gunner
Rotton, Samuel – Master's Mate
    (discharged ill September 1787
    at Rio)
Rowley, John – Able Seaman
Russell, James – Armourer's Mate
Sang, George – Able Seaman
Saunders, John (alias Moore,
    Edward) – Able Seaman
Seally, David – Master's Mate
    (discharged ill 1 September
    1787 at Rio)
Shine, John – Able Seaman
Shortland, John Jnr – 2nd Mate
    (transferred from *Friendship*
    at Rio)
Smith, Benjamin – Able Seaman
Smith, John – Able Seaman
Spicely, John – Able Seaman
Straffen, James – Carpenter
Thomas, Richard – Able Seaman

Thring, James – Able Seaman
Thring, Martha – Able Seaman's
    Wife (died 12 November 1787
    at Cape Town)
Tinney, James – Able Seaman
Titcumb, John – Able Seaman
Tureene, Lawrence – Able Seaman
Walker, David – Able Seaman
Wallis, Alexander – Able Seaman
    (transferred from *Fishburn* at
    Tenerife)
Ward, John – Able Seaman
Watson, Robert – Able Seaman
Webb, Robert – Able Seaman
Webb, Thomas – Able Seaman
Welsh, William – Able Seaman
Wescott, Robert – Able Seaman
Westbrook, William Burton –
    Carpenter's Crew
White, Peter – Sailmaker
White, Thomas – Gunner
Williams, Thomas – Able Seaman
Wilson, James – Able Seaman
Yule, Robert – Able Seaman

Marines and Family
Angell, James – Private
Assell, John – Private
Bacon, Samuel – Private
Bacon, Jane/Elizabeth – Marine's
    Wife
Bacon, Elizabeth – Marine's Child
    (born 1787 at sea, exact date
    unknown)
Bagley, James – Corporal
Bagley, Sarah – Marine's Wife
Bagley, Maria/Marie – Marine's
    Child
Bagnall, Ralph – Private
Batchelor, John – Private
Bates, John – Private

Bull, William – Private

Collins, David – Lieutenant and
Judge Advocate

Dougherty, Arthur – Private

Dougherty, Judah – Marine's Wife

Dougherty, Daniel – Marine's
Child

Dukes, Thomas – Private

Flemming, George – Private

Furzer, James – 1st Lieutenant

Garvin, Thomas – Private

Gilbourne, Andrew – Private

Gilbourne, Margaret – Marine's
Wife

Goodwin, Philip – Private

Gowen, John – Corporal

Gunn, George – Private
(transferred from *Lady Penrhyn*
as Acting Servant to David
Collins)

Halfpenny, Thomas – Private

Heritage, Charles – Private

Hughes, William – Drummer

Hurdle, James – Private

Kennedy, Michael – Private

King, Samuel – Private

McEwan, Patrick – Private

Moulton, William – Private

Murphy, Michael – Private

Parsons, Henry – Private

Petrie, Henry – Sergeant

Prater, Charles – Private (Servant
to Lieutenant Collins)

Proctor, William – Sergeant

Radford, Joseph – Private

Redman, James – Private

Reynolds, Charles – Drummer

Rice, John – Private

Scott, Thomas – Private

Scully, Thomas – Private

Seedhouse, William – Private

Standley, William – Private

Stanfield, Daniel – Private

Tarr, Isaac – Private

Thomas, Edward – Private

Thomas, Samuel – Private

Thomas, Ann – Marine's Wife

Tunks, William – Private

Turner, John – Private

Turner, Susannah – Marine's Wife

West, John – Drummer

Wigfall, Samuel – Private

Williams, James – Private

Williamson, John – Private

Willmott, Robert – Private

Wixted, John – Corporal

NAVAL ESCORTS

HMS *Supply*

Ship type: Brig – naval tender – 8 guns

Dimensions: 170 tons, 70 ft long, 26 ft wide

Launched: Believed to have been built in America about 1759. She became part of the Royal Navy fleet in October 1786.

Master/Captain: Lieutenant Henry Lidgbird Ball RN

Surgeon: James Callam

Fate: Returned to England in April 1792 and was subsequently sold for £500 to Thomas Oldfield, a London coal merchant. She is believed to have been a collier around the Thames River until retired in 1806.

Naval Officers

Phillip, Arthur – Captain RN – Commodore of the Fleet – 1st Governor of NSW (transferred from HMS *Sirius* at sea)

Crew

Barnatt, Thomas – Seaman

Blackburn, David – Ship's Master

Bone, Joseph – Carpenter

Braiden, Samuel – Quartermaster's Mate

Carter, William – Able Seaman

(deserted 12 November 1787 at Cape Town)

Chase, Jacob – Armourer

Davis, James – Seaman (transferred from *Sirius*)

Dempster, John Hamilton – Able Seaman

Dunlap, Gavin – Gunner

Dwire, Dennis – Able Seaman

Farrell, Ambrose – Able Seaman

Frederick, John – Able Seaman

Furvis, John – Seaman

Gould, Peter – Boatswain

Hickey, Jeremiah – Seaman
(deserted 9 November 1787 at
Cape Town)
Hobbs, John – Seaman (discharged
ill 7 July 1787 at Tenerife)
Hoyer, Frederick – Able Seaman
Jackson, Thomas – Able Seaman
(deserted 12 November 1787
at Cape Town)
Jay, Richard – Able Seaman
Jeffries, Joseph – Seaman
Lawson, John – Midshipman
Marlier/Marliez, Barnard – Able
Seaman (transferred from *Sirius*)
Massey, Richard – Gunner's Mate
McDonald, William – Seaman
Mellon, Charles – Seaman
(deserted 12 November 1787 at
Cape Town)
Mooney, Richard – Able Seaman
Moore, Samuel – Ship's Steward
Nicholas, John – Able Seaman
Parker, William – Midshipman
Reid, Robinson – Carpenter
Reid, Thomas – Able Seaman
Robinson, John – Able Seaman
Russell, William – Able Seaman
Smith, Daniel – Able Seaman
Spowers, William –
Quartermaster's Mate
Swesey, John – Seaman
Taylor, William – Seaman
Toberry, James – Able Seaman
(deserted 12 November 1787 at
Cape Town)

Toberry, Joseph – Boatswain's Mate
Tomlinson, Laurence – Able
Seaman
Walton, Jacob – Able Seaman
Waters, Edmund – Clerk
Whitehair, Joseph – Sailmaker

Marines and Family
Dawes, William – 2nd Lieutenant/
Observer
Gore, George – Private
Hoddinott, John – Sergeant
Mathews, James – Private
McMahon, Patrick – Private
Reiley, James – Private
Richardson, Richard – Private
Rogers, James – Private
Rooksby, Joseph – Private
Simms, William – Private
Talbot, Peter – Corporal (died
20 November 1787 at sea)
Thorne, John – Private
Todd, William – Private
Winwood, George – Private
Wise, James – Private
Woodman, Jonathon – Private

Convicts
Haynes, William – Convict/
Artificer (transferred from
Friendship at sea)
Yardsley, Thomas – Convict/
Gardener (transferred from
Friendship at sea)

More details about the ships in the First Fleet can be found at
fellowshipfirstfleeters.org.au
See also Mollie Gillen, *The Founders of Australia:*
A Biographical Dictionary of the First Fleet

List of Provisions

LIVESTOCK AND PROVISIONS

- 10 forges
- 175 steel hand saws
- 700 iron shovels
- 700 garden hoes
- 700 West Indian hoes
- 700 grubbing hoes
- 700 felling axes
- 700 hatchets
- 700 helves for felling axes
- 747,000 nails
- 100 pairs of hinges and hooks
- 10 sets of cooper's tools
- 40 corn mills
- 40 wheelbarrows
- 12 ploughs
- 12 smith's bellows
- 30 grindstones
- 330 iron pots
- 6 carts
- 4 timber carriages
- 14 fishing nets
- 14 chains for timber carriages
- 5448 squares of crown grass
- 200 canvas beds

- 62 chauldrons of coal
- 80 carpenter's axes
- 20 shipwright's axes
- 600 lbs of coarse sugar
- 1001 lbs of Indian sago
- 1 small cask of raisins
- 61 lbs of spices
- 3 hogsheads of vinegar
- 2 barrels of tar
- 1 dozen tin saucepans
- 1 printing press
- type fonts
- 3 dozen flat irons
- candlesticks
- 3 snuffers
- 48 spinning brasses
- 7 dozen razors
- Bible, prayer book etc.
- 6 bullet moulds
- 9 hackies for flax
- 9 hackies pins
- 3 flax dresser brushes
- 127 dozen combs
- 18 coils of whale line

- 6 harpoons
  - 12 lances
  - shoe leather
  - 305 pairs of women's shoes
  - 40 tents for women convicts
  - 6 bundles of ridge poles
  - 11 bundles of stand poles
  - 2 chests of pins and mallets
  - 1 portable canvas house (Gov. Phillip)
  - 18 turkeys
  - 29 geese
  - 35 ducks
  - 122 fowls
  - 87 chickens
  - kittens
  - puppies
  - 4 mares
  - 2 stallions
  - 4 cows
  - 1 bull
  - 1 bull calf
  - 44 sheep
  - 19 goats
  - 32 hogs
  - 5 rabbits
  - Gov. Phillip's greyhounds
  - Rev. John's [Marsden's] cats
  - mill spindles with 4 crosses
  - 2 cases of mill bills and picks
  - 1 case of mill brushes
  - 589 women's petticoats
  - 606 women's jackets
  - 121 women's caps
  - 327 pairs of women's stockings
  - 250 women's handkerchiefs
  - 700 steel spades
  - 175 claw hammers
  - 140 augurs
- 700 gimlets
- 504 saw files
- 300 chisels
- 6 butcher's knives
- 100 pairs of scissors
- 30 box rules
- 100 plain measures
- 50 pickaxes
- 50 helvers
- 700 wooden bowls
- 700 wooden platters
- 5 sets of smith's tools
- 20 pit saws
- 700 clasp knives
- 500 tin plates
- 60 padlocks
- 50 hay forks
- 42 splitting wedges
- 8000 fish hooks
- 48 dozen lines
- 8 dozen lbs of sewing twine
- 12 brick moulds
- 36 mason's chisels
- 6 harnesses for horses
- 12 oxbows
- 3 sets of ox furniture
- 20 bushels of seed barley
- 1 piano
- 10 bushels of India seed corn
- 12 baskets of garden seed
- coarse thread (blue/white)
- transport jack
- ventilators for water and wine
- hoses
- windsails
- 24 spinning whorls
- 1 set of candlestick makers
- carbines
- bulkheads

- beds
- hammocks
- marines' clothes
- fig trees
- bamboos
- sugar cane
- quinces
- apples
- pears
- strawberries
- oak and myrtle trees
- 135 tierces of beef
- 165 tierces of pork
- 50 puncheons of bread
- 116 casks of pease
- 110 frinkins of butter
- 8 bram of rice
- 10 pairs of handcuffs and tools
- 1 chest of books
- 5 puncheons of rum
- 300 gallons of brandy
- 15 tons of drinking water
- 5 casks of oatmeal
- 12 bags of rice
- 140 women's hats
- 1 machine for dress flax
- 252 dozen lbs of cotton candles
- 168 dozen lbs of mould candles
- 44 tons of tallow
- 2 millstones, spindles etc.
- 800 sets of bedding
- 1 loom for weaving canvas
- 2780 woollen jackets
- 5440 drawers
- 26 marquees for married officers
- 200 wood canteens
- 40 camp kettles
- 448 barrels of flour
- 60 bushels of seed wheat
- 381 women's shifts

PLANTS AND SEEDS

- banana
- cocoa
- coffee
- cotton
- eugenia
- guava
- ipecacuanha
- lemon
- orange
- prickly pear
- Spanish reed
- tamarind

List supplied by First Fleet Fellowship Vic

List of Convicts

Family Name	Given Name	Age Leaving England	Gender	Crime	Original Sentence	Transported for (years – 99 = life)	Occupation	Departed on
Abel/Able	Robert	15	M	Assault and highway robbery	Death	7	No trade recorded	*Alexander*
Abel	Mary	30	F	Stealing clothing	Transportation	7	Servant	*Lady Penrhyn*
Abrahams	Esther + child (Ester Rosanna)	20	F	Stealing lace	Transportation	7	Milliner	*Lady Penrhyn*
Abrahams/ Abrams	Henry	26	M	Highway robbery	Death	7	Labourer	*Scarborough*
Adams	John	47	M	Stealing lead from roof	Transportation	7	No trade recorded	*Scarborough*
Adams	Mary	29	F	Stealing clothing	Transportation	7	Servant	*Lady Penrhyn*
Agnew/ Ayners	John	27	M	Stealing lead from roof	Transportation	7	No trade recorded	*Scarborough*
Akers/Acres	Thomas	29	M	Assault and highway robbery	Death	7	No trade recorded	*Charlotte*
Allen	Charles	20	M	Stealing linen	Transportation	7	No trade recorded	*Scarborough*
Allen	John	45	M	Stealing bedding	Transportation	7	Labourer or miller	*Alexander*
Allen/Conner	Mary	28	F	Stealing clothing	Transportation	7	Hawker	*Lady Penrhyn*
Allen	Mary	22	F	Highway robbery	Transportation	7	"A poor unhappy woman of the town" or servant	*Lady Penrhyn*
Allen	Susannah		F	Stealing clothing	Transportation	7	No trade recorded	*Prince of Wales*
Allen	Tamasin/ Jamasin	32	F	Assault and robbery	Transportation	7	Servant	*Lady Penrhyn*

Family Name	Given Name	Age Leaving England	Gender	Crime	Original Sentence	Transported for (years – 99 = life)	Occupation	Departed on
Allen	William	24	M	Assault and robbery	Transportation	7	Labourer	Alexander
Anderson	Elizabeth	32	F	Stealing linen	Transportation	7	Servant	Lady Penrhyn
Anderson	Frances (Fanny)	30	F	Stealing clothing and money	Transportation	7	Dealer	Charlotte
Anderson	John	26	M	Stealing linen	Transportation	7	Seaman	Charlotte
Anderson	John	24	M	Assault and stealing linen	Transportation	7	No trade recorded	Scarborough
Archer/ Forrester	John	31	M	Stealing coach window glass	Transportation	7	No trade recorded	Scarborough
Arscott	John	20	M	Stealing tobacco	Transportation	7	No trade recorded	Scarborough
Atkinson/ Atkins	George	22	M	Stealing clothing	Transportation	7	No trade recorded	Scarborough
Ault	Sarah		F	Stealing bridles and strap irons	Transportation	7	No trade recorded	Prince of Wales
Ayres	John	20	M	Stealing musical instruments	Transportation	7	Shoemaker	Scarborough
Ayres/Eyres/ Hares	William	24	M	Assault and highway robbery	Death	7	Saddler	Friendship
Bails/Bales	Robert	21	M	Assault and highway robbery	Death	14	Labourer and former soldier	Alexander
Baker	Martha	25	F	Highway robbery	Transportation	7	Servant	Lady Penrhyn
Baker	Thomas	23	M	Unknown	Transportation	7	No trade recorded	Charlotte
Baldwin/ Balding	James/ William	32	M	Burglary	Death	7	Chimney sweep	Scarborough
Baldwin/ Bowyer	Ruth	25	F	Stealing silver spoons	Transportation	7	Servant	Prince of Wales
Ball	John	51	M	Stealing livestock (a sheep)	Death	7	No trade recorded	Charlotte
Bannister	George	19	M	Burglary	Transportation	7	No trade recorded	Alexander
Barber	Elizabeth	27	F	Assault and robbery	Death	7	Book stitcher	Friendship
Barford/ Barferd	John	20	M	Stealing a trunk of clothing	Transportation	7	No trade recorded	Alexander
Barland	George	20	M	Stealing a coat	Transportation	7	No trade recorded	Scarborough
Barnes	Stephen		M	Stealing clothing	Transportation	7	No trade recorded	Alexander

Family Name	Given Name	Age Leaving England	Gender	Crime	Original Sentence	Transported for (years – 99 = life)	Occupation	Departed on
Barnett/ Barrett/ Barney	Daniel	30	M	Stealing iron grapplings	Transportation	7	Waterman	*Friendship*
Barnett/ Barnard/ Burton	Henry	43	M	Stealing a parcel	Death	7	No trade recorded	*Alexander*
Barrett	Thomas	29	M	Stealing household goods	Death	99	No trade recorded	*Charlotte*
Barry/Berry	John	19	M	Stealing stockings	Transportation	7	None	*Friendship*
Barsby	George		M	Assault and highway robbery	Death	99	No trade recorded	*Alexander* (died before departure)
Barsby	Samuel	23	M	Stealing material	Death	7	No trade recorded	*Charlotte*
Bartlett	James		M	Stealing rope yarn	Death	7	No trade recorded	*Alexander* (pardoned and released before departure)
Basely/Bazley	John		M	Robbery of clothing	Death	7	Seaman	*Charlotte*
Bason	Elizabeth	30	F	Stealing material	Death	7	No trade recorded	*Charlotte*
Batley/Batly	Oten	23	M	Stealing a watch, seal and chain	Transportation	7	No trade recorded	*Charlotte*
Batley	Walton/ Walter	27	M	Stealing clothing	Transportation	7	Bricklayer	*Friendship*
Baughan/ Bingham	John	33	M	Stealing woolen blankets	Transportation	7	Cabinet maker	*Friendship*
Bayley/Bailey	James	41	M	Burglary	Transportation	7	No trade recorded	*Charlotte*
Bayliss/Busley	John	37	M	Stealing silver	Transportation	7	Silversmith	*Friendship*
Beardsley/ Beadley/ Beazley/ Baizley	Ann	21	F	Stealing clothing	Transportation	5	None	*Friendship*
Beckford	Elizabeth	70	F	Stealing cheese	Transportation	7	Servant	*Lady Penrhyn* (died at sea 12 July)
Bell	William	25	M	Assault and highway robbery	Death	7	Soldier	*Scarborough*

Family Name	Given Name	Age Leaving England	Gender	Crime	Original Sentence	Transported for (years – 99 = life)	Occupation	Departed on
Bellamy	Sarah	17	F	Stealing a purse containing cash and promissory notes	Transportation	7	Servant or weaver	*Lady Penrhyn*
Bellett/Billet	Jacob	21	M	Stealing material and silk	Transportation	7	Silk weaver	*Scarborough*
Benear/ Benier/ Benare/Bines/ Bins/Benner/ Benere/ Binner	Samuel	32	M	Assault and highway robbery	Transportation	7	No trade recorded	*Scarborough*
Bennett	John	19	M	Highway robbery	Transportation	7	No trade	*Friendship*
Best	John	27	M	Burglary	Transportation	7	None	*Friendship*
Bingham/ Mooring/ Biggins	Elizabeth		F	Not recorded	Transportation	7	No trade recorded	*Prince of Wales*
Bird	Elizabeth/ Winifred	45	F	Stealing livestock (a sheep)	Death	7	Servant	*Lady Penrhyn*
Bird	James	39	M	Stealing bags of saltpetre	Transportation	7	Labourer	*Alexander*
Bird	Samuel	25	M	Stealing bags of saltpetre	Transportation	7	No trade recorded	*Alexander*
Bishop	Joseph	23	M	Stealing handkerchiefs	Transportation	7	Fisherman	*Friendship*
Blackhall/ Blackall	William	25	M	Stealing lead from roof	Transportation	7	Labourer	*Alexander*
Blake	Francis	21	M	Stealing clothing and chocolate	Transportation	7	Servant	*Scarborough*
Blanchet	Susannah	24	F	Stealing clothing	Transportation	7	Servant	*Prince of Wales*
Blatherhorn/ Beans/Fisher	William	28	M	Stealing material and handkerchiefs	Death	99	No trade recorded	*Charlotte*
Bloodworth	James	28	M	Not recorded	Transportation	7	Bricklayer	*Charlotte*
Blunt	William	30	M	Burglary	Death	7	Coachman	*Scarborough*
Boggis	William	20	M	Stealing a sheet	Transportation	7	Fisherman	*Scarborough*
Bolton	Mary	29	F	Burglary	Death	7	Servant	*Lady Penrhyn*

Family Name	Given Name	Age Leaving England	Gender	Crime	Original Sentence	Transported for (years – 99 = life)	Occupation	Departed on
Bolton/ Boulton	Rebecca	26	F	Stealing clothing	Transportation	7	Servant	*Prince of Wales*
Bond	Peter	21	M	Stealing household goods	Transportation	7	No trade recorded	*Alexander*
Bond	William	31	M	Stealing household goods	Death	7	No trade recorded	*Charlotte*
Bonner	Jane	22	F	Stealing clothing	Transportation	7	No trade recorded	*Prince of Wales* (died at sea 30 July)
Boyle	John	30	M	Fraud (impersonation)	Death	7	Seaman	*Scarborough*
Bradbury	William	27	M	Stealing a wallet and cash	Death	99	No trade recorded	*Scarborough*
Bradford	John	28	M	Stealing tallow	Transportation	7	No trade recorded	*Charlotte*
Bradley	James	23	M	Stealing a handkerchief	Transportation	7	No trade recorded	*Scarborough*
Bradley	James	24	M	Stealing a handkerchief	Transportation	7	No trade recorded	*Alexander* (died before departure)
Branagan/ Brannagan/ Brannegan/ Branegan	James	32	M	Assault and highway robbery	Death	7	No trade recorded	*Charlotte*
Brand/Bryn	Curtis	23	M	Stealing livestock (2 game cocks)	Transportation	7	None	*Friendship*
Branham	Mary	17	F	Stealing clothing	Transportation	7	Servant	*Lady Penrhyn*
Braund/ Broad/ Brand	Mary	20	F	Highway robbery	Death	7	No trade recorded	*Charlotte*
Brewer	William	34	M	Stealing livestock (a sheep)	Death	7	No trade recorded	*Charlotte*
Brice	William	16	M	Stealing a looking glass	Transportation	7	None	*Friendship*
Brindley	John	27	M	Assault and robbery	Death	7	No trade recorded	*Alexander*
Brough	William	39	M	Burglary	Transportation	7	Labourer	*Alexander* (died at sea 19 May)

Family Name	Given Name	Age Leaving England	Gender	Crime	Original Sentence	Transported for (years – 99 = life)	Occupation	Departed on
Brown	James	22	M	Stealing livestock (a horse)	Transportation	7	Labourer	*Alexander*
Brown	Richard	36	M	Stealing sheep skins	Transportation	7	No trade recorded	*Alexander*
Brown	Thomas	25	M	Stealing silverware	Transportation	7	No trade recorded	*Charlotte*
Brown	Thomas/John	22	M	Stealing a snuff box	Transportation	7	Nurseryman	*Scarborough*
Brown	William	26	M	Assault and highway robbery	Death	7	No trade recorded	*Charlotte* (died at sea 19 September)
Brown	William French	29	M	Stealing cheese	Transportation	7	No trade recorded	*Alexander*
Bruce	Elizabeth	29	F	Stealing linen	Transportation	7	Servant	*Lady Penrhyn*
Bruce	Robert	31	M	Assault and highway robbery	Death	7	No trade recorded	*Charlotte*
Bryant	John	29	M	Highway robbery	Transportation	7	No trade recorded	*Charlotte*
Bryant	Michael	20	M	Receiving stolen goods	Transportation	14	None	*Friendship*
Bryant	Thomas	21	M	Highway robbery	Death	7	Labourer	*Scarborough*
Bryant	William	29	M	Fraud (impersonation)	Death	7	No trade recorded	*Charlotte*
Buckley	Joseph	39	M	Stealing cash	Transportation	7	No trade recorded	*Charlotte*
Bunn/Burn	Margaret	25	F	Stealing 2 handkerchiefs and cash	Transportation	7	Servant	*Lady Penrhyn*
Burdo/ Bordeaux	Sarah	23	F	Stealing cash	Transportation	7	Mantua maker (dressmaker)	*Lady Penrhyn*
Burkitt	Mary/ Martha/ Patience/ Pacence	30	F	Stealing	Transportation	7	Servant	*Lady Penrhyn*
Burley/ Burleigh	James	16	M	Stealing a coat	Transportation	7	No trade recorded	*Alexander*
Burn	Patrick	26	M	Highway robbery	Death	7	Baker	*Friendship*
Burn	Peter	31	M	Stealing casks and alcohol (porter)	Transportation	7	No trade recorded	*Scarborough*
Burn	Simon	33	M	Highway robbery	Death	7	Stocking weaver	*Friendship*

Family Name	Given Name	Age Leaving England	Gender	Crime	Original Sentence	Transported for (years – 99 = life)	Occupation	Departed on
Burne	James	33	M	Assault and highway robbery	Death	7	No trade recorded	*Scarborough*
Burridge	Samuel	61	M	Burglary	Transportation	7	No trade recorded	*Charlotte*
Butler	William	20	M	Stealing lead from building	Transportation	7	Seaman	*Scarborough*
Cable/Kable/ Cabell	Henry	20	M	Burglary	Death	7	Labourer	*Friendship*
Caesar	John	23	M	Stealing cash	Transportation	7	Servant or labourer	*Alexander*
Campbell	James	23	M	Robbery clothing, household goods	Transportation	7	Blacksmith	*Scarborough*
Campbell	James/ George/ John	28	M	Assault and robbery	Death	7	No trade recorded	*Scarborough*
Carey	Ann	21	F	Burglary	Transportation	7	No trade recorded	*Charlotte*
Carney	John	18	M	Burglary	Death	7	No trade recorded	*Scarborough*
Carroll	Mary	36	F	Stealing linen	Transportation	7	Mantua maker (dressmaker)	*Lady Penrhyn*
Carter/ Cartwright	Richard	44	M	Stealing sacks of malt	Transportation	7	Labourer or farmer	*Friendship*
Carty	Francis	31	M	Assault and highway robbery	Death	7	No trade recorded	*Scarborough*
Carver	Joseph	28	M	Stealing silk material	Transportation	7	Labourer	*Alexander*
Castle	James/John	28	M	Stealing watch, chain, seals and handkerchief	Transportation	7	No trade recorded	*Scarborough*
Chaaf	William	24	M	Burglary	Death	7	No trade recorded	*Charlotte*
Chadwick/ Chaddick	Thomas	25	M	Stealing cucumbers, malicious damage	Transportation	7	No trade recorded	*Scarborough*
Chanin	Edward	44	M	Burglary	Death	7	No trade recorded	*Charlotte* (died at sea 8 January)
Childs/ Chields	William	23	M	Stealing lace	Transportation	7	Waterman	*Alexander*
Chinery	Samuel	20	M	Stealing	Transportation	7	No trade recorded	*Charlotte*

Family Name	Given Name	Age Leaving England	Gender	Crime	Original Sentence	Transported for (years – 99 = life)	Occupation	Departed on
Church	William	28	M	Stealing livestock (3 cows)	Death	7	No trade recorded	*Charlotte*
Clare/Clear	George	53	M	Stealing material	Death	7	Shoemaker	*Friendship*
Clark	Elizabeth	20	F	Stealing clothing	Transportation	7	No trade recorded	*Friendship*
Clark/Hosier	James/John/Charles	33	M	Stealing watch, chain and seal	Transportation	7	Butcher or seaman	*Scarborough*
Clarke	John	26	M	Stealing livestock (2 lambs) and mutton	Death	7	No trade recorded	*Charlotte* (died at sea 6 June)
Clarke	William	23	M	Burglary	Death	7	No trade recorded	*Scarborough*
Clayton/Kayton/Hayton	George	23	M	Stealing clothing	Transportation	7	Shoemaker	*Scarborough*
Cleaver	Mary	27	F	Burglary	Transportation	7	No trade recorded	*Charlotte*
Clements	Thomas	23	M	Stealing cash	Transportation	7	No trade recorded	*Scarborough*
Cleugh/Clough/Clugh	Richard	26	M	Stealing cash	Death	7	No trade recorded	*Alexander*
Coffin	John	25	M	Stealing household goods	Transportation	7	Servant	*Charlotte*
Cole	Elizabeth	20	F	Stealing	Transportation	7	Milliner	*Lady Penrhyn*
Cole	Elizabeth	26	F	Burglary	Transportation	7	No trade recorded	*Charlotte*
Cole	William	23	M	Stealing gold watch chain and seal	Transportation	7	No trade recorded	*Scarborough*
Colley	Elizabeth	22	F	Receiving stolen goods	Transportation	14	Servant	*Lady Penrhyn*
Collier/Cully	Richard	22	M	Robbery	Transportation	7	Staymaker	*Scarborough*
Collins/Colling	Joseph	20	M	Stealing linen	Transportation	7	No trade recorded	*Scarborough*
Colman	Ishmael	32	M	Stealing woollen blankets	Transportation	7	No trade recorded	*Charlotte* (died at sea two weeks after departure)
Colpitts	Ann	28	F	Stealing 12 handkerchiefs	Transportation	7	Servant	*Lady Penrhyn*

Family Name	Given Name	Age Leaving England	Gender	Crime	Original Sentence	Transported for (years – 99 = life)	Occupation	Departed on
Conelly	Cornelius	24	M	Assault and highway robbery	Death	7	No trade recorded	*Charlotte*
Connelly	William	26	M	Stealing clothing	Transportation	7	No trade recorded	*Alexander*
Connolly	William	26	M	Burglary	Death	7	No trade recorded	*Scarborough*
Cook	Charlotte	20	F	Stealing clothing	Transportation	7	Tambour worker	*Lady Penrhyn*
Coombes	Ann	27	F	Stealing clothing and household goods	Transportation	7	No trade recorded	*Charlotte*
Cooper	Mary	37	F	Stealing clothing ('petit larceny')	Transportation	7	Charwoman	*Lady Penrhyn*
Copp	James	40	M	Stealing 11 barrels and other goods	Transportation	7	No trade recorded	*Charlotte*
Corden/ Cordell/ Caldwall	James	18	M	Burglary	Death	7	No trade recorded	*Alexander*
Cormick/ Corbet	Edward	24	M	Stealing (2 charges) a 'scarlet cloth cardinal' and sack of wheat	Transportation	7	Labourer	*Alexander*
Cox	James	27	M	Burglary	Death	99	No trade recorded	*Charlotte*
Cox	John Mathew/ Massy	32	M	Stealing lace	Death	99	Seaman	*Scarborough*
Creamer	John	18	M	Not recorded	Transportation	7	No trade recorded	*Charlotte*
Creek/Creeke	Jane	48	F	Stealing feathers, irons and coffee pot	Transportation	7	Charwoman or servant	*Lady Penrhyn*
Cropper	John	31	M	Stealing a trunk of clothing	Transportation	7	No trade recorded	*Alexander*
Cross	John	31	M	Stealing livestock (a sheep)	Death	7	No trade recorded	*Alexander*
Cross	William	23	M	Stealing livestock (fowls and ducks)	Transportation	7	No trade recorded	*Scarborough*
Crowder	Thomas Restell	32	M	Burglary	Death	99	No trade recorded	*Alexander*
Cuckow/ Cook/ Cuckoo/ Cookes	William	38	M	Burglary	Death	7	No trade recorded	*Scarborough*

Family Name	Given Name	Age Leaving England	Gender	Crime	Original Sentence	Transported for (years – 99 = life)	Occupation	Departed on
Cudlip/Norris	Jacob	39	M	Burglary	Death	7	No trade recorded	Scarborough
Cullen/Cullein	James Bryan	33	M	Stealing clothing	Transportation	7	Jockey	Scarborough
Cullyhorn/ Callaghan	John	31	M	Burglary	Death	7	Seaman	Scarborough
Cunningham	Edward	21	M	Stealing a silver mug	Transportation	7	No trade recorded	Scarborough
Cuss	John/ Hannaboy	42	M	Burglary	Death	7	No trade recorded	Charlotte
Daley/Dealey	James	24	M	Stealing clothing	Transportation	7	No trade recorded	Scarborough
Dalton/ Burley/ Burleigh	Elizabeth	20	F	Stealing linen handkerchiefs	Transportation	7	Servant	Lady Penrhyn
Daly	Ann		F	Robbery	Transportation	7	No trade recorded	Prince of Wales
Daniels/ Danniells	Daniel	21	M	Stealing metal cooking utensils	Transportation	7	No trade recorded	Scarborough
Darnell/ Darling/ Dowling	Margaret	20	F	Stealing knives and forks	Transportation	7	No trade recorded	Prince of Wales
Davies/Davis/ Ashley	Sarah	26	F	Stealing silk handkerchiefs	Death	7	Glove maker	Lady Penrhyn
Davis	Aaron	24	M	Stealing jewellery	Transportation	7	No trade recorded	Alexander
Davis	Ann	29	F	Stealing clothing	Transportation	7	Servant	Lady Penrhyn
Davis	Edward	33	M	Burglary	Death	7	No trade recorded	Alexander (died before departure)
Davis	Frances	22	F	Burglary	Death	14	Servant	Lady Penrhyn
Davis	James	27	M	Stealing clothing	Transportation	7	No trade recorded	Scarborough
Davis/Davies	Mary	25	F	Burglary	Death	7	Servant	Lady Penrhyn
Davis	Richard	28	M	Stealing clothing	Transportation	7	Printer	Friendship
Davis	Samuel	17	M	Stealing a silver watch	Transportation	7	No trade recorded	Alexander
Davis	William	57	M	Stealing livestock (a sheep)	Death	7	Tailor	Friendship
Davis	William	23	M	Unknown	Transportation	99	Baker	Alexander

Family Name	Given Name	Age Leaving England	Gender	Crime	Original Sentence	Transported for (years – 99 = life)	Occupation	Departed on
Davison/ Davidson	John	19	M	Burglary	Death	7	No trade recorded	*Scarborough*
Davison/ Davidson	Rebecca	28	F	Stealing cash	Transportation	7	Needleworker	*Lady Penrhyn*
Dawson	Margaret	17	F	Stealing clothing, jewellery and cash	Death	7	Servant	*Lady Penrhyn*
Day	Richard	22	M	Burglary	Transportation	7	Labourer	*Alexander (died at sea 8 December)*
Day	Samuel	21	M	Burglary	Death	14	No trade recorded	*Alexander*
Delany	Patrick	25	M	Assault and highway robbery	Death	7	Soldier	*Friendship (died at sea 23 June)*
Dennison/ Denison/ Deneson	Barnaby	28	M	Intent to rob	Transportation	7	No trade recorded	*Alexander*
Dennison	Michael	19	M	Stealing	Transportation	7	No trade recorded	*Alexander*
Dickenson	Mary	26	F	Stealing clothing	Transportation	7	Barrow woman	*Lady Penrhyn*
Discall/Driscal	Timothy	38	M	Stealing iron grappling and other goods	Transportation	7	No trade recorded	*Scarborough*
Dixon	Mary	41	F	Stealing household goods (2 counts)	Transportation	7	No trade recorded	*Prince of Wales*
Dixon/ Dickson	Thomas	22	M	Stealing livestock (a horse)	Death	7	No trade recorded	*Alexander*
Dodding/ Dodden/ Dorren	James	22	M	Stealing linen	Transportation	7	Seaman	*Friendship*
Douglas	William	24	M	Stealing a silver watch	Transportation	7	No trade recorded	*Alexander*
Dowland/ Doland/ Doolan	Ferdinand	32	M	Stealing livestock (a horse – mare)	Death	7	Dustman	*Scarborough*
Dring	William	19	M	Stealing brandy and clothing	Transportation	7	No trade recorded	*Alexander*
Dudgeon/ Dudgens	Elizabeth	23	F	Stealing cash	Transportation	7	No trade recorded	*Friendship*
Dundas	Jane	29	F	Stealing linen	Transportation	7	Servant	*Prince of Wales*

Family Name	Given Name	Age Leaving England	Gender	Crime	Original Sentence	Transported for (years – 99 = life)	Occupation	Departed on
Dunnage	Joseph	30	M	Stealing a glass window from a carriage/being at large after transportation order	Transportation/ Death	7/99	Seaman	Scarborough
Dutton	Ann	25	F	Stealing a clock, looking glass and locks	Transportation	7	Servant	Lady Penrhyn
Dyer	Leonard	27	M	Intent to rob	Transportation	7	No trade recorded	Alexander
Dykes/Dikes/ Dix	Mary	29	F	Stealing cash	Transportation	7	Staymaker	Lady Penrhyn
Earle/Earl	William	24	M	Burglary	Death	7	No trade recorded	Alexander
Earley/Hurley/ Early/Harley/ Arlly	Rachel	25	F	Stealing tea and silk	Transportation	7	No trade recorded	Friendship
Eaton	Martha	25	F	Receiving stolen goods	Transportation	7	Servant	Lady Penrhyn
Eccles/ Heccles	Thomas	48	M	Burglary	Death	99	Labourer	Scarborough
Edmunds/ Edmonds	William	29	M	Stealing livestock (a heifer)	Death	7	No trade recorded	Alexander
Edwards	William	34	M	Stealing clothing	Transportation	7	Brickmaker	Friendship
Egglestone	George	23	M	Stealing	Transportation	7	Hairdresser or labourer	Alexander
Eggleton/ Eagleton	William	31	M	Stealing clothing	Transportation	7	Labourer	Alexander
Ellam/Elias	Deborah	20	F	Stealing clothing	Transportation	7	No trade recorded	Prince of Wales
Ellam	Peter/Edward	19	M	Stealing clothing	Transportation	7	Labourer	Alexander
Elliott/Trimby	Joseph	20	M	Stealing a tobacco pouch	Transportation	7	Gardener	Friendship
Elliott	William/ Edward	31	M	Stealing clothing food and cash	Transportation	7	No trade recorded	Scarborough
English	Nicholas	17	M	Stealing hair powder	Transportation	7	No trade recorded	Scarborough
Evans	Elizabeth	28	F	Stealing tea	Transportation	7	Servant	Lady Penrhyn

Family Name	Given Name	Age Leaving England	Gender	Crime	Original Sentence	Transported for (years – 99 = life)	Occupation	Departed on
Evans	William	40	M	Stealing livestock (a horse)	Death	7	No trade recorded	*Friendship*
Everett	John	25	M	Stealing livestock (turkeys)	Transportation	7	Labourer	*Alexander* (died before departure)
Everingham	Matthew James	18	M	Stealing books	Transportation	7	Law clerk	*Scarborough*
Farley	William	17	M	Stealing sugar	Transportation	7	No trade recorded	*Friendship*
Farmer	Ann	62	F	Petty stealing	Transportation	7	No trade recorded	*Prince of Wales*
Farrell	Phillip	24	M	Stealing a handkerchief	Transportation	7	Seaman	*Scarborough*
Fenlow/ Findlow	John	21	M	Highway robbery	Transportation	7	Whitesmith (tinsmith)	*Friendship*
Fentum	Benjamin	27	M	Assault and highway robbery	Death	7	No trade recorded	*Scarborough*
Ferguson	John	28	M	Stealing material	Transportation	7	No trade recorded	*Charlotte*
Field	Jane	57	F	Stealing 3 bottles rum and port	Transportation	7	No trade recorded	*Prince of Wales*
Field	William	25	M	Assault and highway robbery	Transportation	7	No trade recorded	*Friendship*
Finicy/ Fillesey/ Tillesby	Thomas	29	M	Stealing shoe buckles	Transportation	7	No trade recorded	*Alexander*
Finn/Phyn	Mary	26	F	Stealing material	Transportation	7	Servant	*Lady Penrhyn*
Fitzgerald	Elizabeth	26	F	Stealing clothing	Transportation	7	Servant	*Lady Penrhyn*
Fitzgerald	Jane	30	F	Not recorded	Transportation	7	No trade recorded	*Charlotte*
Flarty	Phebe	15	F	Stealing clothing	Transportation	7	No trade recorded	*Prince of Wales*
Flinn/Flyn	Edward	27	M	Stealing clothing	Transportation	7	None	*Friendship*
Forbes	Ann	19	F	Stealing material	Death	7	No trade recorded	*Prince of Wales*
Forrester	Robert	28	M	Stealing gold coins	Death	7	No trade recorded	*Scarborough*
Fowkes/ Folkes	Francis		M	Stealing clothing	Transportation	7	Seaman (former midshipman) or clerk	*Alexander*
Fowles	Ann	22	F	Stealing clothing	Transportation	7	Hawker	*Lady Penrhyn*

Family Name	Given Name	Age Leaving England	Gender	Crime	Original Sentence	Transported for (years – 99 = life)	Occupation	Departed on
Fownes	Margaret	45	F	Assault and robbery	Death	7	Servant	*Lady Penrhyn*
Foyle	William	27	M	Burglary	Death	7	No trade recorded	*Charlotte*
Francis	William	24	M	Highway robbery	Transportation	7	No trade recorded	*Alexander*
Francisco	George	22	M	Stealing clothing	Transportation	7	No trade recorded	*Scarborough*
Fraser/ Redchester/ Frazer	Ellen/Eleanor	22	F	Stealing material	Transportation	7	No trade recorded	*Prince of Wales*
Fraser	William		M	Stealing material	Transportation	7	Labourer	*Charlotte*
Freeman	James	19	M	Highway robbery	Death	7	Labourer	*Alexander*
Freeman	Robert	29	M	Attempted highway robbery	Transportation	7	No trade recorded	*Alexander*
Fry	George	25	M	Burglary	Death	7	No trade recorded	*Scarborough*
Fuller	John	35	M	Stealing livestock (a horse)	Death	7	No trade recorded	*Scarborough*
Gabel/ Gambel/ Gable/ Gambol	Mary	37	F	Stealing	Transportation	7	Servant	*Lady Penrhyn*
Gardner/ Gardener	Francis	17	M	Stealing coal	Transportation	7	No trade recorded	*Scarborough*
Garland	Francis	26	M	Assault and highway robbery	Death	7	No trade recorded	*Charlotte*
Garth	Edward	23	M	Stealing livestock (2 cows)	Death	7	No trade recorded	*Scarborough*
Garth/Gough/ Grah/Grates	Susannah	24	F	Stealing cash	Transportation	7	No trade recorded	*Friendship*
Gascoigne/ Gaskins/ Gascking	Olivia/ Olive	24	F	Robbery	Death	7	Servant	*Lady Penrhyn*
Gearing	Thomas	43	M	Burglary, sacrilege	Death	99	Labourer	*Alexander* (died at sea 3 June)
George	Ann	22	F	Assault and robbery	Transportation	7	Shoe binder	*Lady Penrhyn*
Guest/Gess	George	20	M	Stealing livestock (10 pigs, 1 horse)	Death	7	Labourer	*Alexander*

Family Name	Given Name	Age Leaving England	Gender	Crime	Original Sentence	Transported for (years – 99 = life)	Occupation	Departed on
Glenton	Thomas	22	M	Stealing clothing	Transportation	7	Labourer	*Alexander*
Gloster/ Glocester/ Gloucester	William	38	M	Stealing coach glasses	Transportation	7	No trade recorded	*Alexander*
Goodwin	Andrew	20	M	Stealing lead from building	Transportation	7	No trade recorded	*Scarborough*
Goodwin/ Goodwine	Edward	22	M	Stealing material	Transportation	7	No trade recorded	*Scarborough*
Gordon	Daniel/Janel	47	M	Stealing clothing	Transportation	7	No trade recorded	*Alexander*
Gould	John	45	M	Stealing wooden barrels	Transportation	7	No trade recorded	*Charlotte*
Grace	James	18	M	Stealing clothing	Transportation	7	Shoemaker	*Friendship*
Granger	Charles	28	M	'Petit' stealing	Transportation	7	Leather breeches maker	*Friendship*
Gray/Grey	Charles/ Patrick	36	M	Not recorded	Transportation	7	No trade recorded	*Alexander*
Green/ Cowley	Ann	28	F	Stealing china	Transportation	7	Mantua maker	*Lady Penrhyn*
Green	Hannah	31	F	Stealing clothing	Transportation	7	None	*Friendship*
Green	John	61	M	Stealing livestock (a donkey)	Transportation	7	No trade recorded	*Alexander* (died before departure)
Green	Mary		F	Stealing teapot and cups	Transportation	7	No trade recorded	*Prince of Wales*
Greenwell	Nicholas	29	M	Attempted highway robbery	Transportation	7	No trade recorded	*Alexander* (released a day before departure)
Greenwood	Mary	24	F	Assault and highway robbery	Death	7	Servant	*Lady Penrhyn*
Griffiths/ Greefies	Samuel	35	M	Stealing livestock (a sheep)	Death	7	No trade recorded	*Alexander*
Griffiths	Thomas	28	M	Stealing material	Transportation	7	Seaman	*Scarborough*
Groves	Mary	30	F	Stealing cash	Transportation	7	No trade recorded	*Prince of Wales*
Gunther/ Gunter	William	23	M	Not recorded	Transportation	7	No trade recorded	*Alexander*

Family Name	Given Name	Age Leaving England	Gender	Crime	Original Sentence	Transported for (years – 99 = life)	Occupation	Departed on
Hagley/Agley	Richard	42	M	Assault and highway robbery	Death	7	No trade recorded	*Scarborough*
Haines/Haynes	Joseph	18	M	Receiving stolen goods	Transportation	14	No trade recorded	*Alexander*
Hall	Elizabeth	18	F	'Petit' stealing	Transportation	7	Servant	*Lady Penrhyn*
Hall	John	29	M	Stealing butter	Transportation	7	No trade recorded	*Charlotte*
Hall	Joseph	31	M	Assault and highway robbery	Death	14	No trade recorded	*Charlotte*
Hall	Margaret	22	F	Stealing jewellery and cash	Death	7	None	*Friendship*
Hall	Samuel		M	Burglary	Death	7	Carpenter	*Alexander*
Hall/Hammond	Sarah	46	F	Stealing clothing	Transportation	7	Hawker	*Lady Penrhyn*
Hamilton	Maria	33	F	Stealing clothing	Transportation	7	Lace weaver	*Lady Penrhyn*
Hamlyn/Hamlin	William	59	M	Assault and attempted highway robbery	Transportation	7	No trade recorded	*Charlotte*
Handford/Hanford	John	27	M	Stealing an iron bar	Transportation	7	No trade recorded	*Alexander*
Handland/Gray	Dorothy	61	F	Perjury	Transportation	7	Old clothes woman, dealer	*Lady Penrhyn*
Harben/Harbine	Joseph	21	M	Stealing	Transportation	7	No trade recorded	*Alexander*
Harper/Harpur	Joshua	34	M	Stealing bedding and curtains	Transportation	7	No trade recorded	*Scarborough*
Harris	John	27	M	Stealing silver spoons	Death	99	Wax chandler	*Scarborough*
Harris	William	32	M	Stealing clothing	Transportation	7	Labourer	*Alexander*
Harrison	Joseph	26	M	Burglary	Death	7	No trade recorded	*Scarborough*
Harrison	Joseph	27	M	Not recorded	Transportation	7	No trade recorded	*Scarborough*
Harrison	Mary	34	F	Assault and malicious damage	Transportation	7	Silk winder	*Lady Penrhyn*
Harrison	Mary	25	F	Stealing bills of exchange	Transportation	7	Servant	*Prince of Wales*
Hart	Catherine	19	F	Stealing clothing	Transportation	7	Servant	*Lady Penrhyn*

Family Name	Given Name	Age Leaving England	Gender	Crime	Original Sentence	Transported for (years – 99 = life)	Occupation	Departed on
Hart	Frances	36	F	Receiving stolen clothing	Transportation	7	Mantua maker	*Friendship/ Charlotte*
Hart	John	28	M	Stealing a silver cup	Transportation	7	No trade recorded	*Alexander* (died before departure)
Hart	John	46	M	Stealing a basket of food	Transportation	7	Porter, ex-sergeant	*Scarborough*
Hartley	John	50	M	Stealing livestock (poultry)	Transportation	7	No trade recorded	*Alexander* (died at sea 5 August)
Harwood/ Howard	Esther	36	F	Stealing a silver watch and cash	Transportation	7	Oyster seller or servant	*Lady Penrhyn*
Hatch	John	47	M	Stealing wheat	Transportation	7	No trade recorded	*Alexander* (died before departure)
Hatcher	John	37	M	Burglary	Transportation	7	No trade recorded	*Alexander*
Hatfield	William	30	M	Assault with intent to rob	Transportation	7	No trade recorded	*Alexander*
Hatheway/ Hathaway	Henry	22	M	Assault and highway robbery	Death	7	Labourer	*Alexander*
Hatton/ Hattom	Joseph	39	M	Stealing material	Transportation	7	Hawker and pedlar	*Scarborough*
Hawkes	Richard	36	M	Stealing hemp yarn	Transportation	7	Labourer	*Alexander*
Haydon/ Hadon/ Haidon	John	31	M	Highway robbery	Death	7	No trade recorded	*Charlotte*
Hayes	Dennis	20	M	Assault and attempted robbery	Transportation	7	No trade recorded	*Alexander*
Hayes	John	22	M	Robbery	Transportation	7	Labourer	*Scarborough*
Haynes/ Haines	William	32	M	Assault and highway robbery	Death	7	Cabinet maker	*Friendship*
Hayward	Elizabeth	14	F	Stealing clothing	Transportation	7	Apprentice clog [cloak?] maker	*Lady Penrhyn*
Heading	James	30	M	Stealing livestock (4 horses)	Death	99	Labourer	*Alexander*
Headington/ Heddington/ Eddington	Thomas	29	M	Robbery	Transportation	7	Labourer	*Alexander*

Family Name	Given Name	Age Leaving England	Gender	Crime	Original Sentence	Transported for (years – 99 = life)	Occupation	Departed on
Henley/ Handy/ Handley	Cooper	33	M	Assault and highway robbery	Death	7	Weaver	*Friendship*
Henry	Catherine	36	F	Stealing muslin shawls	Transportation	7	Hawker	*Lady Penrhyn*
Herbert	Jane	40	F	Stealing a promissory note	Transportation	7	Servant	*Prince of Wales*
Herbert	John	20	M	Stealing silk handkerchief	Transportation	7	No trade recorded	*Scarborough*
Herbert	John	26	M	Assault and highway robbery	Death	7	No trade recorded	*Charlotte*
Hervey/ Harvey	Elizabeth	30	F	Burglary	Death	14	No trade recorded	*Friendship*
Hill	John	28	M	Burglary	Death	99	Labourer	*Alexander*
Hill	John	34	M	Stealing linen handkerchief	Transportation	7	No trade recorded	*Scarborough*
Hill	Mary	20	F	Stealing a watch, gold seal and key	Transportation	7	Servant	*Lady Penrhyn*
Hill	Thomas	29	M	Stealing clothing	Transportation	7	No trade recorded	*Scarborough*
Hill	Thomas	28	M	Stealing a silver watch	Transportation	7	Leather breeches maker	*Friendship*
Hilt/Hitt	William	17	M	Housebreaking	Death	99	No trade recorded	*Charlotte*
Hindle/Ingle/ Engle	Ottiwell/ Ottawel/ Oataway		M	Stealing a silver watch	Transportation	7	Weaver	*Alexander*
Hindley	William	21	M	Stealing clothing	Transportation	7	Labourer	*Alexander*
Hippsley/ Hipesley	Elizabeth	30	F	Stealing a silver watch and cash	Transportation	7	Needleworker	*Lady Penrhyn*
Hogg	William	39	M	Forgery	Transportation	14	Silversmith	*Scarborough*
Holland	William	31	M	Stealing silver teaspoons and other goods	Transportation	7	No trade recorded	*Charlotte*
Hollister	Job	21	M	Stealing tobacco	Transportation	7	No trade recorded	*Alexander*
Hollogin/ Holligin	Elizabeth		F	Stealing clothing	Transportation	7	No trade recorded	*Prince of Wales*
Holloway	James	27	M	Stealing a silk handkerchief	Transportation	7	No trade recorded	*Scarborough*

Family Name	Given Name	Age Leaving England	Gender	Crime	Original Sentence	Transported for (years – 99 = life)	Occupation	Departed on
Holmes	Susannah	22	F	Burglary	Death	14	None	Friendship
Holmes	William	24	M	Burglary	Death	7	No trade recorded	Scarborough
Horne	Henry	24	M	Assault and robbery	Transportation	7	Seaman	Alexander
Hortopp	James	34	M	Burglary	Death	7	No trade recorded	Charlotte
Howard	John	24	M	Assault and attempted highway robbery	Transportation	7	No trade recorded	Scarborough
Howard	Thomas	32	M	Stealing	Transportation	7	No trade recorded	Scarborough
Howell/ Hawell	Thomas	28	M	Stealing livestock (4 hens)	Transportation	7	Labourer	Alexander
Hubbard	William	19	M	Stealing a bedsheet	Transportation	7	Plasterer	Scarborough
Hubbard/ Husband	William	24	M	Burglary	Death	7	No trade recorded	Scarborough
Hudson	John	13	M	Stealing	Transportation	7	Chimney sweep	Friendship
Huffnell	Susannah	22	F	Stealing clothing	Transportation	7	Servant	Lady Penrhyn
Hughes	Frances Ann	32	F	Not recorded	Transportation	7	No trade recorded	Prince of Wales
Hughes	Hugh	26	M	Stealing lead from a building	Transportation	7	Wheelwright	Alexander
Hughes	John	21	M	Assault and highway robbery	Death	7	Labourer	Scarborough
Hughes	Thomas	24	M	Stealing livestock (a horse)	Death	7	None	Friendship
Humphreys	Edward	21	M	Stealing clothing	Transportation	7	Dustman	Scarborough
Humphreys	Henry	21	M	Stealing a winch and other goods	Transportation	7	No trade recorded	Charlotte
Humphries/ Humfries	Mary	30	F	Assault and highway robbery	Death	14	Servant	Lady Penrhyn
Hurley	Jeremiah	23	M	Stealing clothing	Transportation	7	No trade recorded	Scarborough
Hussey	Samuel/ James	33	M	Stealing livestock (two horses)	Death	7	None	Friendship
Hylids/Illid/ Eylidd	Thomas	32	M	Robbery	Transportation	7	Ship's carpenter	Scarborough
Inett	Ann	30	F	Burglary	Death	7	Mantua maker	Lady Penrhyn

Family Name	Given Name	Age Leaving England	Gender	Crime	Original Sentence	Transported for (years – 99 = life)	Occupation	Departed on
Ingram/ Ingraham	Benjamin	18	M	Stealing linen handkerchief	Transportation	7	No trade recorded	*Scarborough*
Irvine/Irvin	John	26	M	Stealing a silver cup	Transportation	7	Surgeon	*Scarborough*
Jackson	Hannah	30	F	Stealing material	Transportation	7	No trade recorded	*Charlotte*
Jackson	Jane	30	F	Stealing silver watch, key, seal and cash	Transportation	7	Servant	*Lady Penrhyn*
Jackson	Mary	21	F	Stealing cash	Transportation	7	Hawker	*Lady Penrhyn*
Jackson	William	25	M	Burglary	Transportation	7	No trade recorded	*Alexander* (died before departure)
Jacobs	David	27	M	Stealing clothing	Transportation	7	No trade recorded	*Scarborough*
Jacobs	John	21	M	Assault and highway robbery	Death	7	No trade recorded	*Scarborough*
Jemmison/ Jamison/ Jammison/ Jameson	James/John	27	M	Stealing clothing	Transportation	7	None	*Friendship*
Jeffries	John	26	M	Stealing a silver watch, steel chain and brass key	Transportation	7	Labourer	*Alexander*
Jeffries	Robert	31	M	Stealing livestock (8 ducks, 9 hens)	Transportation	7	No trade recorded	*Alexander* (died on day of departure)
Jenkins	Robert	55	M	Stealing clothing	Transportation	7	Labourer	*Alexander*
Jenkins	William	24	M	Assault with intent to rob	Transportation	7	No trade recorded	*Charlotte*
Jepp/Jeff/ Gepp	John	27	M	Robbery	Transportation	7	Master butcher	*Alexander*
Johns	Stephen	19	M	Stealing livestock (5 sheep)	Death	7	No trade recorded	*Scarborough*
Johnson	Catherine	17	F	Stealing material	Transportation	7	No trade recorded	*Prince of Wales*
Johnson	Charles	23	M	Stealing a linen handkerchief and piece of ribbon	Transportation	7	Labourer	*Alexander* (died at sea 31 May)
Johnson	Edward	29	M	Stealing silver	Transportation	7	No trade recorded	*Charlotte*

Family Name	Given Name	Age Leaving England	Gender	Crime	Original Sentence	Transported for (years – 99 = life)	Occupation	Departed on
Johnson	Mary	23	F	Stealing material	Transportation	7	No trade recorded	Prince of Wales
Johnson	William	24	M	Assault and highway robbery	Death	7	Labourer	Scarborough
Jones	Edward	23	M	Stealing watch pieces	Transportation	7	No trade recorded	Alexander
Jones	Francis		M	Stealing clothing	Transportation	7	No trade recorded	Alexander
Jones	John	26	M	Stealing (details not clear because of confusion with names)	Transportation	14	No trade recorded	Charlotte
Jones	Margaret	38	F	Receiving stolen goods	Transportation	7	No trade recorded	Charlotte
Jones	Richard	34	M	Stealing livestock (4 cattle)	Death	7	Miller	Friendship
Jones	Thomas	23	M	Burglary	Death	14	Bricklayer	Friendship
Jones	Thomas	21	M	Stealing a silver tankard	Transportation	7	No trade recorded	Alexander
Jones	William	21	M	Stealing a purse and cash	Transportation	7	Stocking weaver	Friendship
Josephs	Thomas	27	M	Assault and highway robbery	Death	7	No trade recorded	Scarborough
Keeling/ Kellan	John Herbert	22	M	Stealing a sword	Death	99	Seaman	Scarborough
Kelly	Thomas	23	M	Stealing a silver mug and spoons	Transportation	7	Servant	Alexander
Kennedy	Martha	31	F	Assault and robbery	Transportation	7	Pinheader	Prince of Wales
Kidner/Kidney	Thomas	23	M	Stealing Irish linen	Transportation	7	No trade recorded	Alexander
Kilby	William	51	M	Stealing livestock (poultry)	Death	99	Labourer	Alexander
Kilpack/ Killpack	David	27	M	Stealing livestock (poultry)	Death	99	Sawyer	Scarborough
Kimberly	Edward	22	M	Stealing material	Transportation	7	No trade recorded	Scarborough
King	John	33	M	Stealing clothing	Transportation	7	Brickmaker	Scarborough
Knowler/ Nowland	John	25	M	Robbery	Transportation	7	Labourer	Alexander

Family Name	Given Name	Age Leaving England	Gender	Crime	Original Sentence	Transported for (years – 99 = life)	Occupation	Departed on
La Rue/Larne/ Lu Riew/ Larew	James	21	M	Unknown	Transportation	7	No trade recorded	*Charlotte*
Lambeth	John	24	M	Stealing cash	Death	7	Blacksmith	*Friendship*
Lane	William	33	M	Stealing assorted foods and barrels	Transportation	7	Labourer	*Scarborough*
Langley	Jane	22	F	Stealing cash	Transportation	7	No trade recorded	*Lady Penrhyn*
Lankey	David	24	M	Stealing a silk handkerchief	Transportation	7	Tailor	*Scarborough*
Larah/Zarah	Flora/Laura		F	Stealing a mahogany tea chest and cash	Transportation	7	No trade recorded	*Prince of Wales*
Lavell/Lovell	Henry	23	M	Forgery	Death	99	Ivory turner	*Friendship*
Lawrell	John	27	M	Stealing silver teaspoons	Transportation	7	No trade recorded	*Scarborough*
Lawrence/ Laurence	Mary	30	F	Stealing silver tableware and jewellery	Transportation	7	Servant	*Lady Penrhyn*
Laycock/ Haycock/ Haylock	Caroline	22	F	Unknown	Transportation	7	No trade recorded	*Prince of Wales*
Le Grove	Stephen	29	M	Stealing timber	Death	7	Waterman	*Friendship*
Leary	Jeremiah	22	M	Housebreaking	Death	14	No trade recorded	*Friendship*
Leary	John	24	M	Assault and highway robbery	Death	7	No trade recorded	*Scarborough*
Lee/Lees	Elizabeth	24	F	Stealing wine and spirits	Transportation	7	Servant cook	*Lady Penrhyn*
Legg/Legge	George	24	M	Stealing a gold watch and other goods	Transportation	7	Shoemaker	*Charlotte*
Lemon	Isaac	25	M	Stealing livestock (a horse)	Death	7	Labourer	*Alexander* (died before departure)
Leonard/ Leonell	Elizabeth	33	F	Assault and robbery	Death	7	Servant	*Lady Penrhyn*
Levy	Amelia/Mary	19	F	Stealing silk handkerchiefs	Transportation	7	Furrier	*Lady Penrhyn*

Family Name	Given Name	Age Leaving England	Gender	Crime	Original Sentence	Transported for (years – 99 = life)	Occupation	Departed on
Levy	Joseph	21	M	Stealing a copper kettle	Transportation	7	No trade recorded	Scarborough
Lewis	Sophia	29	F	Stealing handkerchiefs, coat and cash	Transportation	7	Servant	Lady Penrhyn
Lightfoot	Samuel	23	M	Stealing clothing	Transportation	7	No trade recorded	Charlotte
Limeburner	John	32	M	Housebreaking	Death	7	No trade recorded	Charlotte
Limpus	Thomas	26	M	Stealing a cambric handkerchief	Transportation	7	No trade recorded	Charlotte
Lisk/List/Liske	George	28	M	Assault	Transportation	7	Watchmaker	Scarborough
Lloyd/Loyd/Lyde	John	22	M	Stealing cash	Transportation	7	None	Friendship
Lock	Elizabeth	23	F	Burglary	Death	7	Servant	Lady Penrhyn
Lockley/Lockly/Lockey	John	22	M	Assault and highway robbery	Death	7	Watchmaker	Alexander
Long	Joseph	27	M	Stealing a silver watch	Death	7	No trade recorded	Alexander
Long	Mary		F	Assault and highway robbery	Death	99	No trade recorded	Prince of Wales
Longstreet	Joseph	32	M	Stealing wool	Transportation	7	No trade recorded	Alexander (died at sea 19 July)
Love	Mary	60	F	Receiving stolen goods	Transportation	14	Servant	Lady Penrhyn
Lucas	Nathaniel	23	M	Stealing clothing	Transportation	7	Carpenter	Scarborough
Lynch	Ann	40	F	Receiving stolen goods	Transportation	14	No trade recorded	Charlotte
Lynch	Humphrey	24	M	Assault and highway robbery	Death	7	Tailor	Alexander
Lyne/Lane	Richard	26	M	Stealing a watch and other goods	Transportation	7	No trade recorded	Scarborough
MacClean	Edward	43	M	Stealing clothing	Death	7	Labourer	Scarborough
Maclean/Mclean	Francis	19	M	Burglary	Death	7	Labourer	Alexander
Maclean	Thomas	18	M	Burglary	Death	7	Labourer	Alexander

Family Name	Given Name	Age Leaving England	Gender	Crime	Original Sentence	Transported for (years – 99 = life)	Occupation	Departed on
Macentire/ Macintire/ Mcintire	John	32	M	Assault and robbery	Death	7	No trade recorded	*Alexander*
Mackey/ Mackie/ Mackrie	James	25	M	Stealing clothing	Transportation	7	Weaver	*Friendship*
Mansfield	John	17	M	Stealing livestock (8 pigs)	Transportation	7	Labourer	*Alexander*
Mariner	William	24	M	Burglary and sacrilege	Death	7	Labourer	*Alexander*
Marney/ Marriner/ Mariner	William	28	M	Stealing clothing and cash	Transportation	7	No trade recorded	*Scarborough*
Marriott/ Merrit// Marriot	Jane		F	Stealing clothing	Transportation	7	Servant	*Prince of Wales*
Marrott/ Merritt/ Marriott	John	35	M	Burglary	Death	7	Labourer	*Alexander*
Marshall	Joseph	33	M	Receiving stolen goods	Transportation	14	No trade recorded	*Scarborough*
Marshall	Mary	29	F	Stealing linen handkerchiefs	Transportation	7	Servant	*Lady Penrhyn*
Marshall	Mary	19	F	Assault and robbery	Death	99	Servant	*Lady Penrhyn*
Martin	Abraham	42	M	Stealing an iron gate and fence	Transportation	7	No trade recorded	*Charlotte*
Martin	Ann	17	F	Stealing silk handkerchiefs	Transportation	7	Servant	*Lady Penrhyn*
Martin/ Martyn	James	26	M	Stealing iron bolts	Transportation	7	No trade recorded	*Charlotte*
Martin	John	29	M	Stealing clothing	Transportation	7	No trade recorded	*Alexander*
Martin/ Mather	Mary		F	Stealing clothing	Transportation	7	No trade recorded	*Prince of Wales*
Martin/ Martyn	Stephen	38	M	Stealing boots and spurs	Transportation	7	No trade recorded	*Alexander*
Martin	Thomas	22	M	Stealing linen and clothing	Transportation	7	Weaver	*Charlotte*

Family Name	Given Name	Age Leaving England	Gender	Crime	Original Sentence	Transported for (years – 99 = life)	Occupation	Departed on
Mason	Betty/ Elizabeth	22	F	Stealing a purse and gold coins	Death	14	None	*Friendship*
Mason/Gibbs	Susannah	49	F	Stealing clothing	Transportation	7	No trade recorded	*Prince of Wales*
Mather/ Matthews	Ann	14	F	Stealing clothing	Transportation	7	No trade recorded	*Prince of Wales*
Matson	Thomas	27	M	Stealing a lead pump	Transportation	7	Labourer	*Alexander*
May	Richard	24	M	Burglary	Death	7	No trade recorded	*Alexander*
Mccabe	Eleanor	24	F	Assault and robbery	Transportation	7	Hawker	*Lady Penrhyn*
McCormack/ McCormick	Mary	33	F	Receiving stolen goods	Transportation	7	None	*Friendship*
McDale/ McDeed/ Dade/Deane	Richard	33	M	Stealing gold coins	Death	7	Shoemaker	*Friendship*
McDonald	Alexander	29	M	Stealing clothing	Transportation	7	Servant	*Alexander*
McDonaugh	James	35	M	Stealing a lead pump	Transportation	7	Labourer	*Alexander*
McGrah/ McGrath	Redman/ Redmond	30	M	Stealing household goods	Transportation	7	None	*Friendship*
McLaughlin/ McLellan/ McLennan/ MacLaulin	Charles	15	M	'Pettit' stealing of a purse and cash	Transportation	7	No trade recorded	*Alexander*
McNamara	William	24	M	Stealing clothing	Death	7	Seaman	*Friendship*
Meech/ Meach	Jane	29	F	Stealing iron chains	Transportation	7	No trade recorded	*Charlotte*
Messiah/ Massias	Jacob	16	M	Stealing a silver watch, seal and brass key	Transportation	7	No trade recorded	*Scarborough*
Middleton	Richard	27	M	Stealing livestock (a horse)	Death	7	No trade recorded	*Scarborough*
Midgley	Samuel	21	M	Burglary	Death	7	No trade recorded	*Alexander*
Miles/Moyle	Edward	25	M	Stealing clothing	Transportation	7	No trade recorded	*Scarborough*
Mills/Hill	Mathew/ John	24	M	Highway robbery	Death	7	No trade recorded	*Friendship*

Family Name	Given Name	Age Leaving England	Gender	Crime	Original Sentence	Transported for (years – 99 = life)	Occupation	Departed on
Milton	Charles	34	M	Stealing copper	Transportation	7	Labourer	Alexander
Mitchcraft/ Beachcroft	Mary	16	F	Assault and robbery	Transportation	7	Servant	Prince of Wales
Mitchell	Mary	19	F	Stealing	Transportation	7	Servant	Lady Penrhyn
Mitchell	Nathaniel	36	M	Stealing cheese and other goods	Transportation	7	No trade recorded	Charlotte
Mobbs	Samuel	23	M	Stealing a cotton handkerchief	Transportation	7	Plasterer	Scarborough
Mollands/ Mullins	John	21	M	Stealing cash	Transportation	7	No trade recorded	Scarborough
Mood	Charles	25	M	Not recorded	Transportation	7	No trade recorded	Scarborough
Moore/ Ransmore	William	29	M	Stealing clothing	Transportation	7	No trade recorded	Scarborough
Moran/ Moorin/ Moreing/ Moseing/ Morin	John	32	M	Stealing 2 silver tablespoons	Transportation	7	No trade recorded	Scarborough
Morgan	Richard	25	M	Assault and stealing a metal watch	Transportation	7	No trade recorded	Alexander
Morgan	Robert	24	M	Stealing a silk handkerchief	Transportation	7	Plasterer's assistant	Scarborough
Morgan	William	19	M	Stealing household goods	Transportation	7	Bricklayer's labourer	Scarborough
Morley/ Mawley	Joseph	26	M	Assault and highway robbery	Death	7	Silk dyer	Friendship
Morris	Peter	28	M	Stealing clothing	Transportation	7	No trade recorded	Alexander
Morrisby	James/John	30	M	Stealing an iron bar	Transportation	7	Blacksmith or soldier	Scarborough
Mortimer	John	54	M	Stealing mutton	Transportation	7	No trade recorded	Charlotte
Mortimer	Noah	26	M	Stealing mutton	Transportation	7	No trade recorded	Charlotte
Morton/ Moulton	Mary	20	F	Stealing 17 handkerchiefs	Transportation	7	Servant	Lady Penrhyn
Moseley/ Morley	John	29	M	Fraud (impersonation)	Death	99	No trade recorded	Scarborough

Family Name	Given Name	Age Leaving England	Gender	Crime	Original Sentence	Transported for (years – 99 = life)	Occupation	Departed on
Mould	William	28	M	Stealing household goods	Transportation	7	Brazier	*Scarborough*
Mowbray/ Moubrey	John	25	M	Stealing silver watch	Death	7	No trade recorded	*Alexander* (died at sea 24 December)
Mulcock/ Mocock/ Mullock/ Molock/ Mulcock	Jesse	25	M	Stealing livestock (a horse)	Death	7	No trade recorded	*Alexander*
Mullens	Hannah/ Hanna	27	F	Forgery	Death	99	Servant	*Lady Penrhyn*
Mullis/Mullot	Stephen	25	M	Robbery	Transportation	7	Caulker	*Charlotte*
Munro	Lydia/Letitia	17	F	Stealing material	Death	14	No trade recorded	*Prince of Wales*
Murphy	James	44	M	Assault and highway robbery	Death	7	Shoemaker	*Friendship*
Murphy	William		M	Assault	Transportation	7	No trade recorded	*Alexander*
Neal	James	18	M	Stealing sugar	Transportation	7	No trade recorded	*Friendship*
Neale/Neal	John	33	M	Stealing a gold watch, chain, seals and key	Transportation	7	No trade recorded	*Scarborough*
Needham	Elizabeth	25	F	Stealing clothing	Transportation	7	Servant or needleworker	*Lady Penrhyn*
Nettleton	Robert	29	M	Stealing a silk handkerchief, scissors and snuffers	Transportation	7	No trade recorded	*Alexander*
Nicholls	John	27	M	Stealing assorted barber's tools and aids	Transportation	7	Servant	*Scarborough*
Norton	Phebe	31	F	Stealing household goods	Transportation	7	Servant	*Lady Penrhyn*
Nowland/ Newland	John	32	M	Highway robbery	Transportation	7	Shoemaker	*Scarborough*
Nunn	Robert	28	M	Stealing clothing	Transportation	7	No trade recorded	*Scarborough*
Nurse	John	17	M	Burglary	Transportation	7	No trade recorded	*Scarborough*
O'craft/ Oakraft	John	38	M	Stealing clothing and money	Transportation	7	No trade recorded	*Charlotte*

Family Name	Given Name	Age Leaving England	Gender	Crime	Original Sentence	Transported for (years – 99 = life)	Occupation	Departed on
Ogden	James	19	M	Stealing a purse, pieces of gold and silver	Transportation	7	Labourer	Alexander
Okey	William	19	M	Burglary	Death	7	Labourer	Alexander
Oldfield	Isabella	25	F	Stealing pieces of material	Transportation	7	None	Friendship
Oldfield	Thomas	24	M	Stealing 3 pieces of material	Transportation	7	Labourer or woollen dresser	Friendship
Opley/Hopley	Peter	19	M	Stealing clothing	Transportation	7	Butcher	Alexander
Orford/ Aweford/ Alford/ Hartford/ Oxford	Thomas	25	M	Stealing clothing	Transportation	7	No trade recorded	Alexander
Osborne/ Jones	Elizabeth	30	F	Stealing cash	Transportation	7	Servant	Lady Penrhyn
Osborne/ Osborn/ Hosburn	Thomas	23	M	Stealing clothing	Transportation	7	No trade recorded	Alexander
Owen	John	18	M	Stealing 18 table knives and forks	Transportation	7	No trade recorded	Scarborough
Owen	Joseph	67	M	Receiving stolen goods	Transportation	14	None	Friendship
Owles	John	35	M	Aiding a prison escape	Transportation	7	No trade recorded	Alexander
Page	Paul		M	Burglary	Death	7	No trade recorded	Alexander
Paget	Joseph	26	M	Not recorded	Transportation	7	Seaman	Scarborough
Palmer	John Henry	22	M	Fraud (forgery)	Death	99	Law clerk	Alexander (died at sea 12 January)
Pare/Pane	William	47	M	Burglary	Death	7	No trade recorded	Alexander
Parish	William		M	Assault and attempted highway robbery	Transportation	7	Seaman	Alexander
Parker	Elizabeth	23	F	Burglary	Transportation	7	No trade recorded	Friendship
Parker	John	25	M	Assault and highway robbery	Death	7	Apprentice ivory turner	Alexander
Parker	Mary	28	F	Stealing clothing	Transportation	7	Servant	Lady Penrhyn

Family Name	Given Name	Age Leaving England	Gender	Crime	Original Sentence	Transported for (years – 99 = life)	Occupation	Departed on
Parkinson/ Partington	Jane	22	F	Stealing material	Transportation	7	Milliner	*Friendship* (died at sea after leaving Cape Town)
Parr	William		M	Fraud (cheating a shopkeeper)	Transportation	7	No trade recorded	*Alexander*
Parris	Peter	27	M	Burglary	Death	7	No trade recorded	*Scarborough*
Parry	Edward	57	M	Robbery of cord and bag	Transportation	7	Labourer	*Alexander* (died before departure)
Parry	Sarah	28	F	Assault and robbery of silver watch, steel chain, seal and key	Death	99	Milliner	*Lady Penrhyn*
Parsley	Ann	15	F	Stealing clothing	Transportation	7	No trade recorded	*Prince of Wales*
Partridge/Rice	Richard	30	M	Stealing clothing	Death	99	No trade recorded	*Scarborough*
Partridge	Sarah	22	F	Stealing lengths of silk	Death	7	Mantua maker	*Lady Penrhyn*
Peat/Peet	Charles	28	M	Assault and highway robbery	Death	99	No trade recorded	*Scarborough*
Peaulet/ Peallet/ Powlett/Pulet/ Powlett	James		M	Stealing a silver watch, metal chain and gold seal	Transportation	7	No trade recorded	*Scarborough*
Peck	Joshua	31	M	Stealing	Transportation	7	No trade recorded	*Scarborough*
Penny/Pinney/ Pinkey	John	32	M	Stealing clothing	Transportation	7	Jeweller	*Friendship*
Percival/ Percivall	Richard	23	M	Stealing household goods	Transportation	7	No trade recorded	*Scarborough*
Perkins	Edward	57	M	Stealing livestock (a rooster)	Transportation	7	Labourer or brickmaker	*Friendship*
Perrott/ Parrett/ Bearcroft/ Parkins	Edward		M	Stealing clothing	Transportation	7	No trade recorded	*Alexander*
Petherick/ Pederick/ Patrick/ Pedrick	John	39	M	Stealing clothing	Transportation	7	Labourer or miner	*Friendship*

Family Name	Given Name	Age Leaving England	Gender	Crime	Original Sentence	Transported for (years – 99 = life)	Occupation	Departed on
Petrie	John	22	M	Stealing clothing	Transportation	7	Soldier or servant or tailor	Alexander
Pettitt/Petit	John	29	M	Stealing musical instruments	Transportation	7	Shoemaker	Scarborough
Peyton	Samuel	19	M	Stealing	Transportation	7	Stonemason	Alexander
Phillimore	Richard/William	33	M	Stealing livestock (6 sheep)	Death	7	No trade recorded	Scarborough
Phillips	Mary	33	F	Burglary	Death	7	No trade recorded	Charlotte
Phillips	Richard	22	M	Stealing lead from a building	Transportation	7	No trade recorded	Scarborough
Pigott/Pickett	Samuel	26	M	Stealing material	Death	7	No trade recorded	Charlotte
Piles	Mary	20	F	Stealing	Transportation	7	Servant	Lady Penrhyn
Pinder	Mary	21	F	Not recorded	Transportation	7	No trade recorded	Prince of Wales
Pipkin	Elizabeth		F	Stealing a silver watch	Transportation	7	No trade recorded	Prince of Wales
Pontie	John	27	M	Stealing lace	Death	99	No trade recorded	Scarborough
Poole	Jane	19	F	Burglary	Death	7	No trade recorded	Charlotte
Poore/Power/Poor	William	21	M	Stealing livestock (26 hens)	Transportation	7	No trade recorded	Charlotte
Pope	David	34	M	Stealing lead from a roof	Transportation	7	No trade recorded	Alexander
Powell	Ann	35	F	Stealing clothing	Transportation	7	Servant or charwoman or washerwoman	Lady Penrhyn
Power	John	24	M	Stealing timber	Transportation	7	No trade recorded	Alexander
Price	James	26	M	Burglary	Transportation	7	No trade recorded	Alexander
Price	John	22	M	Stealing livestock (a goose)	Transportation	7	No trade recorded	Alexander
Prior/Fryer	Catherine	24	F	Highway robbery	Death	7	No trade recorded	Charlotte
Prior	Thomas	31	M	Stealing livestock (poultry)	Transportation	7	Labourer	Alexander
Pritchard	Thomas	22	M	Stealing lead from a roof	Transportation	7	Labourer	Friendship
Pugh	Edward	22	M	Stealing clothing	Transportation	7	Carpenter	Friendship

Family Name	Given Name	Age Leaving England	Gender	Crime	Original Sentence	Transported for (years – 99 = life)	Occupation	Departed on
Pulley/ Powley/ Pooley	Elizabeth	24	F	Burglary	Death	7	No trade recorded	*Friendship*
Radford/ Redford/ Ratford	William	25	M	Stealing	Death	7	No trade recorded	*Alexander*
Ramsay	John	25	M	Assault and highway robbery	Death	7	Seaman or labourer	*Scarborough*
Randall/ Reynolds	John	22	M	Stealing a steel watch chain	Transportation	7	Labourer	*Alexander*
Raymond/ Reymond	George	31	M	Stealing bedding	Transportation	7	No trade recorded	*Scarborough*
Read/Reed	Ann	22	F	Assault and highway robbery	Death	99	Fishmonger or servant	*Lady Penrhyn*
Read/Reed	William	31	M	Stealing clothing linen and cash	Transportation	7	No trade recorded	*Scarborough*
Reardon/ Bartlett	Bartholomew	62	M	Stealing a hair trunk	Transportation	7	No trade recorded	*Scarborough*
Repeat	Charles	20	M	Burglary	Death	7	Button stamper	*Alexander*
Rice	John	27	M	Burglary	Death	7	Rope maker	*Charlotte*
Richards	David	23	M	Stealing clothing	Transportation	7	Ivory turner	*Scarborough*
Richards	James	23	M	Stealing spirits and livestock (a horse – a mare)	Death	7	Labourer	*Alexander*
Richards	James	20	M	Stealing livestock (a horse – a gelding)	Death	7	No trade recorded	*Scarborough*
Richards	John	56	M	Burglary	Death	7	Stonecutter	*Scarborough*
Richardson	Hardwicke		M	Stealing clothing	Transportation	7	Seaman	*Alexander*
Richardson	James	20	M	Assault and highway robbery	Transportation	7	Labourer	*Alexander*
Richardson/ Mann	John	27	M	Stealing household goods	Transportation	7	No trade recorded	*Scarborough*
Richardson/ Richards	Samuel	21	M	Stealing silk	Transportation	7	Seaman	*Scarborough*
Richardson	William	25	M	Assault and highway robbery	Death	7	No trade recorded	*Alexander*

Family Name	Given Name	Age Leaving England	Gender	Crime	Original Sentence	Transported for (years – 99 = life)	Occupation	Departed on
Rickson	William	21	M	Robbery	Transportation	7	Labourer	*Scarborough*
Risby	Edward	29	M	Robbery	Transportation	7	Weaver	*Alexander*
Roach	Henry	26	M	Assault and highway robbery	Death	7	No trade recorded	*Charlotte*
Roberts	John		M	Stealing a japanned hand-board	Transportation	7	No trade recorded	*Alexander*
Roberts	William	31	M	Stealing yarn	Transportation	7	No trade recorded	*Scarborough*
Robins	John	27	M	Stealing a silver watch	Transportation	7	No trade recorded	*Charlotte*
Robinson	George	17	M	Burglary	Transportation	7	No trade recorded	*Scarborough*
Robinson	George	38	M	Stealing a purse and cash	Death	7	No trade recorded	*Alexander*
Robinson	Joseph/ Thomas	24	M	Stealing brandy and clothing	Death	7	No trade recorded	*Alexander*
Robinson	William	24	M	Assault and highway robbery	Death	7	Seaman	*Charlotte*
Rogers	Daniel	33	M	Stealing clothing	Transportation	7	Labourer	*Alexander*
Rogers	Isaac	25	M	Assault and highway robbery	Death	14	No trade recorded	*Alexander* (died at sea 22 July)
Rolt	Mary	29	F	Not recorded	Transportation	7	No trade recorded	*Prince of Wales*
Romaine/ Romain	John	21	M	Stealing clothing	Transportation	7	No trade recorded	*Scarborough*
Roman/ Knowland/ Ronan/ Rowland	Andrew	32	M	Fraud (impersonation)	Death	7	Seaman	*Friendship*
Rope	Anthony	28	M	Stealing clothing	Transportation	7	Labourer	*Alexander*
Rosson	Isabella	33	F	Stealing clothing	Transportation	7	Laundress, mantua maker	*Lady Penrhyn*
Rowe	John	30	M	Stealing clothing	Transportation	7	No trade recorded	*Scarborough*
Rowe	William	32	M	Stealing cash	Transportation	7	No trade recorded	*Scarborough*
Ruffler	John	27	M	Stealing livestock (a horse – a gelding)	Death	99	No trade recorded	*Scarborough*

Family Name	Given Name	Age Leaving England	Gender	Crime	Original Sentence	Transported for (years – 99 = life)	Occupation	Departed on
Ruglass/ Ruggles	John	22	M	Assault and highway robbery	Death	99	No trade recorded	Scarborough
Ruse/Ruce	James	28	M	Burglary	Death	7	Farmer	Scarborough
Russell/Russel	John	64	M	Stealing	Transportation	7	Seaman	Scarborough
Ruth	Robert	22	M	Assault and highway robbery	Death	7	Seaman	Charlotte
Ryan	John	23	M	Stealing clothing	Transportation	7	Silk weaver	Friendship
Saltmarsh	William	17	M	Robbery	Transportation	7	Labourer	Alexander
Sampson	Peter		M	Stealing linen	Transportation	7	No trade recorded	Scarborough
Sandlin/Lines/ Sandland/ Sandilon/ Lynes	Ann	30	F	Stealing	Transportation	7	Needleworker	Lady Penrhyn
Sands	William	27	M	Stealing livestock (a horse – a mare)	Transportation	7	No trade recorded	Alexander (died before departure)
Saunderson	Thomas	22	M	Burglary	Transportation	7	No trade recorded	Alexander
Scattergood	Robert	35	M	Stealing livestock (2 geese)	Transportation	7	Labourer	Alexander (died before departure)
Scott	Elizabeth		F	Stealing bridles, straps and stirrups	Transportation	7	No trade recorded	Prince of Wales
Selshire	Samuel	23	M	Assault and highway robbery	Death	7	No trade recorded	Scarborough
Seymour	John	26	M	Stealing timber from a forest nursery	Transportation	7	No trade recorded	Scarborough
Sharp	George	39	M	Stealing cash	Death	7	No trade recorded	Alexander (died at sea 24 September)
Shaw	Joseph	35	M	Stealing linen material	Death	7	No trade recorded	Alexander
Sheers/Shiers	James	40	M	Assault and highway robbery	Death	99	No trade recorded	Scarborough
Shephard/ Haydon/ Eaton/ Sheppard/ Hayden	Mary	22	F	Highway robbery	Death	7	No trade recorded	Charlotte

Family Name	Given Name	Age Leaving England	Gender	Crime	Original Sentence	Transported for (years – 99 = life)	Occupation	Departed on
Shepherd/ Sheppard	Robert	32	M	Stealing sacks of flour	Transportation	7	No trade recorded	*Alexander*
Sherman/ Shearman	William	25	M	Stealing livestock (turkeys)	Transportation	7	No trade recorded	*Alexander*
Shore	John	37	M	Stealing material	Transportation	7	Calenderer, cloth glazer	*Alexander*
Shore	William	19	M	Burglary	Death	7	No trade recorded	*Alexander*
Sidaway/ Sideway	Robert	29	M	Stealing material	Death	99	Watchcase maker	*Friendship*
Silverthorn	John	24	M	Assault and highway robbery	Death	7	Weaver	*Alexander*
Slater	Sarah	30	F	Stealing clothing	Death	7	Watch chain maker	*Lady Penrhyn*
Small	John	26	M	Assault and highway robbery	Death	7	Ex-marine	*Charlotte*
Smart	Daniel	32	M	Stealing wool	Transportation	7	No trade recorded	*Alexander*
Smart	Richard	23	M	Stealing wool	Transportation	7	No trade recorded	*Alexander* (died at sea 24 May)
Smith	Ann	30	F	Stealing a pewter pint pot	Transportation	7	Nurse	*Lady Penrhyn*
Smith	Ann		F	Stealing	Transportation	7	No trade recorded	*Charlotte*
Smith	Ann		F	Stealing material	Transportation	7	Nurse	*Prince of Wales*
Smith	Catherine	35	F	Stealing a silver watch and seal	Transportation	7	Hawker	*Lady Penrhyn*
Smith	Catherine		F	Stealing a silver watch	Transportation	7	No trade recorded	*Prince of Wales*
Smith	Edward	30	M	Burglary	Death	7	No trade recorded	*Charlotte*
Smith	Edward	30	M	Stealing a handkerchief	Transportation	7	No trade recorded	*Scarborough*
Smith	Hannah	29	F	Stealing clothing	Transportation	7	No trade recorded	*Charlotte*
Smith	James	20	M	Stealing livestock (a horse – a mare)	Death	7	Dustman	*Scarborough*
Smith	John	35	M	Robbery	Transportation	7	Seaman	*Scarborough*
Smith	John	23	M	Assault and highway robbery	Death	7	No trade recorded	*Charlotte*

Family Name	Given Name	Age Leaving England	Gender	Crime	Original Sentence	Transported for (years – 99 = life)	Occupation	Departed on
Smith	Mary	25	F	Stealing clothing	Death	7	Mantua maker	Lady Penrhyn
Smith	Thomas	30	M	Stealing a length of material	Transportation	7	No trade recorded	Scarborough
Smith	Thomas	24	M	Stealing assorted goods	Death	7	No trade recorded	Alexander (died at sea 4 July)
Smith	William	29	M	Burglary	Death	7	No trade recorded	Scarborough
Smith	William		M	Not recorded	Transportation	7	No trade recorded	Alexander
Smith	William	21	M	Stealing an iron grappling and other goods	Transportation	7	No trade recorded	Scarborough
Smith	William	31	M	Burglary	Death	7	No trade recorded	Charlotte
Snailham/ Snaleham/ Snailam/ Strachan	William	21	M	Stealing clothing (2 separate charges)	Transportation	7	No trade recorded	Scarborough
Sparkes	Henry/ Thomas	29	M	Assault and highway robbery	Death	7	No trade recorded	Scarborough
Spence	John	28	M	Stealing tea	Transportation	7	No trade recorded	Friendship
Spencer	Daniel	24	M	Receiving stolen goods	Transportation	14	No trade recorded	Charlotte
Spencer/ Spence	Mary	19	F	Stealing clothing	Transportation	5	No trade recorded	Prince of Wales
Springham	Mary	21	F	Stealing cash and a snuff box	Transportation	7	Hawker	Lady Penrhyn
Springmore	Charlotte	30	F	Assault and malicious damage	Transportation	7	Silk winder	Lady Penrhyn
Squires/ Squire	James	33	M	Stealing livestock (4 cocks, 5 hens) and other goods	Transportation	7	No trade recorded	Charlotte
Stanley	William	47	M	Stealing livestock (killing a sheep)	Death	7	No trade recorded	Alexander
Stanton/ Ebden/Ibden/ Abdin/Eldon	Thomas	27	M	Stealing livestock (horses – geldings) (2 charges)	Death	7	No trade recorded	Scarborough
Stephens/ Morris	John	22	M	Stealing clothing	Transportation	7	No trade recorded	Charlotte

Family Name	Given Name	Age Leaving England	Gender	Crime	Original Sentence	Transported for (years – 99 = life)	Occupation	Departed on
Stewart/ Stuart	James	30	M	Stealing bedding	Transportation	7	No trade recorded	*Scarborough*
Stewart/ Stuart	Margaret	25	F	Stealing (shoplifting from several shops)	Transportation	7	Hawker	*Charlotte*
Stogdell/ Stockdale	John	25	M	Receiving stolen goods	Transportation	14	Servant	*Alexander*
Stokoe	John	34	M	Stealing cash	Death	7	No trade recorded	*Alexander*
Stone	Charles	20	M	Stealing clothing	Transportation	7	No trade recorded	*Alexander*
Stone	Martin	23	M	Burglary	Death	7	No trade recorded	*Alexander* (died before departure)
Stow/Stowe	James	25	M	Stealing clothing	Transportation	7	No trade recorded	*Alexander*
Stretch	Thomas	33	M	Burglary	Death	7	Labourer or miller	*Friendship*
Strong	James	34	M	Stealing bedding	Transportation	7	Fiddler	*Alexander*
Summers/ Summer	John	34	M	Stealing a knapsack	Transportation	7	No trade recorded	*Alexander*
Taylor	Henry	33	M	Stealing iron bars and railing	Transportation	7	Stocking weaver	*Friendship*
Taylor	Joshua	19	M	Stealing a handkerchief	Transportation	7	Labourer	*Alexander*
Taylor	Sarah	32	F	Assault and robbery (2 charges)	Transportation	7	Servant	*Prince of Wales*
Teague	Cornelius	41	M	Burglary	Transportation	7	No trade recorded	*Scarborough*
Tenhel/ Tenchall/ Tennyhill/ Tenihile/ Tenninghill/ Hill/Daniel	John	19	M	Stealing spices	Transportation	7	None	*Friendship*
Tennant	Thomas Hilton	27	M	Stealing	Transportation	7	Currier	*Alexander*
Thackery	Elizabeth	20	F	Stealing handkerchiefs	Transportation	7	None	*Friendship*
Thodie/Ives/ Thoudy/ Thody	James	28	M	Stealing clothing	Death	7	Plasterer	*Friendship*

Family Name	Given Name	Age Leaving England	Gender	Crime	Original Sentence	Transported for (years – 99 = life)	Occupation	Departed on
Thomas	Elizabeth	20	F	Stealing clothing	Transportation	7	No trade recorded	*Prince of Wales*
Thomas	James	23	M	Stealing copper	Transportation	7	No trade recorded	*Alexander*
Thomas	James/ Richard	22	M	Assault and stealing a handkerchief	Death	7	No trade recorded	*Scarborough*
Thomas	John	23	M	Stealing copper	Transportation	7	No trade recorded	*Scarborough*
Thompson	James	40	M	Stealing 2 silver teaspoons	Transportation	7	Haymaker	*Scarborough*
Thompson	William	31	M	Stealing clothing	Transportation	7	No trade recorded	*Scarborough*
Thompson	William/ Jeremy	33	M	Stealing livestock (a horse – a mare)	Death	7	No trade recorded	*Alexander*
Thornton	Ann	32	F	Stealing clothing	Transportation	7	Servant	*Lady Penrhyn*
Till/Tilley	Thomas	23	M	Burglary	Death	7	Chimney sweep	*Scarborough*
Tilley	Thomas	41	M	Robbery of cloth and bag	Transportation	7	Labourer	*Alexander*
Timmins/ Tunmins	Thomas	19	M	Stealing livestock (a horse – a mare)	Death	7	No trade recorded	*Alexander*
Todd	Nicholas		M	Stealing clothing	Transportation	7	No trade recorded	*Scarborough*
Trace	John	33	M	Stealing mutton	Transportation	7	No trade recorded	*Charlotte*
Trippett	Susannah	21	F	Stealing metal watch, key and chain	Transportation	7	Artificial flower maker	*Lady Penrhyn*
Trotter	Joseph	25	M	Stealing copper stills	Transportation	7	Waterman	*Alexander*
Tucker	Moses	35	M	Fraud (false pretences)	Transportation	7	Labourer or carpenter	*Friendship*
Turner	John	28	M	Stealing livestock (a horse – a gelding)	Death	7	No trade recorded	*Scarborough*
Turner	John	47	M	Stealing a cask of beer	Transportation	7	Shipwright	*Friendship*
Turner	Ralph	38	M	Stealing material	Transportation	7	Labourer	*Alexander* (died before departure)
Turner	Thomas	47	M	Assault and highway robbery	Death	7	None	*Friendship*

Family Name	Given Name	Age Leaving England	Gender	Crime	Original Sentence	Transported for (years – 99 = life)	Occupation	Departed on
Turner/Wilkes	Mary	21	F	Stealing clothing	Transportation	7	Servant	*Lady Penrhyn*
Tuso/Tuzo/Toozo	Joseph	17	M	Assault and highway robbery	Death	99	No trade recorded	*Scarborough*
Twineham/Twyman/Twyneham	William	24	M	Stealing clothing	Transportation	7	No trade recorded	*Alexander* (died before departure)
Twyfield/Dawley	Ann	29	F	Assault and highway robbery	Death	7	Servant	*Lady Penrhyn*
Twyfield/Phyfield/Fyfield	Roger	27	M	Burglary	Death	7	Labourer	*Friendship*
Tyrrell	William	28	M	Stealing an iron bar	Transportation	7	No trade recorded	*Alexander*
Underwood	James	44	M	Stealing livestock (5 sheep)	Death	14	Shipwright	*Charlotte*
Usher	John	18	M	Stealing linen material	Transportation	7	Jeweller	*Alexander*
Varndell	Edward	28	M	Stealing livestock (2 horses – mares)	Death	7	Labourer	*Alexander*
Vickery	William	25	M	Stealing cash	Transportation	7	No trade recorded	*Charlotte*
Vincent	Henry	27	M	Stealing cash and a barrel of dried fruit	Transportation	7	No trade recorded	*Scarborough*
Wade/Cockran/Coclin/Cacklane	Mary	32	F	Stealing material from a bleaching ground	Death	14	Second-hand dealer	*Lady Penrhyn*
Wager	Benjamin	21	M	Stealing clothing	Transportation	7	Servant	*Alexander*
Wainwright/Eccles/Mainwright	Ellen/Esther	18	F	Stealing clothing	Transportation	7	No trade recorded	*Prince of Wales*
Walbourne/Walburn/Waldbourn	James	22	M	Stealing a handkerchief	Transportation	7	No trade recorded	*Scarborough*
Walker	John	22	M	Stealing clothing	Transportation	7	Carpenter	*Scarborough*
Wall	William	23	M	Stealing clothing	Transportation	7	Labourer	*Alexander*
Walsh	William	34	M	Stealing silverware	Transportation	7	Waiter	*Scarborough*
Ward	Ann	20	F	Stealing clothing	Transportation	7	Servant	*Lady Penrhyn*

Family Name	Given Name	Age Leaving England	Gender	Crime	Original Sentence	Transported for (years – 99 = life)	Occupation	Departed on
Ward	John	17	M	Not recorded	Transportation	7	No trade recorded	*Alexander (died at sea 29 June)*
Ware/Wear	Charlotte	25	F	Assault and robbery	Transportation	7	None	*Friendship*
Waterhouse	William	34	M	Robbery	Transportation	7	Labourer	*Alexander*
Watkins	Mary	21	F	Robbery	Transportation	7	No trade recorded	*Friendship/ Charlotte*
Watson	John	33	M	Stealing	Transportation	7	Hawker	*Alexander*
Watson	Thomas	18	M	Stealing	Death	7	No trade recorded	*Charlotte*
Welch	John	57	M	Stealing cash	Death	7	No trade recorded	*Alexander*
Welch	John	24	M	Stealing linen sheets	Transportation	7	Servant	*Scarborough*
Welch	John Coen	27	M	Theft of household goods	Death	99	No trade recorded	*Scarborough*
Welsh/Welch	James	28	M	Stealing livestock (a sheep)	Death	7	Labourer	*Alexander*
West	George	19	M	Assault and robbery	Transportation	7	Soldier	*Alexander (died at sea 13 January)*
Westlake	Edward		M	Stealing mutton	Transportation	7	No trade recorded	*Charlotte*
Westwood	John	35	M	Stealing a snuff box	Transportation	7	Servant	*Scarborough*
Wheeler	Samuel	28	M	Stealing household goods	Transportation	7	Brickmaker	*Alexander*
Whitaker	George	27	M	Assault and highway robbery (4 charges)	Death	7	Labourer	*Alexander*
White/Wight	James		M	Highway robbery	Death	7	No trade recorded	*Scarborough*
Whiting/ Whiteing	William	25	M	Stealing livestock (a sheep)	Death	7	No trade recorded	*Alexander*
Whitton/ Whitten	Edward	36	M	Assault and highway robbery	Death	99	Labourer	*Scarborough*
Wickham	Mary	35	F	Receiving stolen goods	Transportation	14	No trade recorded	*Charlotte*
Widdicombe/ Weddicomb	Richard	23	M	Stealing a winch and other goods	Transportation	7	No trade recorded	*Charlotte*

Family Name	Given Name	Age Leaving England	Gender	Crime	Original Sentence	Transported for (years – 99 = life)	Occupation	Departed on
Wilcocks/ Wilcox	Samuel	25	M	Stealing clothing and other goods	Transportation	7	No trade recorded	*Alexander*
Wilding/ Warren	John	37	M	Stealing a watch and 2 gold cases	Death	7	Labourer	*Scarborough*
Willcocks/ Wilcocks	Richard	25	M	Assault with intent to rob	Transportation	7	No trade recorded	*Charlotte*
Williams	Charles	25	M	Stealing clothing	Transportation	7	No trade recorded	*Scarborough*
Williams	Daniel	48	M	Stealing livestock (cattle – 2 oxen, 2 heifers)	Death	7	No trade recorded	*Friendship*
Williams	Frances		F	Burglary (2 counts)	Death	7	No trade recorded	*Prince of Wales*
Williams	James	20	M	Stealing clothing	Transportation	7	No trade recorded	*Scarborough*
Williams	John	43	M	Stealing steel	Transportation	7	No trade recorded	*Charlotte*
Williams	John	18	M	Burglary	Death	7	Labourer	*Scarborough*
Williams/ Floyd	John	32	M	Burglary	Death	7	No trade recorded	*Scarborough*
Williams	Mary	39	F	Stealing clothing	Transportation	7	Needleworker	*Lady Penrhyn*
Williams/ Creamer	Peter	23	M	Assault and highway robbery	Death	7	Seaman	*Charlotte*
Williams	Robert	24	M	Stealing livestock (2 horses – mares)	Death	7	No trade recorded	*Scarborough*
Wilson	Charles	26	M	Stealing clothing and cash	Death	99	No trade recorded	*Scarborough*
Wilson	John		M	Stealing material	Transportation	7	No trade recorded	*Alexander*
Wilson	Mary	47	F	Stealing clothing	Transportation	7	No trade recorded	*Prince of Wales*
Wilson	Peter	20	M	Stealing cash	Transportation	7	Silk weaver	*Alexander*
Wilton/ Whilton/ Wilson	William	43	M	Stealing livestock (18 turkeys)	Transportation	7	No trade recorded	*Alexander* (died before departure)
Wisehammer	John	18	M	Stealing snuff	Transportation	7	None	*Friendship*
Wood	George	23	M	Stealing clothing	Transportation	7	No trade recorded	*Alexander*
Wood/Brand	Lucy	33	F	Stealing jewellery and cash	Transportation	7	Lace maker	*Lady Penrhyn*
Wood	Mark	24	M	Stealing clothing	Transportation	7	Shoemaker	*Friendship*

Family Name	Given Name	Age Leaving England	Gender	Crime	Original Sentence	Transported for (years – 99 = life)	Occupation	Departed on
Woodcock	Francis	48	M	Stealing livestock (a sheep)	Death	14	Labourer	*Friendship*
Woodcock	Peter	24	M	Stealing a silver watch, metal chain and gold seal	Transportation	7	No trade recorded	*Scarborough*
Woodham	Samuel	20	M	Assault and highway robbery	Death	99	No trade recorded	*Scarborough*
Woolcott/ Woolcot	John	47	M	Burglary	Death	99	No trade recorded	*Charlotte*
Worsdell/ Wordale	William	58	M	Stealing iron bolts	Transportation	7	No trade recorded	*Scarborough*
Wright	Ann	33	F	Stealing clothing	Transportation	7	Servant	*Lady Penrhyn* (died before departure)
Wright	Benjamin	18	M	Stealing a silk handkerchief	Transportation	7	No trade recorded	*Scarborough*
Wright	James	25	M	Highway robbery (3 charges)	Death	7	No trade recorded	*Scarborough*
Wright	Joseph	22	M	Stealing lead from a roof	Transportation	7	No trade recorded	*Scarborough*
Wright	Thomas	22	M	Stealing livestock (3 pigs)	Transportation	7	Labourer	*Alexander*
Wright	William		M	Stealing a watch and gown	Transportation	7	No trade recorded	*Scarborough*
Yardsley/ Yasley	Thomas	28	M	Stealing clothing and wheat (3 charges)	Transportation	7	Gardener	*Scarborough*
Yeats/Yates	Nancy	19	F	Burglary	Death	7	Milliner	*Lady Penrhyn*
Young	John	25	M	Stealing clothing	Transportation	7	No trade recorded	*Alexander*
Young	Simon	25	M	Fraud (impersonation)	Death	7	Seaman	*Scarborough*
Youngson/ Youngster	Elizabeth	15	F	Burglary	Death	7	Laundress	*Prince of Wales*
Youngson	George	13	M	Burglary	Transportation	7	No trade recorded	*Prince of Wales*

Table takes Portsmouth, 13 May 1787, as departure point.

Compiled with the assistance of Brian McDonald, based on the University of Wollongong table firstfleet.uow.edu/download.html and tables in Mollie Gillen's *The Founders of Australia: A Biographical Dictionary of the First Fleet* (with appendices by Yvonne Browning and Michael Flynn).

ROB MUNDLE O.A.M. is a bestselling author, journalist and competitive sailor whose family heritage is with the sea, dating back to his great-great-grandfather, who was the master of square-riggers.

For over forty years, Rob has combined his passions for sailing and writing. He has written twelve books – including the international bestseller *Fatal Storm* – reported on more than thirty-five Sydney-to-Hobart yacht races (and competed in three), and covered seven America's Cups, four Olympics and numerous international events.

He is the winner of many sailing championships, has been a competitor in local and international contests, and has sailed everything from sailboards and 18-foot skiffs through to supermaxi yachts and offshore multihulls.

He was awarded an Order of Australia Medal in the Queen's Birthday Honours List 2013 for services to sailing and journalism.

His most recent book is *Flinders: The Man Who Mapped Australia*.